Sports Illustrated

BASKETBALL'S GREATEST

O'NEAL
34

Sports Illustrated

BASKE

GREA

SHAQUILLE O'NEAL

NO.
5

CENTER

PHOTOGRAPH BY JOHN W. MCDONOUGH

TBALL'S

TEST

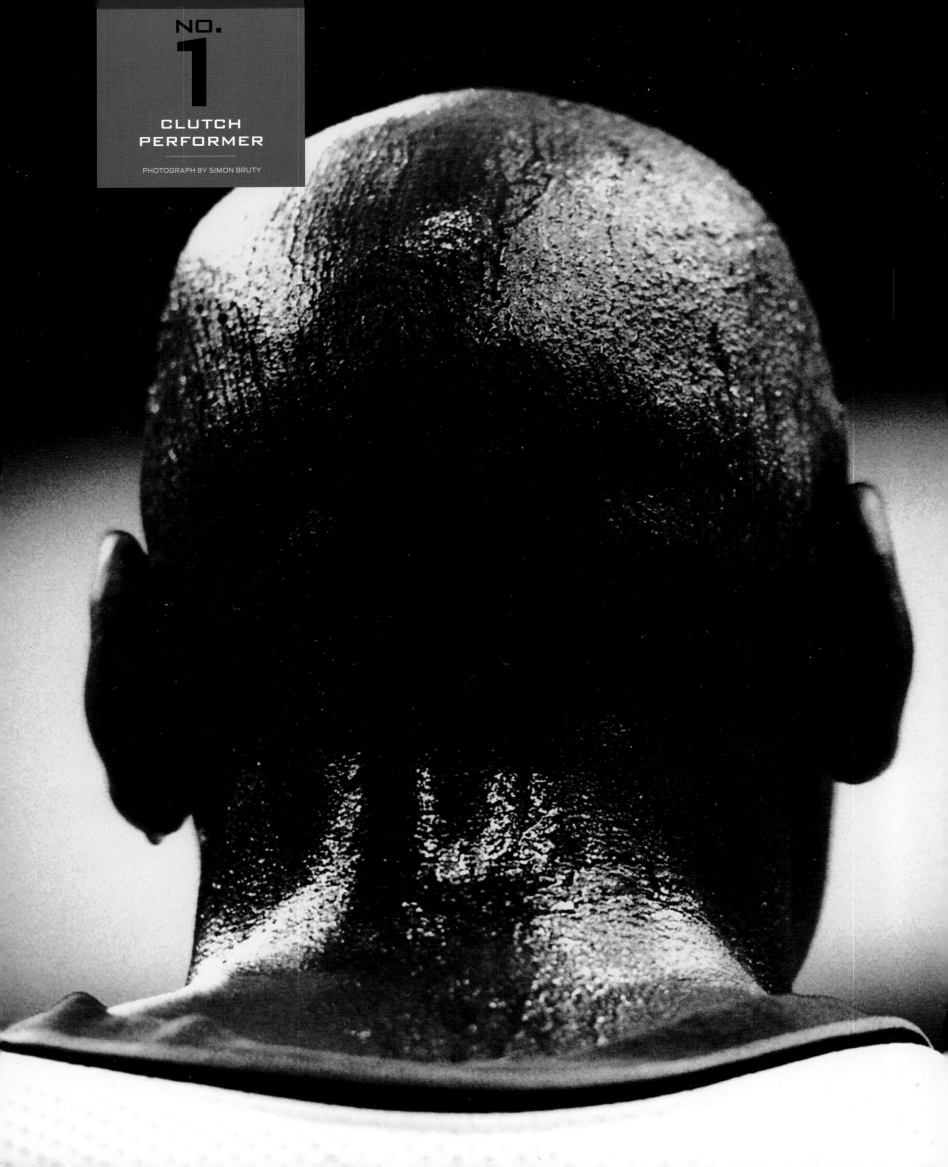

CONTENTS

INTRODUCTION 6

Man to Man Talk BY BILL SYKEN
One-on-one matchups reveal much about the specific nature of this sport . . . . . .

BEST POINT GUARDS 22

Simple and to the Point BY PHIL TAYLOR
John Stockton played the game the same way he lived his life 27

BEST SHOOTING GUARDS 38

Air to the Throne BY JACK McCALLUM
Michael Jordan drew rare accolades after he had won just one title 42

BEST SMALL FORWARDS 54

The King Earns a Ring BY LEE JENKINS
LeBron James quieted the naysayers the only way he could 59

BEST POWER FORWARDS 70

A Kid Shall Lead Them BY LEIGH MONTVILLE
Kevin Garnett's career was launched in one intently watched workout 77

BEST CENTERS 86

The Stuff of Dreams BY LEIGH MONTVILLE
A playoff performance showcased Hakeem Olajuwon's brilliance 93

BEST COACHES 102

The Republic of Pop BY JACK McCALLUM
Gregg Popovich has built a culture of success in San Antonio 111

BEST SIXTH MEN 118

Pining for Playing Time BY MICHAEL FARBER
Toni Kukoc, like many sixth men, would rather have started 131

BEST THREE-POINT SHOOTERS . . . 134

Tougher Than You Think BY MICHAEL SILVER
Steve Kerr showed rare resiliency in becoming an alltime great 141

BEST REBOUNDERS 150

Stop Jivin' Me, Coach BY FRANK DEFORD
Moses Malone's pronouncement began a new era in basketball 157

BEST CLUTCH PERFORMERS 166

A Can't Miss Proposition BY JACK McCALLUM
Reggie Miller relived a great fourth quarter at Madison Square Garden . . 177

BEST DEFENDERS 182

Whatever You Try Will Fail BY S.L. PRICE
Tim Duncan has known how to use his stoicism as a weapon 193

MOST ENTERTAINING PLAYERS . . . 198

Did He Just Say That? BY JACK McCALLUM
Charles Barkley has led the most enjoyable studio show in sports 211

BEST GAMES 214

Anatomy of a Miracle BY LEE JENKINS
The seconds were magnified before Ray Allen's big three-pointer 220

The Spirit Was Willis BY FRANK DEFORD
Willis Reed set the tone for Game 7 simply by taking the court 225

BEST SINGLE-SEASON TEAMS 236

Green, Plus a Touch of Red BY JACK McCALLUM
Larry Bird's Celtics dominated, with help from Bill Walton 243

BEST FRANCHISES 252

Cuckoo for His Team BY RICK REILLY
Dedicated fan Jack Nicholson has led the star parade at Lakers games . . 257

BEST OF THE REST 270

Slam Dunks	272	Moments	281
Uniforms	276	Draft Surprises	282
Courtside Characters	278	International Scenes	283
Quotes	280	The Full Results	284

BILL SYKEN *Editor* / STEVEN HOFFMAN *Creative Director*

CRISTINA SCALET *Photo Editor* / KEVIN KERR *Copy Editor* / JOSH DENKIN *Designer*

PORTER BINKS *Photo Researcher* / STEFANIE KAUFMAN *Project Manager*

MAN TO MAN TALK

THE GAME'S GREATEST ONE-ON-ONE CLASHES ANCHOR THE RANKINGS IN THIS BOOK AND REVEAL MUCH ABOUT THE SPECIFIC NATURE OF BASKETBALL

BY BILL SYKEN

IEW THE CLIP REPEATEDLY AND IT CAN feel as if you are watching not a spontaneous play on a basketball court, but rather a dance that has been carefully choreographed. It's not just how the two men move in relation to one other. It's that their steps tell a clear and simple story, that of one man's control over the other.

The eyes first go to the tall man in the red uniform. He's dribbling the ball in the corner, facing the basket and eyeing the even taller man in front of him, whose uniform is white with black trim. There are a few feet of space between them. The man in red then lunges forward as he crosses his dribble over to his left hand. The man in white responds, closing the distance between them while raising his hands high, his body straight up. The two men take a couple of steps in concert, and then the man in red stops and holds the ball chest high with two hands. He quickly raises the ball with his left hand but instead of shooting, he brings the ball down, pivots so his back is to the basket and around again. He rises as if to shoot. The man in white leaps high and forward, the full 235 pounds of his body weight hurtling helplessly away from the basket.

Olajuwon's dominance in 1995 was defining.

THE MAN IN RED, HIS GOAL ACHIEVED, ducks under the man in white and easily lays the ball up and in. If this is indeed a dance, the man in red is clearly leading. "I tell ya, [Hakeem] Olajuwon has David Robinson just bamboozled," the television announcer sputters.

The play lives on in highlights, a snapshot of the dismantling of Robinson's Spurs by Olajuwon's Rockets in the 1995 Western

The Game 7 duel between Wilkins and Bird elevated both men.

Conference finals. It is a signature moment for one Hall of Fame career—Houston was plowing toward its second straight NBA championship—and a diminishing one for another. But the play is of interest here because it reveals something distinctive about the task of ranking basketball's greatest, and about the nature of the game itself.

This book is the third in a series from SI, following FOOTBALL'S GREATEST and BASEBALL'S GREATEST. But in BASKETBALL'S GREATEST, our panelists are for the first time comparing players who, at least within positional rankings, competed directly against one another. Peyton Manning and Tom Brady, for all the times they've played each other, have never tried to sack one another or intercept each other's passes. Mickey Mantle, Willie Mays and Duke Snider all played centerfield at the same time—and for a period in the same city, to boot—and at one time or another they chased down one of the others' fly balls. But they never stared each other down the way pitchers and batters do. Mays never had the chance to dominate Mantle one on one, the way Olajuwon so memorably did against Robinson.

It's that head-to-head competition that grounds many of the rankings in this book. Because when you get right down to it, the career achievements of Olajuwon and Robinson are strikingly similar. Each center transformed his franchise the moment he arrived in the NBA. Each won two championships, though they all came with qualifiers—Olajuwon won his first ring while Michael Jordan was taking a baseball sabbatical and his second the year Jordan returned and played only a partial season, and Robinson didn't get his until he was joined in the San Antonio frontcourt by another iconic big man, Tim Duncan. The career stats for Olajuwon and Robinson are nearly identical. Olajuwon's points/rebounds/blocked shots averages are 21.8/11.1/3.1. Robinson's are 21.1/10.6/3.0. Even trivialities fail to differentiate them. They both played in Texas and—fun fact alert!—until Akeem changed his name to Hakeem, they had the same number of letters in both their first and last names.

When our panel voted, there was general consensus that among the alltime centers, Olajuwon and Robinson belonged squarely in the middle of the pack—not quite up there with the likes of Bill Russell, but definitely ahead of Bill Walton. But despite being so close, on the ballots which compared the two men, Olajuwon was listed ahead of Robinson every time. It's the power of the highlight. Everyone saw it with their own eyes, the pecking order among equals: Olajuwon was better than Robinson.

PEYTON MANNING AND TOM
BRADY, FOR ALL THE TIMES
THEY'VE PLAYED EACH OTHER,
HAVE NEVER TRIED TO SACK
ONE ANOTHER OR INTERCEPT
EACH OTHER'S PASSES.

The Russell-Chamberlain debate is about team success versus stats.

NOT ALL THE PLAYERS IN THIS BOOK competed as directly as Olajuwon and Robinson. But many did, at least for a while. Among our top 10 point guards you can make a chain of overlapping seasons from the early days of the NBA (Hall of Famer Bob Cousy, ranked sixth on our list, was a Celtics rookie in 1950) to today (the Clippers' Chris Paul is No. 10). True, the meaning of those degrees of separation varies. The weakest link in the point guard chain is the 1979–80 season, which overlaps a rookie Magic Johnson with the career coda of Walt Frazier, who played only three games in a best-forgotten stint with the Cavaliers. But the comparison of contemporaries helped when rating, say, Magic and John Stockton. Because they played in roughly the same era, we know which one dominated the league and transformed the game—in fact it's clear that Magic is the top point guard ever: SI's panel was unanimous there. But imagine if Stockton had played a few decades earlier (as his earthbound game and short shorts suggested he should have). Might we not be tempted to look at the NBA records Stockton owns—most career assists, most career steals—and argue that he's the best point guard ever?

In some cases personal clashes defined both players for the better. Think about the storied shootout between Boston's Larry Bird and Atlanta's Dominique Wilkins in Game 7 of the 1988 Eastern Conference semifinals (No. 8 in our 10 Greatest Games category). In that game Wilkins proved he was more than a Human Highlight Film, shooting a variety of pull-ups and jumpers while scoring 47 points in 43 minutes with zero turnovers. Bird answered Wilkins with his own array of turnarounds and long-range jump shots, scoring 20 in the fourth quarter and 34 on the day. It's of note that Bird was pushed to this great performance not by his famed rival, Magic Johnson, but a fellow Top 10 small forward.

The funny thing is that even though Wilkins's team lost, that performance helped separate him from other great scoring forwards such as Bernard King and Alex English, each of whom received consideration from our panel but did not make the Top 10. Wilkins was truly burnished in defeat. And what if the refs had called a couple more fouls that day for Atlanta (the Hawks went to the line only 12 times and made 11 free throws, the only clanger coming on Wilkins's intentional miss with the Hawks down by three late) or had not ruled a Doc Rivers block on Danny Ainge a goaltend, a call that Rivers still disputes? The Hawks, who lost 118–116, could easily have come out on top, and what would we think of Wilkins then? We might well place him a couple steps higher on the alltime ladder for having bested the greatest small forward ever.

N O TEAM SPORT HAS AS STRONG A one-on-one tradition as basketball: The mano a mano battle is at the heart of the game, from driveways and schoolyards all the way to the world's most famous arenas. And yet the tension between individual play and the majesty of the team game—five players working in unison—defines the greatest and most enduring of all basketball debates: Bill Russell versus Wilt Chamberlain.

The two centers were near contemporaries: Russell began his career with the Celtics in 1956, and Chamberlain joining the NBA three years later with the Philadelphia Warriors. In an age when basketball was dominated by big men, they were the true titans. Their names are all over the NBA record books—though, for the most part, in different sections. Chamberlain piled up the points and rebounds (though his Boston counterpart also had few peers on the boards). But it was Russell's Celtics who usually walked away with the titles.

The Russell-Chamberlain debate can still spark the fire of veteran fans. Go into the local YMCA one weekday afternoon and visit the steam room just as the old-timers are clearing out after their weekly run on the hardwood. You might hear fragments of the ancient arguments echoing off the walls:

"50 points for a season."

"11 championships"

"Led the league in assists one year, because he felt like it."

"Team, not stats."

"His whole team was Hall of Famers."

"He was a winner."

"No one roots for Goliath."

Our panelists have voiced an opinion on Russell versus Chamberlain, though it is not a unanimous one. Nor will our ranking end the debate, in this or any category in BASKETBALL'S GREATEST. In some cases, no matter how many games are played and how much evidence you have, the dance just goes on and on. ∎

HOW WE RANKED THEM

These Top 10 lists bring together the expert opinions of seven writers and editors whose knowledge of the game runs deep

F OR THIS BOOK SI WRITERS AND EDITORS were polled before the 2013–14 season and asked to submit Top 10 lists in 15 categories. Votes were tallied with 10 points awarded for a first-place vote, nine points for a second-place vote and so on. Voters were also asked to justify their selections, and those comments appear with each Top 10 player. In most cases, if one panelist had a player ranked higher than the others, he was asked to speak on that player's behalf.

For players who bridged positions, such as a power forward-center (say, Tim Duncan) or a hybrid guard (Oscar Robertson), it was left to voters to decide at which position they merited Top 10 consideration. To force definitions on such players would be neater, but it would cut off an important aspect of the debate. Similarly, it was left to panelists to decide whether one season coming off the bench, or 10, was the criterion for being named one of the game's greatest sixth men. The definition of what makes an athlete entertaining was left up to the panelists as well. In the parlance of the game, we let them play.

THE PANELISTS

CHRIS BALLARD *SI Senior Writer*
MARK BECHTEL *SI Senior Editor*
LEE JENKINS *SI Senior Writer*
CHRIS MANNIX *SI Senior Writer*
JACK McCALLUM *SI Special Contributor*
IAN THOMSEN *former SI Senior Writer*
ALEXANDER WOLFF *SI Senior Writer*

CHARLES BARKLEY

NO.
3

POWER
FORWARD

PHOTOGRAPH BY JOHN W. MCDONOUGH

John Stockton

NO.

2

POINT GUARD

PHOTOGRAPH BY TRENT NELSON/
THE SALT LAKE TRIBUNE

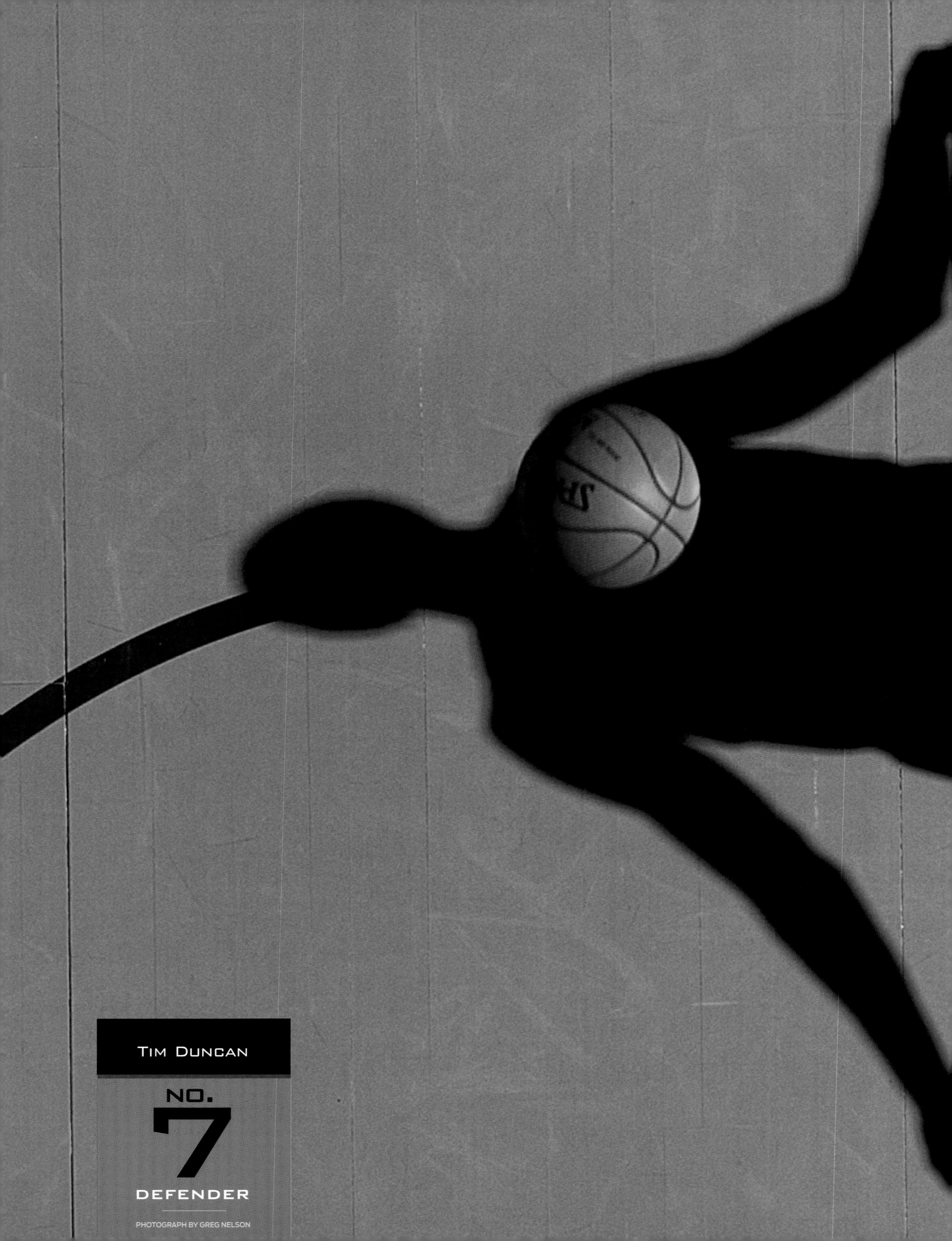

TIM DUNCAN

NO. 7

DEFENDER

PHOTOGRAPH BY GREG NELSON

NBA Co

TBALL'S

TEST

10 THE

BEST POINT GUARDS

"THE MODERN NBA POINT GUARD FLOWS FROM TWO DISTINCT PROTOTYPES," WROTE JACK MCCALLUM IN SI IN 2007. "THE BOB COUSY MODEL IS SMALL AND CEREBRAL, A CREATURE OF QUICKNESS AND SAVVY, DARTING AROUND THE DANGEROUS BIG MEN WHO CAN DO HIM HARM. THE OSCAR ROBERTSON MODEL IS OVERSIZED AND FORCEFUL, DOMINANT IN BODY AS WELL AS MIND, AT HOME IN BOTH THE PERIMETER AND THE PAINT." AMONG THOSE ENDORSING THIS ANALYSIS WAS STEVE NASH, WHOM MCCALLUM PLACED FIRMLY IN THE COUSY TRADITION. "AS LONG AS YOU ALLOW FOR SOME VARIANTS WITHIN THE MODELS, [THE THEORY] HAS A LOT OF TRUTH TO IT," NASH SAID.

IF YOU WERE TO SORT THESE TOP 10 POINT GUARDS ALONG THOSE LINES, THE COUSY CAMP WOULD HOLD SWAY, EVER SO SLIGHTLY.

BUT THE PLAYER WHO LEADS THE PACK DOESN'T BELONG TO EITHER GROUP. MCCALLUM ACKNOWLEDGED IN HIS STORY THAT HIS CATEGORIES OVERSIMPLIFIED REALITY BY LEAVING OUT "BRANCHES OF THE EVOLUTIONARY TRAIL THAT ARE DEAD ENDS," BY WHICH HE CHIEFLY MEANT MAGIC JOHNSON, WHO WAS 6' 9", COULD GRAB BOARDS, LEAD THE SHOWTIME FAST BREAK, DIRECT THE HALF-COURT OFFENSE AND SCORE FROM ALL OVER THE FLOOR. MAGIC WAS A CATEGORY UNTO HIMSELF, WHICH IS WHY HE ARRIVES TO THESE RANKINGS IN A PLACE OF HIGH DISTINCTION.

1

MAGIC JOHNSON

LAKERS 1979–1991, 1995–1996

❝ A quarterback who at 6' 9" could see over the defense, rebound with the big boys, score inside and outside, light up the town and sell out the arena with a smile? They threw away the mold. ❞ —JACK McCALLUM

▸ THREE-TIME NBA MVP
▸ RETIRED AS ASSISTS LEADER

LIKE BILL WALTON, Magic threw a scoring pass from the high post to Michael Cooper. Then, like Dave Cowens, he used position to get a rebound, dribbled upcourt and hit a jumper from the foul line. Next, he drove to the hoop. "That time I wanted to dunk it, like Kareem," he said. "But I saw Darryl Dawkins coming and I thought, well, I better change to something a little more . . ."—he flashed his elfin smile—". . .magical." So he did. He hung in the air, double-pumped, made the layup and drew the foul. Magical. He was everywhere. He did everything. "What position did I play?" he said. "Well, I played center, a little forward, some guard. I tried to think up a name for it, but the best I came up with was C-F-G Rover." Which means that a rookie played one of the greatest games in NBA playoff history at all five positions—center, point guard, shooting guard, small forward and power forward.

—*John Papanek, SI, May 26, 1980*

Magic personified Showtime in Los Angeles.

JAZZ 1984–2003

Stockton dishes to his favorite target, Malone.

PHOTOGRAPH BY JOHN W. MCDONOUGH

2
JOHN STOCKTON

" On top of running fast breaks, hitting clutch shots and executing the pick-and-roll with Karl Malone as if they had invented it, Stockton was respected for his willingness to sacrifice his body for a screen. " —CHRIS MANNIX

▸ NBA CAREER LEADER IN ASSISTS AND STEALS
▸ PLAYED EVERY GAME IN 17 OF 19 SEASONS

THROUGHOUT ALL those seasons of flawlessly conducting the Jazz offense, he never claimed to know more than the coach. To the end he looked over at Jerry Sloan on most half-court possessions. "Why wouldn't I?" he said when I asked him about it last season. "He's the coach. He runs the team."

—Jack McCallum, SI, May 12, 2003

SIMPLE AND TO THE POINT

John Stockton, whose wedding announcement quietly declared that he was "employed in Salt Lake City," had a gift for avoiding complication in his game and his life

BY PHIL TAYLOR

NO ONE CAN DO MORE than guess at John Stockton's world view, because part of his philosophy is that he doesn't articulate his philosophy. If we had really been paying attention, no questions would be necessary. We would know that he hasn't changed—not his hairstyle, not his wardrobe, not his personality—because there has been no need. We would know that what he's all about is stripping away the excess, getting down to what's important. "When you're doing it right," he says, "it looks simple."

He's talking about basketball. Or is he? The reason he doesn't go in the air for a no-look, behind-the-back fancy dish when a simple chest pass will do is the same reason he makes other choices. If simple works, why change? If the Jazz franchise fits you like your favorite pair of khakis, why even think about playing anywhere else? Why even have an agent? Just figure out a salary you think is fair, tell the owner to do the same thing, and meet somewhere in the middle. If you've always worn your shorts a little snug and no longer than mid-thigh, why change just because everyone else is letting them billow down around the knees? If the hometown girl you began dating in college will give you a lifetime, no-cut contract, why go looking elsewhere? Marry her and settle down. If you've never been happier than you were in the neighborhood you grew up in, why not get yourself a house right next door to your parents' and re-create your childhood for your five kids? "You don't do anything just because other people do," Stockton says. "My father taught me that."

The interviews, the agents, the autograph seekers he's been known to duck—Stockton doesn't avoid them because he's shy. He avoids them because they complicate things. "You know, people say to me sometimes that John looks so serious out there, like he's not having any fun," says Karl Malone. "I tell them not to worry about John. He's enjoying himself on the court, and I don't know anybody who's happier with his life than he is. That son of a gun has it all figured out."

Stockton's game is structured, measured. He has created precious few moments appropriate for video montages. If Dominique Wilkins is the Human Highlight Film, Stockton is the Human Instructional Video. There are guys playing pickup at the Y who can give you a flashier show, if that's what you're looking for. "I think I saw him go behind the back against Bobby Hurley once, a couple of years ago," says teammate Greg Foster. "That's about as Showtime as John gets." His work has to be seen over long stretches to be truly understood, because it's the cumulative effect of all those perfectly timed decisions, one after another after another, that illustrates his greatness.

Stockton has never liked a fuss, especially when it was over him. When he was in high school, he wouldn't even let his parents buy him a letter jacket. In fact he never wore anything that would let people know he was an athlete. When he got married he made sure that the wedding announcement in *The Spokesman-Review* said only that the groom was "employed in Salt Lake City."

As you walk down North Hamilton Street in Spokane, the red lettering on the white sign is visible in the distance: Jack and Dan's Tavern. As you get closer, you can see the tiny shamrocks that dance around the letters. It's the sight that Little Johnny, as some of the neighborhood old-timers still call him, saw every day as he pedaled over from school to see his dad, the Jack of Jack and Dan's. First he came from grammar school at St. Aloysius, a few blocks away on East Boone Avenue, and later from high school at Gonzaga Prep, about a mile away. "When he was small, he'd show up at that door at 4:30 every day, and sometimes I'd give him a quarter to get french fries from the Dairy Queen across the street," Jack says, coming out from behind the bar and wiping his hands on his apron. "When it was time to go home, he'd sit on the handlebars of the bike, and I'd ride him back to the house." His eyes look off into the distance for a moment as a slight smile crosses his face. "Those are some good memories," Jack finally says. "Thanks for bringing them up."

Connect the dots on a Spokane city map—St. Al's, Jack and Dan's, Gonzaga Prep, Gonzaga University and the Stockton family home around the corner from the tavern on North Superior Street—and you have the borders inside which the first 22 years of John Stockton's life were neatly contained.

There are a couple of pieces of Jazz decorations in Jack and Dan's—one sent by a fan in Utah and another made by one of Jack's neighbors—but there's no picture of John, no memorabilia that indicates the co-owner has a famous son. "I know he wouldn't like it," Jack says. "I don't even have to ask him." This way John can walk into the tavern when he comes to town and feel like he has stepped back into Spokane, circa 1975. When he made it to the NBA, John told the owner of the house next door to his parents' to let him know if he ever wanted to sell. A few years later the owner did, and now John and his family spend much of their summers in an unassuming home on the same street where he grew up.

Today the quick, young point guards are getting by him with greater frequency, and the day is coming when Stockton will take his permanent leave from the NBA. You want to honor him in a way that he will appreciate? Don't make a speech, don't give him a plaque, don't block his exit, even if it's just to shake his hand. ∎

3

ISIAH THOMAS

"With his small stature and big smile, Isiah Thomas looked miscast as a scoring point with a remorseless streak. But he had the game and guts to take on Michael Jordan's Bulls, and he led Detroit to back-to-back titles." —ALEXANDER WOLFF

▸ 12-TIME ALL-STAR
▸ 1990 NBA FINALS MVP

THOMAS WAS the honored guard of these Finals. Not only did he engineer the Pistons' offense, but he emerged as a most formidable defender too. Only in Game 5 did Thomas permit his Portland quarterback counterpart, Terry Porter, to get in the flow. Porter did not choke. Isiah choked him.

—Jack McCallum, SI, June 25, 1990

The Chicago native had tough battles with the Bulls.
PHOTOGRAPH BY MANNY MILLAN

4

OSCAR ROBERTSON

ROYALS 1960–1970
BUCKS 1970–1974

" At 6' 5", he blew up the existing notion of what a point guard was supposed to look like. And he remains the only man to average a triple double for a season. " —MARK BECHTEL

▸ CAREER AVERAGES OF 25.7 POINTS, 7.5 REBOUNDS AND 9.5 ASSISTS
▸ SIX-TIME NBA ASSISTS LEADER

"I AM proud if I can be consistent," Robertson says. "I hope I'm always consistent because, look, that's what makes a pro." He has been almost eerily consistent. In eight years as a pro he has never averaged less than 28.3 points a game or more than 31.4, and in six of the eight years his average varied less than a point. In assists and free throws he has maintained the same level of consistency. He is like a .333 hitter who arrived at that figure by going 1 for 3 with one walk in every game of the season. It would be reasonable to suppose that somewhere along the line a scorer of Robertson's stripe would put absolutely everything together and come up with a 65-or 75-point game. "That will just never happen," Robertson says, a bit appalled. "Never. What would that possibly prove?"

—Frank Deford, SI, December 9, 1968

Robertson also received votes at shooting guard.

PHOTOGRAPH BY JAMES DRAKE

MUST BE 21 TO
CHASE ALCOHOL
HEAT
HEAT
6
KIDD
2
ARROYO
8
BOSH
1
WADE
3
TERRY
65

5

JASON KIDD

MAVERICKS 1994–1997, 2008–2012,
NETS 2001–2008
TWO TEAMS THROUGH 2013

> " He turned average forwards and shooting guards into All-Stars. Shawn Marion and Richard Jefferson should be tithing him part of their career earnings in perpetuity. An excellent defender in his prime, he morphed into a surprisingly accurate outside shooter in the sunset of his career. " —CHRIS BALLARD

> ▸ SECOND IN NBA CAREER ASSISTS AND STEALS
> ▸ 10-TIME ALL-STAR

HIS GENIUS reveals itself best on the move; he sees patterns where others see chaos. With New Jersey up 77–69 and only three seconds left on the shot clock, Kidd drives to the basket. He must shoot—anyone else would shoot— but as he jumps he sees Kerry Kittles standing alone at the top of the key. At the last second Kidd flings the ball to Kittles, who drops in the killing three. Under Kidd's watchful eye, there's always an extra pass, and each teammate gets at least one moment good enough for the 11 p.m. highlights. "Jason deserves a lot of credit: They're playing together," Knicks guard Allen Houston says of the Nets. "Nobody cares who scores; it's a total team. That's very rare."

—S.L. Price, SI, January 28, 2002

Kidd's Mavericks upended Miami (left) in the 2011 Finals.

PHOTOGRAPHS BY GREG NELSON

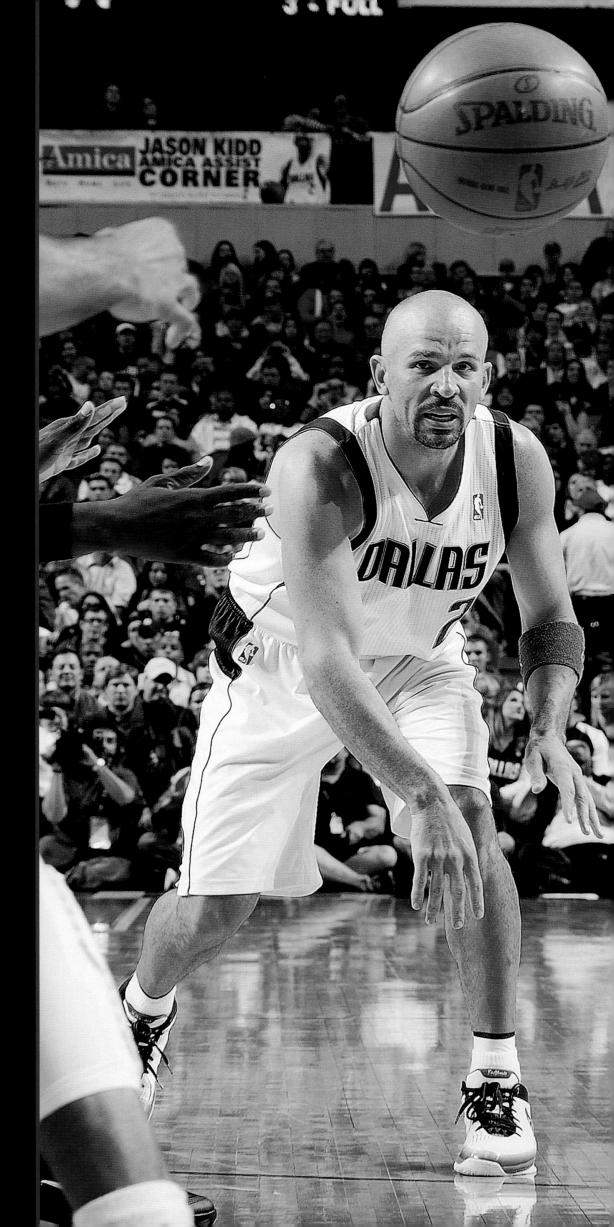

6

BOB COUSY

CELTICS 1950–1963
ROYALS 1969–1970

Cousy was a pioneer when it came to dazzling passes.

PHOTOGRAPH BY JOHN G. ZIMMERMAN

" The 6' 1" Cousy was the NBA's first magician, the original point guard with an unprecedented flair that attracted new audiences to pro basketball. His open-court playmaking was crucial to the Celtic dynasty. " —IAN THOMSEN

‣ EIGHT-TIME NBA ASSISTS LEADER
‣ 1956–57 NBA MVP

LIKE NOBODY ELSE in the game, Cousy can open up a seemingly clogged court by appearing to focus in one direction, simultaneously spotting a seemingly unreachable teammate in another area, and quickly turning him into a scoring threat with a whiplash pass.

—*Herbert Warren Wind, SI, January 9, 1956*

7

STEVE
NASH

SUNS 1996–1998, 2004–2012
MAVERICKS 1998–2004
LAKERS 2012–PRESENT

> " One of the best pure passers ever, he is equally adept with either hand. He brings a soccer player's mind-set to the game, circling behind the basket, employing change of pace and forever looking for teammates making runs. Many forget that he's also one of the game's great shooters, a multiple 40/50/90 guy. " —CHRIS BALLARD

▸ TWO-TIME NBA MVP
▸ SIX-TIME NBA ASSISTS LEADER

NASH'S DEFINING SKILL may be his exceptional body control. Consider a move he makes in the first quarter of the game against Dallas. Nash drives by Josh Howard to the left and, upon gaining a step, does something counterintuitive: He slows down. This throws Howard off-balance and creates contact. Nash can now extend his left hand away from his body, rather than up, to release an uncontested shot. "If I just run and put it straight off the glass, he can beat me in pretty easily," Nash explains. "But if I dictate when the race starts and stops, I have a chance to beat him." Furthermore, because Nash has slowed the play he does not commit to it, he keeps his passing angles open, and it is harder for his defender to take a charge.

—Chris Ballard, SI, April 23, 2007

Nash could drive or drill it from deep.

PHOTOGRAPH BY JOHN W. MCDONOUGH

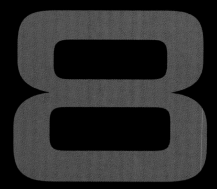

8

WALT FRAZIER

KNICKS 1967–1977
CAVALIERS 1977–1980

" Nicknamed Clyde after one half of the folk-hero bank robbing team of Bonnie and Clyde, Frazier ran an offense like a CEO and played D like a jewel thief. " —JACK McCALLUM

▸ CAREER AVERAGES OF 18.9 POINTS, 5.9 REBOUNDS AND 6.1 ASSISTS
▸ NAMED TO SEVEN NBA ALL-DEFENSIVE TEAMS

THE MAN WHO keeps the ball moving, the one with the handsome face framed by the mossy sideburns is Frazier. His teammates call him Clyde, a nickname derived from his penchant for the kind of wide-brimmed hats and pinstripes Warren Beatty wore in that movie. As his team's triggerman, Clyde penetrates the opposition's perimeter with the tempo of a soft-shoe man, full of hitches and hesitations, working to win the precious half-step advantage he needs in order to unbalance the defense and force it into retreat. If somebody converges to double-team him, it only means that another Knick is already free somewhere, and Clyde may be even better than that other Frazier, the one who fights out of Philadelphia, when it comes to hitting the open man.

—*Jerry Kirshenbaum, SI, December 8, 1969*

The Knicks were champs with Frazier at the helm.

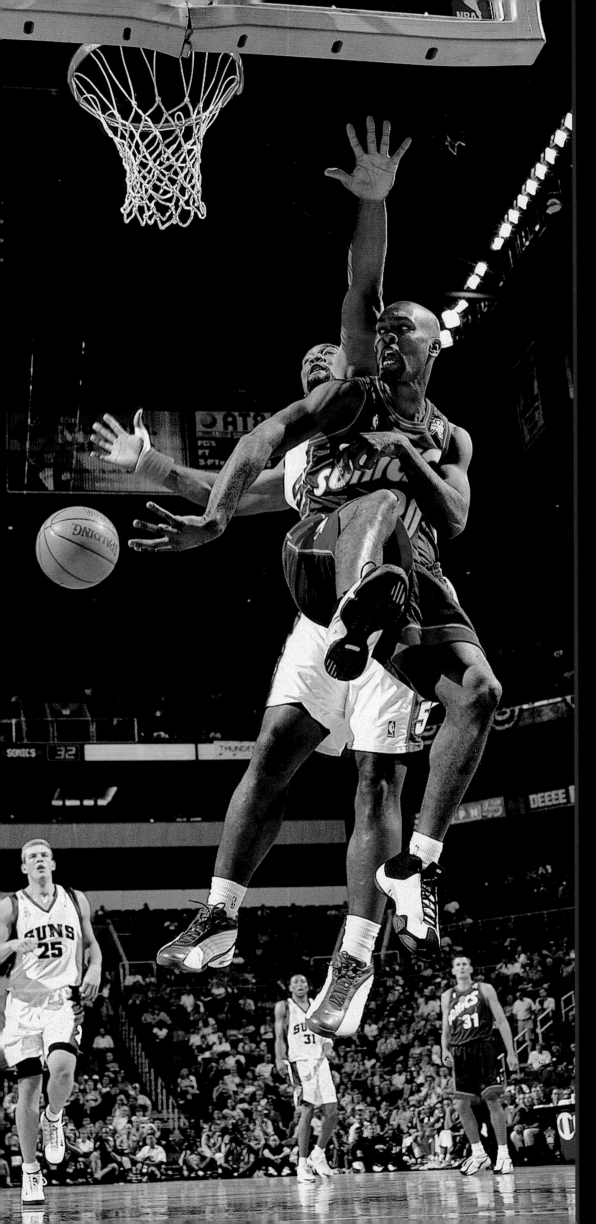

9

GARY PAYTON

SONICS 1990–2003
FOUR TEAMS THROUGH 2007

" As the only point guard who ever won a Defensive Player of the Year award, Payton ranks as arguably the best defender at his position. Brash and cocky, "The Glove"—a nickname bestowed on him during the 1993 playoffs—was a prolific scorer too. " —CHRIS MANNIX

▸ NINE-TIME ALL-STAR
▸ SEVEN SEASONS AVERAGING 20-PLUS POINTS

LIKE A POOL SHARK on a hot streak, Payton is capable of dropping in points in bunches. But he is more effective in the role of playmaker, drawing the double team and then delivering the perfect pass—a Seattleite dish, as it were—to a cutter or an open shooter. Yet Payton, an all-defensive first-team selection for six straight years, may be at his best when opponents have the ball. Surely the league's only player who routinely throws head fakes on defense, Payton is a master at juking as if to double-team, then dropping back like a free safety to intercept a pass. "I think one reason he's so frustrating to play against is that he gets it done on both ends," says teammate Vernon Maxwell. "He scores on you and then turns right around and starts playing some of the best defense in the NBA."

—L. Jon Wertheim, SI, December 20, 1999

Payton knew how to make teammates better.

PHOTOGRAPH BY JOHN W. MCDONOUGH

HORNETS 2005–2011
CLIPPERS 2011–PRESENT

Paul's arrival brought the Clippers a needed intensity.

PHOTOGRAPH BY JOHN W. MCDONOUGH

10

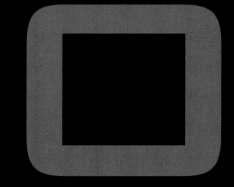

CHRIS PAUL

" Paul is a lion-hearted leader, grinning off the court while driving his teammates on it. CP3 surely isn't the strongest, fastest or most accurate point guard of his era, but he may be the smartest. " —LEE JENKINS

▸ THREE-TIME NBA ASSISTS LEADER
▸ SIX-TIME NBA STEALS LEADER

AT 6 FEET, Paul is nine inches shorter than Magic, but they carry themselves the same way, taskmasters disguised as cheerleaders. "These are people who have the ability to blend everybody around them together," Lamar Odom says, "whether they're taking you to dinner or kicking your ass."

—Lee Jenkins, SI, March 25, 2013

10 THE
BEST SHOOTING GUARDS

IN THE MOVIE *MEAN GIRLS*, LINDSAY LOHAN'S CHARACTER CADY EXPLAINS THAT SHE LIKES MATH BECAUSE "IT'S THE SAME IN EVERY COUNTRY." BASKETBALL'S TRADITION OF DEFINING PLAYERS' POSITIONS BY NUMBER—ONE FOR POINT GUARD, TWO FOR SHOOTING GUARD ETC.—OFFERS THE PROMISE OF MATHEMATICAL CLARITY. BUT IT'S A PROMISE THAT IS NOT KEPT, BECAUSE IN BASKETBALL THE NUMBERS DON'T ALWAYS STAND FOR THE SAME THING.

CONSIDER OSCAR ROBERTSON, WHO WAS HIS TEAM'S QUARTERBACK, BUT WHO PLAYED STRONG INSIDE AND IN THREE SEASONS HAD MORE REBOUNDS THAN ASSISTS (THOUGH HE HAD BOTH IN PRODIGIOUS QUANTITY). WHEN A PLAYER FILLS UP THE STAT SHEET LIKE HE DID, HE DEFIES CATEGORIZATION. INSTEAD OF A NUMBER, PLAYERS LIKE HIM SHOULD HAVE THEIR OWN SYMBOL, PERHAPS AN AMPERSAND. OTHER LEADING AMPERSANDS MIGHT INCLUDE LEBRON JAMES, AND . . . WELL, THERE'S NOT TOO MANY OF THEM, REALLY.

BUT OUR VOTING WENT BY THE TRADITIONAL POSITIONS, AND WHILE SOME PANELISTS DEEMED ROBERTSON AN ALLTIME GREAT POINT GUARD, OTHERS DECIDED HE WAS A TOP SHOOTING GUARD, AND THUS DOES HE EARN A SPOT IN BOTH TOP 10 LISTS. ROBERTSON WAS AMONG A HANDFUL OF PLAYERS TO RECEIVE VOTES AT MULTIPLE POSITIONS, BUT NO ONE ELSE FINISHED AS STRONGLY IN TWO OF THEM.

1

MICHAEL JORDAN

BULLS 1984–1993, 1994–1998
WIZARDS 2001–2003

" The most self-evident pick on any of these lists. Rings, scoring, defense, competitive fire. Perhaps most impressive, he adapted his game seamlessly as he aged. " —CHRIS BALLARD

▸ FIVE-TIME NBA MVP
▸ SIX-TIME NBA FINALS MVP

THINK WHAT a player would have to do to be regarded as Jordan's equal. He would have to construct dramatic book-ends on his basketball life by sinking championship-winning shots at the beginning of his college career (as North Carolina's Jordan did as a freshman in 1982) and at the end of his pro career (as the Chicago Bulls' Jordan did to beat the Utah Jazz in Game 6 of the NBA Finals last spring). He would have to win a championship trifecta with one style of play (take-it-to-the-hoop acrobatics) and then three more titles with a different style (controlled fadeaway jump shooting)—the basketball equivalent of writing a comedy as good as *Twelfth Night* and a tragedy as good as *Hamlet*. He would have to put his imprint not only on the game but also on the culture. And he would have to accomplish all that . . . without acting like a jerk.

—*Jack McCallum, SI, January 25, 1999*

His Airness led the NBA in scoring 10 times.

PHOTOGRAPH BY JOHN W. MCDONOUGH

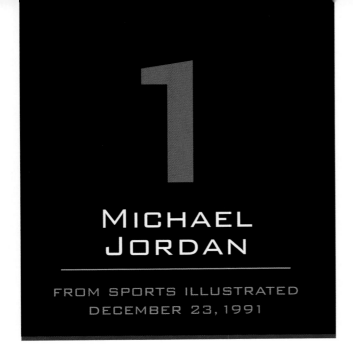

1

MICHAEL JORDAN

FROM SPORTS ILLUSTRATED
DECEMBER 23, 1991

AIR TO THE THRONE

Michael Jordan was already inspiring the loftiest of praise, including SI's Sportsman of the Year award, after he had won only the first of his six championships

BY JACK McCALLUM

T THE RELATIVELY tender age of 28, he stands alone on the mountaintop, unquestionably the most famous athlete on the planet and one of its most famous citizens of any kind. We've heard it so often that it's now a cliché, though nonetheless accurate: He transcends sports.

He will earn about $25 million in 1992, only $3.8 million of it from his day job—the rest, an astonishing $21.2 million, from a flood of endorsements. His name and his face are on sneakers, sandwiches, soft drinks and cereal boxes, to mention just a few items. He has a lovely and loving wife, two adorable sons and a relationship with his parents that is so good, the sappiest sitcom wouldn't touch it. He is bothered somewhat by tendinitis and a bone spur in his left knee but is otherwise in outstanding health. He has trouble off the tee from time to time, but his handicap is still in single figures and any number of professional tutors are at his beck and call.

And, so, despite a few esthetic drawbacks—near baldness, skinny legs, overly long basketball trunks and the continuing tendency to stick out his tongue—we honor Michael Jeffrey Jordan as our Sportsman of the Year for 1991.

It is a virtual certainty that since the award originated in 1954, no athlete has been as popular on a worldwide scale as Jordan is now and, for that matter, has been for the last several years. He has surpassed every standard by which we gauge the fame of an athlete.

"He has a level of popularity and a value as a commercial spokesman that is almost beyond comprehension," says Nova Lanktree, director of the Burns Sports Service in Chicago, an organization that has been lining up athletes for commercials and tracking their popularity for more than two decades. "It is a singular phenomenon. It never happened before and may not ever happen again."

Although it is the singularity of Jordan that is so often celebrated—no one dunks, smiles or sells sneakers the way he does—it is no coincidence that he is being honored by SI only after his *team*, the Chicago Bulls, won a championship. Jordan's seven-year NBA career has been, curiously, both a rocket to stardom and a struggle for vindication. To many NBA observers, the Bulls had to win it all before Jordan could conclusively prove that he was more than a high-flying sideshow or a long, loud ring of the cash register. They did. And so he did.

Superstars should be judged, first and foremost, for their consistency, their ability to produce over the long haul, as Jordan most assuredly has. But the most unforgettable of the breed also offer a collection of moments, rare and incandescent, and Jordan has given us a wide assortment of those: writhing and twisting his way through the Celtics to score 49 and 63 points at Boston Garden in the 1986 playoffs; exploding for 40 points to win the MVP award at his "home" All-Star game at Chicago Stadium in '88; dribbling the length of the floor, pulling up and hitting a 14-foot jump shot to send Game 3 of last year's Finals, which the Bulls went on to win, into overtime.

Is Jordan the greatest ever? A definitive answer is impossible, of course, as it has been whenever the question has been applied to Wilt Chamberlain, Oscar Robertson, Larry Bird or Magic Johnson. But a case can certainly be made. Of that distinguished quartet, only Chamberlain could begin to match Jordan's pure athleticism, but put that aside for a moment and consider his skills and the way he plays the game:

Jordan is now a better shooter than Bird, not from long range, certainly, but from 20 feet in. "I don't do much shooting in the summer anymore, so I don't completely understand it myself," says Jordan. "But it's a fact. Everything about it—my mechanics, when to take the shot, the release—feels better and smoother."

He is not a better passer than the Magic of the 1980s, but were the Bulls, like the Lakers, a fast-break team and were Jordan, like Magic, a point guard, he very well might be. And in half-court situations, when called upon to give up the ball under pressure and find the open man at the last conceivable second, he is without peer.

Jordan never put up rebounding numbers from the backcourt like those of Robertson, who averaged 7.5 per game over 14 seasons. But the Big O played in an era when, at 6' 5", he was often among the bigger players on the floor, while Jordan, in the era of the seven-footer, is no worse than the second-best rebounding guard in today's game (behind the Portland Trail Blazers' Clyde Drexler). Jordan and Robertson are similar in a way, dynamic, demanding and fearless leaders who command nothing less than total respect on the floor. But Robertson, though a superb athlete, was subject to the laws of gravity (as Jordan is not) and was never nearly as exciting.

Can Jordan dominate a game in the manner of Chamberlain— he of the 100- point game and the 50.4-point scoring average (in 1961–62)? Not when today's double-teaming and trapping can take the ball out of one man's hands for long stretches of the game. But by dint of nonstop effort, a *rage* to play that Wilt never possessed, Jordan comes close. "Every single game, Jordan plays every single play like it's his last," says Los Angeles Clippers guard Doc Rivers. Then, too, Wilt never provided the level of anticipation that Jordan does merely

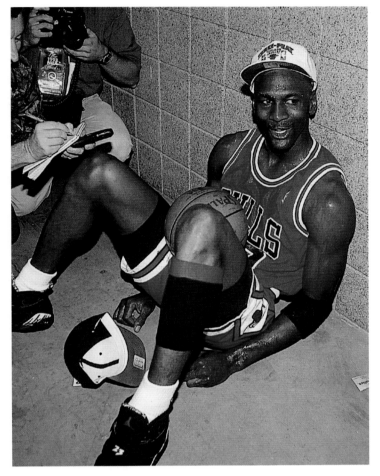

Only after winning it all could Jordan let himself take it easy.

by touching the ball. Out comes the tongue, from side to side goes the head, and down goes the ball in a hard dribble. *What's going to happen? What will he do now?* Julius Erving came close to inspiring that same edge-of-the-seat drama, but the Doctor never had Jordan's offensive repertoire, lacking mainly the pull-up jumper that makes the contemporary Jordan more unstoppable than ever.

"Michael—he's the best," says San Antonio Spurs coach Larry Brown. "I grew up with Connie Hawkins. I saw Julius at his peak. No one went through the ACC like David Thompson. I love Magic and Larry. But Michael, as far as what I've seen. . . . " Brown stops and shakes his head. "I'd pay money to see him play. I'd pay money to see him *practice*."

There are times when his teammates would no doubt pay money so that Jordan would *not* practice. His almost psychotic competitiveness in even the most casual practice situation has caused some strain over the years, much of which has been chronicled in *The Jordan Rules*, the best-seller written by the *Chicago Tribune*'s Sam Smith. But, ultimately, what hath it wrought? A much grittier Chicago team, that's certain.

Jordan is, as usual, playing superbly. Never mind the scoring, a category in which he has led the NBA for the last five seasons and in which he is leading again. He and forwards Scottie Pippen and Horace Grant

have become like a Bermuda Triangle on defense, swallowing up offenses with their court-covering capabilities, and that is why Chicago is clearly the best team in the NBA. Jordan's detractors would theorize that he has now stepped back and given players like Pippen and Grant the chance to breathe and make a name for themselves. But in point of fact, Jordan's own will to succeed, as thorny as it may sometimes be, has inspired his teammates to reach their potential.

"I look forward to playing now, more than ever," Jordan said recently, relaxing in his hotel suite in Berkeley, Calif., before a game against the Golden State Warriors. "It's the only place I can get relief from what's happening off the court. It's always been that way to a certain extent, but it's even more so now. Basketball is my escape, my refuge. It seems that everything else is so . . . so busy and complicated."

Busy he's used to. Complicated, maybe not. For perhaps the first time in his life, Jordan is sensing a backlash against his fame, a subtle dissatisfaction with the whole idea of Michael Jordan. He has heard it in all the talk about *The Jordan Rules*, he has read it in letters to the editor, read it between the lines. "Signs are starting to show that people are tired of hearing about Michael Jordan's positive image and Michael Jordan's positive influence," said Mr. Positive Image and Positive Influence. "Five, six, seven years at the pinnacle of success, and it's got to start turning around."

There are not many 28-year-old multimillionaires who are forced into such introspection about their images, and in all likelihood, a more cautious, less childlike Jordan will evolve out of his self-examination. David Burns, president of Burns Sports Service, says he doesn't see any backlash against Jordan: "He's as wildly popular as ever and still worth every dollar any advertiser wants to pay him." But Jordan feels it is better to hear the whistle in the distance than to get run over by the train, and as a remedy for overkill, he's talking about reducing his off-the-court commitments, taking a step back, becoming a more private person.

"I don't need my name in lights to keep going," says Jordan. "I know people think I do, but I don't. If you told me in college that within a year my face would be all over the world and millions of people would know my name, I'd have said you were crazy. I certainly didn't turn it down when it came my way, but I didn't ask for it, either."

He sure got it, though, and now any conversation about him tends to sound like a global marketing report. Remember the cynical bumper sticker that came along in the Acquisitive Eighties? THE ONE WITH THE MOST TOYS IN THE END WINS. Well, Jordan has the most toys. Game's over. He's won. So, let's just enjoy the world's best basketball player at the height of his powers.

The game, after all, is what made Jordan what he is today, and fortunately, the game is still what he lives and breathes for. He may talk about stepping out of the spotlight, but it's not going to happen for a while, not so long as there's a competitive muscle twitching in his body. The view from the mountaintop is breathtaking, and there's no place that Michael Jordan would rather be. Look up and revel in him, for his equal will not soon be along. ∎

PHOTOGRAPH BY MANNY MILLAN

LAKERS 1996–PRESENT

Bryant's career scoring average is 25.5 points.

" No star of the new millennium was more committed to fulfilling the standards of Michael Jordan. Bryant thrived on conflict, peaking with his 2010 Game 7 victory over the rival Celtics for his fifth title—one more than rival Shaquille O'Neal. " —IAN THOMSEN

▸ FOURTH IN CAREER POINTS
▸ 2007–08 NBA MVP

KOBE BRYANT

UNLIKE CHAMBERLAIN, Bryant often had to bring up the ball, free himself on screens, and dribble this way and that to create space and get off shots. Wilt's 100-point night was all roast beef and potatoes; Kobe's 81-point night was a smorgasbord, with six layups or dunks, and 22 jumpers that came from all angles.

—Jack McCallum, SI, January 30, 2006

3

JERRY WEST

LAKERS 1960–1974

" Classic form made him the model for the league's logo, but also masked inner turmoil—perfectionism, feelings of unworthiness, nerves that led him to throw up before games. He won only one title as a player, but bagged many more as an executive. " —ALEXANDER WOLFF

▸ CAREER AVERAGES OF 27.0 POINTS, 5.8 REBOUNDS AND 6.7 ASSISTS
▸ 14-TIME ALL-STAR

WHEN WEST first came to the Lakers he was more or less a one-handed shooter; opposing guards played him a full step to his right. But he has worked out that weakness in long lonely hours on the court. He has the quickest shot in the game—it takes no more than half a pick to get him free. He moves exceptionally well without the ball. Because of his speed West makes everything look rather routine. Against Oscar Robertson in the first half of the recent All-Star Game at St. Louis, West made a full head-and-shoulder fake to the left, crossed over with his left leg and suddenly had a step and a half on Oscar—and sank his shot. It looked almost too simple. "You never really stop West," says the Celtics' Red Auerbach. "You try any number of ways—play him close, loose, keep him away from the ball, and even then he'll get his 25 or 30 points."

—John Underwood, SI, February 8, 1965

West was a relentless and unforgiving perfectionist.
PHOTOGRAPH BY LONG PHOTOGRAPHY INC.

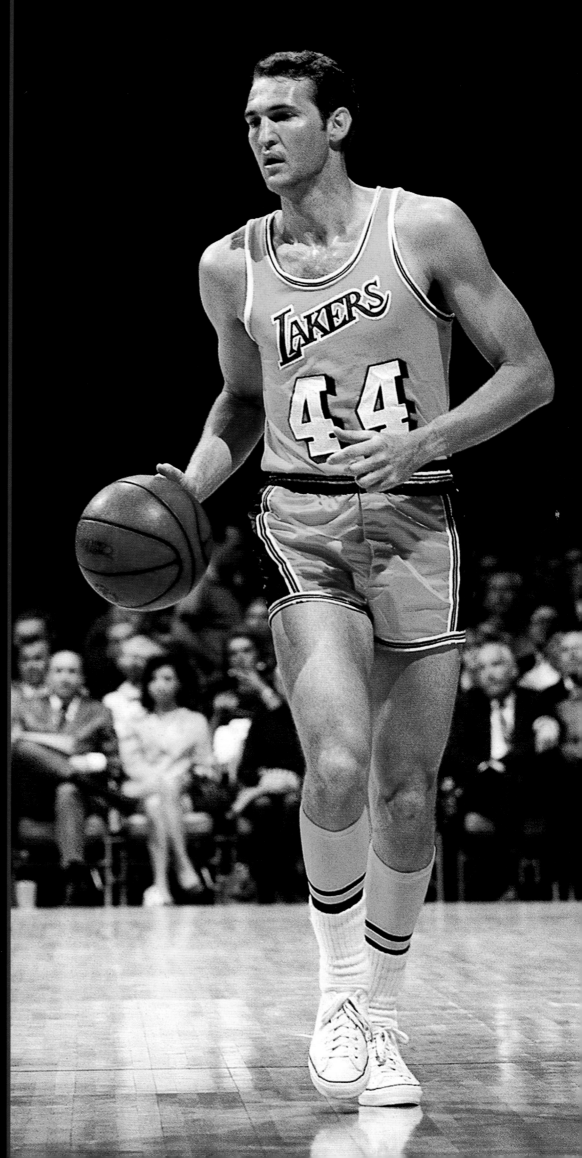

4

DWYANE WADE

"He attacks defenses like Jim Brown with both elusive speed and straight-ahead strength. D-Wade has had several nicknames, but when he led the pre-LeBron Heat to the 2006 title, you could have called him Michael." —JACK McCALLUM

▸ 2008-09 NBA SCORING CHAMPION
▸ 2006 NBA FINALS MVP

AT EVERY pivotal point in Miami's oddly flawed playoff run, Wade had lifted his play to a personal high. But in those final four games—with every Dallas player, coach and fan keying on him—he punctuated a rise unlike any the league has seen, averaging 39.2 points, 8.2 rebounds, 3.5 assists and 2.5 steals.

—*S.L. Price, SI, December 11, 2006*

Wade attacked the rim with athleticism and abandon.

PHOTOGRAPH BY GREG NELSON

CLYDE DREXLER

BLAZERS 1983–1995
ROCKETS 1995–1998

" A slithery driver and elegant dunker, he was unstoppable in the open floor and beautiful to behold at the rim. Drexler carried Portland to the Finals twice and teamed with Hakeem Olajuwon to win it for Houston in '95. " —LEE JENKINS

▸ CAREER AVERAGES OF 20.4 POINTS, 6.1 REBOUNDS AND 5.6 ASSISTS
▸ 10-TIME ALL-STAR

HE'S KEENLY aware that his natural ability has been a cudgel with which his detractors have knocked his play. "He's got talent," they would say, "but he doesn't know how to channel it." That criticism still drives Drexler crazy. Placidly crazy, but crazy nevertheless. "Athleticism is something you work on," says Drexler. "I came out of college with a 43-inch vertical jump, and I think I could still reach that on a day when I'm totally injury-free. But don't you think I worked on that jump every single day? I was a gym rat, just like any of those other guys who supposedly didn't have much natural ability. The guys I consider superior athletes are people like Jerry Rice, Michael [Jordan] and Hakeem Olajuwon, guys who are obviously naturally talented but who also have a high skill level. I'd like to be considered in their class."

—Jack McCallum, SI, May 11, 1992

There's a reason he was nicknamed The Glide.

PHOTOGRAPH BY JOHN W. MCDONOUGH

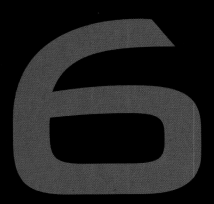

6

ALLEN IVERSON

" Who needs practice? Around the new millennium, nobody was more exciting to watch than Philadelphia's one-man show, a 6-foot dervish with cornrows who hurled himself into men a full foot taller and often found a way through them. " —LEE JENKINS

- 2000–01 NBA MVP
- FOUR-TIME NBA SCORING CHAMPION

IVERSON IS the quickest player the league has ever seen, quicker than Tiny Archibald, quicker than Calvin Murphy, quicker even than Rickey Green, who had quickness and not much else. What Michael Jordan did to the notion of space, Iverson does to speed. He dropped 31 on the Lakers' Nick Van Exel in a Sixers win in Los Angeles on Jan. 4, and X is still not sure Iverson wasn't just a rumor. There's so much Iverson still needs to learn, but for pure, raw rush nobody this side of Jordan is more fun to watch. Jordan's teammate Ron Harper once said that Iverson is so quick, "I have to rub my eyes." Sixers assistant Mo Cheeks, the human blur who helped lead Philly to the 1983 NBA title, says, "In my prime, I think I'd have to give Allen a half step. Maybe a step." And Chicago Bulls coach Phil Jackson has said, "I'd pay to watch Allen play."

—Rick Reilly, SI, March 9, 1998

Though just 165 pounds, Iverson was fearless in the lane.

PHOTOGRAPHS BY BOB ROSATO

7

Gervin possessed a great first step.

PHOTOGRAPH BY MANNY MILLAN

"The Iceman wasn't a gunner; he was a lethal scorer. He could put it in the bucket from anywhere, and in each of the four seasons he won the scoring crown, he shot at least 50% from the floor." —MARK BECHTEL

AS HIS MONIKER implies, Gervin does all this marvelous stuff while appearing to be in a deep coma—face expressionless, eyelids drooping, the Iceman to the letter. It is difficult to distinguish between when he is pushing hard and when he is sleeping on the job, so smooth and graceful are his movements.

—*Curry Kirkpatrick, SI, March 6, 1978*

▸ CAREER AVERAGE OF 25.1 POINTS
▸ 12-TIME ALL-STAR

GEORGE GERVIN

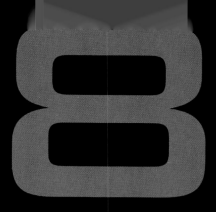

OSCAR ROBERTSON

ROYALS 1960–1970
BUCKS 1970–1974

" He wasn't just the first great all-around player. He was the finest scoring guard the league had ever seen and, by averaging a triple double one year, the first to show that you could dominate from the backcourt. " —ALEXANDER WOLFF

▸ 1961–62 AVERAGES:
30.8 POINTS, 12.5 REBOUNDS AND 11.4 ASSISTS
▸ 1963–64 NBA MVP

THE BIG O was the first guard who took defenders where he wanted to go, using his well-muscled 220 pounds to back them down, his head always up, looking for cutters, wary of double teams, waving teammates to open spots or maybe carving out space to release his deadly jumper, held in one hand, far above his head, virtually unblockable. The astonishing thing about Robertson's stats is not only that he averaged [a triple double] in 1961–62 but also that he came so close to that triple-double standard so many other times. In '63–64 he missed a season triple double because he averaged "only" 9.9 rebounds. Consider: In his first eight seasons Robertson never averaged fewer than 29.2 points and 9.5 assists, and in his first five seasons he never averaged fewer than nine rebounds.

—Jack McCallum, SI, July 15, 2002

The Big O said he never looked at stat sheets.

PHOTOGRAPH BY WALTER IOOSS JR.

9

SAM JONES

CELTICS 1957–1969

" Arguably one of the most effective clutch shooters in NBA history, Jones was also low-key: He was defined by stealthy movement without the ball, and he had an uncanny bank shot and a humility atypical of scorers. " —IAN THOMSEN

▸ CAREER PLAYOFF AVERAGE OF 18.9 POINTS
▸ FIVE-TIME ALL-STAR

K.C. JONES gives me the ball at the top of the key. He rolls up alongside me, and we both stand stock-still for a split second; we are setting up a double screen for Sam Jones. Around comes Sam, and I hand him the ball. Sam jumps and plops in an easy one. Next time we get the ball, K.C. gives it to me at the top of the key. He rolls up alongside me, and we both stand still for a second. Here is Sam, going to beat hell, and he starts around us. I quickly hand the ball back to K.C, who wheels and cuts in for the basket. Sure, you can call this plain old-fashioned basketball tactics. But we have so many options to this play. I call it psychology. Now, over on their bench, the coach leaps up and yells, "Who the devil is guarding Jones?" and they all look a little embarrassed, including those who are not sure which Jones he means. I don't suppose we can take credit for that, but it helps too.

—Bill Russell with Bob Ottum, SI, October 25, 1965

Jones played on 10 title teams.

PHOTOGRAPH BY WALTER IOOSS JR.

Miller loved to get under an opponent's skin.

PACERS 1987–2005

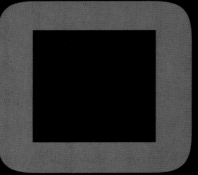

10
REGGIE MILLER

" Few shooters could do as much with as little space as Miller, whose eight points in 8.9 seconds against the Knicks in the 1995 playoffs ranks as one of the NBA's most memorable moments. " —CHRIS MANNIX

▸ CAREER PLAYOFF AVERAGE OF 20.6 POINTS
▸ SIX CONFERENCE FINALS APPEARANCES

"WHAT MAKES Reggie special," says Indiana assistant Rick Carlisle, "is this combination of things that goes on inside of him. He's got the gunslinger's mentality, the I-can-make-anything attitude, but he's also a man with a self-discipline that's totally directed toward getting him ready to play."

—*Jack McCallum, SI May 22, 2000*

10

THE

BEST SMALL FORWARDS

IF ALL OUR TOP SMALL FORWARDS GATHERED FOR A DINNER, TWO PLAYERS WHO WERE DIFFERENT STYLISTICALLY MIGHT FIND MUCH TO COMMISERATE ABOUT: LEBRON JAMES AND RICK BARRY. THE TITLE FOR THEIR CONVERSATION: "DECISIONS, DECISIONS."

LONG BEFORE JAMES, TO MUCH JEERING, TOOK HIS TALENTS FROM CLEVELAND TO SOUTH BEACH, BARRY MADE ANOTHER SCORNED JOURNEY, EVEN IF HIS TRAVELS DIDN'T TAKE HIM VERY FAR—AT FIRST ANYWAY. WHEN BARRY LEFT THE SAN FRANCISCO WARRIORS FOR THE ABA'S OAKLAND OAKS, BECOMING THE FIRST STAR TO SIGN WITH THE NEW LEAGUE, HE WAS SEEN AS "THE EPITOME OF THE DISLOYAL MONEY GRUBBER," AS RON REID WROTE IN SI. TO MAKE MATTERS WORSE, WHEN THE OAKS FRANCHISE DIED AND WAS EVENTUALLY REBORN AS THE VIRGINIA SQUIRES, BARRY BALKED AND INSULTED HIS NEW HOME. "I DON'T WANT [MY SON] TO GO DOWN THERE TO SCHOOL AND LEARN TO SPEAK WITH A SOUTHERN ACCENT," BARRY TOLD SI IN 1970. "HE'LL COME HOME FROM SCHOOL SAYING, 'HI Y'ALL, DAAD.' I SURE DON'T WANT THAT." IN SHORT, HIS DECISION MADE JAMES'S LOOK SMOOTHLY MANAGED BY COMPARISON.

LIKE JAMES, BARRY DID WIN A RING, THOUGH HIS CAME ONLY AFTER HE RETURNED TO THE NBA AND THE WARRIORS. ONE OF THESE TWO FORWARDS WOULD DEFINITELY HAVE BEEN BETTER OFF STAYING AT HOME.

1

LARRY BIRD

CELTICS 1979–1992

" He wasn't fast, but in-your-yard quick. That off-the-shoulder jumper looked blockable, but always seemed to get cleanly away. " —ALEXANDER WOLFF

▸ THREE-TIME NBA MVP
▸ CAREER AVERAGES OF 24.3 POINTS, 10.0 REBOUNDS AND 6.3 ASSISTS

PISTONS COACH Chuck Daly remembers Bird's drilling a jumper in front of the Detroit bench two seasons ago, then stepping back and "knocking me ass over tin cups. I think he did it purposely. He's just a tough guy. He has almost the perfect attitude." Even before he made 11 straight in the three-point shootout at the All-Star Game, Bird, in all likelihood, had the contest won in the locker room when he told the seven other competitors, "All right, who's playing for second?" When your boasts are empty, you're a weenie and a stiff. When you back them up, you're a legend. Bird has become a legend. "I can still see Larry getting on the bus after a shootaround," remembers teammate Rick Carlisle, "and saying, 'Well, we just got done shooting basketball. Now it's time to go to our free hotel, have a free meal, then play the game. It's a tough life.' To Larry, this is special. He loves it. He couldn't imagine doing anything else."

—Jack McCallum, SI, March 3, 1986

Bird helped revive, and personify, Celtic pride.

2

LeBron James

CAVALIERS 2003–2010, 2014–
HEAT 2010–2014

❝ Hyped like no amateur in sports history, The King has lived up to all the acclaim. He has revolutionized the idea of what a basketball star can do, becoming an adept ballhandler and passer with a ferocious post game and lethal shot. ❞ —LEE JENKINS

▸ FOUR-TIME NBA MVP
▸ CAREER AVERAGES OF 27.5 POINTS, 7.2 REBOUNDS AND 6.9 ASSISTS

"THE GAME IS a house, and some players only have one or two windows in their house because they can't absorb any more light," says Mike Krzyzewski, head coach of Team USA. "When I met LeBron, he only had a few windows, but then he learned how beautiful the game can be, so he put more windows in. Now he sees the damn game so well, it's like he lives in a glass building. He has entered a state of mastery. There's nothing he can't do. He's one of the unique sports figures of all time, really, and he's right in that area where it's all come together." A voracious mind has caught up with a supreme body. The marriage is a marvel. "He has no position," says an NBA scout. "His position is to do whatever he wants. There's never been anything like it."

—*Lee Jenkins, SI, December 10, 2012*

James won his first title against the Thunder in 2012.

PHOTOGRAPH BY GREG NELSON

THE KING EARNS A RING

No player entered the NBA with greater expectations than LeBron James, and none had as many naysayers to silence when he finally won his first championship

BY LEE JENKINS

JAMIE EPSTEIN AND SHAUN Kolnick were married last Saturday night at the Ritz Carlton in Coconut Grove, Fla., and when the young couple arrived at the grand ballroom, they spotted an uninvited guest on the terrace. LeBron James sat among the swaying palm trees, his two sons climbing over him like help defenders, seven-year-old LeBron Jr. on his lap and five-year-old Bryce Maximus on his knee. Members of the wedding party, about 20 deep in tuxedos and gowns, fought to press their noses to the window.

Jamie and Shaun took the requisite photographs with bridesmaids, groomsmen and relatives, but on their mantel one snapshot will dwarf the rest. As James posed between Jamie and Shaun with a giant grin, he offered his congratulations and they offered their mazel tovs, because all of them were experiencing a rite of passage. All of them were getting a ring.

James has grown in front of the world's eyes, from a prodigy in Akron to a colossus in Cleveland to a polarizing sun god in Miami. At 4:15 a.m. last Saturday, as James struggled to sleep, he felt himself enter a new stage. "It just finally hit me," he wrote in a text message to Maverick Carter, his childhood friend and business manager. "I'm a champion." Twelve hours later, James sat under overcast skies on the Ritz terrace, wearing a white T-shirt with the slogan EARNED NOT GIVEN and sipping a Sprite. He was still sleepless and in no hurry to nap. "I'm having all my best dreams wrapped into one," he said.

Pressure remains, the burden of the supernaturally gifted, but in a different form. All the breathless questions that hounded James since the Cleveland days—Can you close a game? Can you lead a team? Can you win a title?—are gone, sunk at the bottom of Biscayne Bay. Twenty-nine teams should be very afraid, because James has breached the championship levee, just as Michael Jordan did in 1991. Jordan was 28, and he won five more titles in the next seven years, even with a break for baseball. James is 27, and for the first time he will get to play without a baboon on his back. "With freedom," Heat president Pat Riley says.

The reality show that kicked off two years ago—"when I sat up there and decided I was going to take my talents to South Beach"—reached its climax as he gathered his teammates at American Airlines Arena before Game 5 of the NBA Finals against Oklahoma City. "This is what I told them," he says. "If someone came to you right now and told you, 'If you don't win tonight you won't see your family again,' how would you play? Approach this game like your family is in danger. How bad do you want to see your family again?"

James became the first player in nine years to clinch a championship with a triple double, a feat that evoked John Stockton and Karl Malone—if they inhabited one body. Here was a 6' 8", 250-pound point guard cast as a power forward, beating two and three defenders with drives and dishes, whichever he was in the mood to choose. In Game 5 he scored 26 points with 11 rebounds and 13 assists, eight of which led to three-pointers by five different teammates, accounting for 60 points in a 121–106 throttling of the Thunder.

LeBron was sure he would sob like Michael Jordan ("I remember him with the trophy," he says), but he responded more like Magic Johnson. ("I remember him spraying champagne and yelling, 'Yeah!'") James hopped up and down on the sideline, the way college football players do before kickoff, and unleashed a smile that no one but family and friends have glimpsed since the whole Decision fiasco. "I know why it came out so big," James says. "I've been waiting for it a long time."

He punctuated one of the best regular seasons in the modern era with one of the best playoffs, leading the Heat with 30.3 points, 9.7 rebounds and 5.6 assists, while shooting 50% and guarding everyone from Carmelo Anthony to Rajon Rondo, Russell Westbrook to Kevin Durant. But after James retreated to the locker room, where teammates bathed him in a Budweiser—Dom Perignon cocktail, he caught a scare. He couldn't find his Finals MVP trophy.

"Where's my trophy?" James hollered, rummaging through his locker. "I left it right here!" On the way to the press conference, where the MVP trophy was waiting all along, he relaxed a bit. "It's just an individual award, anyway," he says. "It's not the one that matters." He took the Larry O'Brien Trophy from the podium and cradled it like a third son, and when friends offered to help carry it down a hallway, he waved them off.

James united with Dwyane Wade and Chris Bosh in Miami in July 2010 and perhaps no team in sports history has come under more scrutiny than the Heat. When James and coach Eric Spoelstra brushed shoulders, it was Bump Gate. When players broke down in the locker room, it was *The Crying Game*. The Mavericks beat Miami in the Finals last June, and the catcalls amplified.

But this season the Heat grew comfortable in its tropical Petri dish, and no one found it all that strange when 30 cameras filmed James as he dressed. "In my quiet time, I do think to myself, This is crazy," James says. "But it comes with the territory. You have to embrace it." At the arena before Game 5 his uniform was laid out on the floor at his locker. James pumped up the stereo and bopped his head to Young Jeezy. The cameras stared at him, and he stared back, lost in the lenses. They would never look at him the same. "It's the way this world works," Spoelstra says. "You can't win unless you win." ∎

3

JULIUS ERVING

SQUIRES 1971–1973
NETS 1973–1976
76ERS 1976–1987

No player soared as gracefully as Dr. J.

PHOTOGRAPH BY NEIL LEIFER/NBAE/GETTY IMAGES

" Every high flyer since the mid-'70s—Jordan, Dominique, LeBron—owes a debt to The Doctor, whose in-air artistry would be the stuff of legend if it weren't on film. He won a championship at age 33 and dunked at age 63. " —JACK McCALLUM

▸ THREE-TIME ABA MVP
▸ 1980–81 NBA MVP

HE TOOK took to rebounding one-handed with an arm extended so he could propel himself downcourt to start the break. There was never anything like the young Julius in the open court—huge strides eating up the hardwood, mammoth hands swallowing up the ball before slamming it through the hoop.

—Peter Carry, SI, May 4, 1987

4

SCOTTIE PIPPEN

BULLS 1987–1998, 2003–2004
TWO OTHER TEAMS

" When deifying Michael Jordan, remember this: Jordan's Bulls didn't get past the first round until Pippen arrived. Polished on both ends, and with a feathery jump shot and a willingness to defer, Pippen was the perfect second superstar. " —CHRIS MANNIX

▸ SIX NBA TITLES
▸ SEVEN-TIME ALL-STAR

THE CAREER of Scottie Pippen will no doubt be defined by a single act: his refusal to reenter a 1994 playoff game because he wasn't being given the last shot. While that moment of pique or fear or whatever it was means something, it should not mean everything. Pippen was a second banana with top-banana skills. Judging purely on versatility, the pride of Central Arkansas—who could shoot, rebound, pass and defend—had few peers. Michael Jordan's status as first among equals was confirmed when the 1992 Dream Team prepared for and played in the Olympics, but Pippen was arguably the second-best player on that team. Yet once Jordan left Pippen's universe, Pippen never won another title. Some are meant to follow, not lead, and after a while, Pippen seemed to know that's how he would always be most comfortable.

—*Jack McCallum, SI, October 18, 2004*

The versatile Pippen averaged 16.6 points per game.

5

ELGIN BAYLOR

LAKERS 1958-1972

" He could score, rebound and pass. An early prototype of the later do-it-all forwards, Baylor was one of the great scorers of his generation (once averaging 38-plus points a game) yet never seemed selfish. " —CHRIS BALLARD

‣ CAREER AVERAGES OF 27.4 POINTS, 13.5 REBOUNDS AND 4.3 ASSISTS
‣ EIGHT NBA FINALS APPEARANCES

BAYLOR'S INCALCULABLE asset is that he can play any position on the court in a sport which, like most others, has largely been taken over by experts in each department. At 6' 5", he gives anyone (including Boston center Bill Russell) a battle for the tip-off. He brings the ball upcourt and sets up plays with the speed and deception of a backcourtman like Bob Cousy. His strength, agility and willingness to match muscle under the boards enable him to rebound with the best. He has every shot in the book and has demonstrated the imagination to invent new ones. Finally, like the stopper every baseball team needs to win an important game on pitching alone, Baylor has repeatedly held the rival high-scoring star to a bare minimum of points through tenacious defensive play.

—Jeremiah Tax, SI, April 6, 1959

Baylor was Top 5 in MVP voting seven times.

PHOTOGRAPHS BY LONG PHOTOGRAPHY INC. (LEFT) AND RUSS HALFORD

6
JOHN HAVLICEK

> " He'll always be remembered for *that* steal, which is apt, because it was the epitome of Havlicek as a player: always in the right spot, always around at the end of a game, always coming up a winner. " —MARK BECHTEL

› EIGHT NBA TITLES
› CAREER AVERAGES OF 20.8 POINTS AND 6.3 REBOUNDS

IN THE THREE years during which Ohio State won one NCAA championship and lost two in the finals, Havlicek drew them all: Lenny Chappel of Wake Forest, Terry Dischinger of Purdue, Cotton Nash of Kentucky. "We even put him on a couple of centers," says coach Fred Taylor. "He'd get upset if he didn't think he was guarding the best." And Havlicek made a discovery: "I knew from the first time I played this game that the toughest guy to score on was the guy who kept after me all the time, nose-to-nose, basket-to-basket. The opposite is also true. The toughest guy to defend against is the guy who keeps running. Who never lets up. Never lets you relax. Who sneaks one in on you the first time you drag your feet. I never worried about the physical part, killing myself running or anything like that. I read once where a doctor said you'd pass out before you did any real damage. I never passed out."

—John Underwood, SI, October 28, 1974

Havlicek made eight NBA All-Defensive teams.

7

RICK BARRY

WARRIORS 1965–1967, 1972–1978
FOUR TEAMS THROUGH 1980

" No forward was a better passer,
free throw shooter, instinctive scorer or
defender—"Larry Bird," one scout
said of Barry, "before there was a
Larry Bird." " —ALEXANDER WOLFF

▸ CAREER AVERAGES OF
24.8 POINTS, 6.7 REBOUNDS
AND 4.9 ASSISTS
▸ SEVEN FREE THROW TITLES

AS LONG AS he scores 30, 40, even
50 points a game, Barry must
be prepared to face accusations
about gunning. Coach Bill Sharman
defends Barry. "Selfish?" Sharman
says. "They always say the shooter
is selfish. That's his job—to shoot.
Did they ever say Russell was
selfish for taking all the rebounds?"

—*Frank Deford, SI, February 13, 1967*

Barry led the Warriors to a title in 1975.

PHOTOGRAPH BY FRED KAPLAN

LAKERS 1982–1994

Worthy shot 54.4% over 143 postseason games.

PHOTOGRAPH BY RICHARD MACKSON

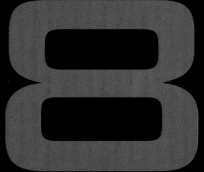

" Oh-so-smooth James sometimes got lost in the Showtime circus of the 1980s Lakers. But Magic Johnson always knew where to find him, especially in the postseason, where the Carolina product routinely increased his production. " —JACK McCALLUM

▸ CAREER PLAYOFF AVERAGE OF 21.1 POINTS
▸ 1988 NBA FINALS MVP

JAMES WORTHY

A FEW PEOPLE still feel Los Angeles blundered in the 1982 draft by taking Worthy over Atlanta's Dominique Wilkins, who led the NBA in scoring this year. "Wilkins missed over a thousand shots this season," coach Pat Riley points out. "James has barely taken a thousand shots."

—Bruce Newman, SI, May 19, 1986

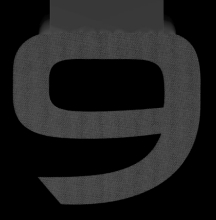

9

DOMINIQUE WILKINS

HAWKS 1982–1994
FOUR TEAMS THROUGH 1999

" The Human Highlight Film's run as one of the league's elite scorers and most electrifying players elevated the Hawks to their most sustained period of excellence in Atlanta, with four consecutive 50-plus win seasons. " —MARK BECHTEL

▸ CAREER AVERAGE OF
  24.8 POINTS
▸ NINE-TIME ALL-STAR

SAY THE NAME Dominique Wilkins and what comes to mind is a half-out-of-control, uncoachable dunking machine. He is a showman, no doubt, not a well-rounded player. He just scores. So check this out: In his ninth season Wilkins is now a complete player, or at least as close to one as he is ever likely to be. Which is pretty darn close, within hand-checking distance of Michael Jordan, Larry Bird and Magic Johnson, the guys who win all the big trophies. For the first time in his career Wilkins is ranked in the top 20 in the NBA in categories (three-point shooting, rebounding and steals) other than scoring. And then there are those amazing assists, amazing because in years past giving the ball to Wilkins was like giving the ball to an eight-year-old street urchin—it was gone for good.

—*Rick Telander, SI, March 4, 1991*

Wilkins and the rim often saw eye-to-eye.

PHOTOGRAPH BY NATHANIEL S. BUTLER/NBAE/GETTY IMAGES

10

PAUL
PIERCE

CELTICS 1998–2013
NETS 2013–PRESENT

❝ His loyalty was rewarded when Kevin Garnett and Ray Allen joined him in Boston. That's when "The Truth" emerged: His scoring and playmaking earned him the championship and MVP of the 2008 Finals. ❞ —IAN THOMSEN

▸ 10-TIME ALL-STAR
▸ CAREER AVERAGE OF
21.3 POINTS

IN GAME 1 [of the 2008 Finals] he left the court with a knee injury, but he returned to hit two three-pointers and give Boston the lead for good. In Game 2 he led the Celtics in scoring and held off L.A.'s desperate comeback with two key free throws and a block. With Boston down 18 at the half of Game 4, Pierce demanded that coach Doc Rivers let him guard Kobe Bryant, then dogged the Lakers guard relentlessly, blocked one of his jumpers and held him to 6-of-15 shooting, and the Celtics fought all the way back to win. George Karl is 57 and has seen the greatest, from Russell to Jordan, produce the kind of basketball that can make a coach swoon. He was in the building for the Celts' miraculous comeback and saw it up close. "Probably the best half of basketball I can remember one player playing," Karl says.

—S.L. Price, SI, December 8, 2008

Pierce memorably topped Bryant in 2008.

PHOTOGRAPH BY BOB ROSATO

10 THE

BEST POWER FORWARDS

OF ALL THE POSITIONS ON THE FLOOR, THE POWER FORWARD MAY BE THE MOST NEBULOUS. THOSE DRAWING VOTES IN THIS CATEGORY INCLUDED WES UNSELD, WHO IS 6' 7" BUT USUALLY REFERRED TO AS A CENTER, AND KEVIN DURANT, WHO IS 6' 9" AND IS GENERALLY DEFINED AS A SMALL FORWARD—AND WHO ACTUALLY PLAYED SHOOTING GUARD AT THE BEGINNING OF HIS CAREER UNDER COACH P.J. CARLESIMO.

THE QUESTION OF WHICH PLAYERS REALLY BELONG HERE ULTIMATELY DECIDED THE VOTE FOR BEST EVER. TIM DUNCAN WAS SELECTED NO. 1 BY FIVE OF SEVEN PANELISTS. AND YET HE FINISHES SECOND TO KARL MALONE BECAUSE ONE PANELIST PLACED DUNCAN IN ANOTHER CATEGORY, INSISTING THAT DUNCAN WAS TRULY A CENTER—AND NOT JUST WHEN HE WAS PLAYING ALONGSIDE RASHO NESTEROVIC OR FABRICIO OBERTO, BUT DAVID ROBINSON AS WELL (AND, DOUBLING DOWN ON HIS BET, THE PANELIST GAVE ROBINSON A VOTE AT POWER FORWARD).

ONE INFORMED FIGURE SHARES THIS PANELISTS' VIEW: SPURS COACH GREGG POPOVICH, WHO, ANSWERING A QUESTION BEFORE THE 2012–13 FINALS ON WHOM HE WAS STARTING AT CENTER, ANSWERED "TIM DUNCAN, LIKE WE HAVE FOR THE LAST 15 YEARS." THE BEAUTY OF THE IMPERTURBABLE DUNCAN IS THAT IT'S HARD TO IMAGINE HE CARES HOW HE'S CATEGORIZED, SO LONG AS HIS TEAM WINS.

1

KARL MALONE

JAZZ 1985–2003
LAKERS 2003–2004

" A lunch-bucket player, Malone would reach into that pail for his bread-and-butter, the pick-and-roll, which he and John Stockton ran to perfection. As he aged, The Mailman got better at everything, from defense to free throw shooting. " —ALEXANDER WOLFF

▸ TWO-TIME NBA MVP
▸ CAREER AVERAGES OF
25.0 POINTS, 10.1 REBOUNDS

THE QUESTION isn't whether Malone belongs in the NBA paint—the question is who belongs in there with him. "It's where men are made," says the 6' 9", 256-pound Malone. "If you're a boy, you should be home with mom. In the paint, either put up or shut up. I want to play all 48. I don't want nobody coming in for Karl Malone." "Yes, I can see him saying that," says Michael Cooper of the Lakers. "When you're as strong as Darryl Dawkins and run the floor like Byron Scott . . . when you're the fastest big man ever to play, I think you're allowed." "He runs the court like a small man, then overpowers bigger people," says Golden State Warriors coach Don Nelson. "Is there a more dominant power forward in the game today? If there is, I'd like to see him."

—Ralph Wiley, SI, November 7, 1988

The Mailman made four All-Defensive teams.

SPURS 1997—PRESENT

Duncan battled the Heat in consecutive NBA Finals.

PHOTOGRAPH BY JOHN W. MCDONOUGH

" Not even Bill Russell had a longer run than Duncan has. He has elevated the Spurs to championship contention throughout his tenure. No power forward was more dominant across the board as a defender, scorer, playmaker and rebounder. " —IAN THOMSEN

DUNCAN HAS emerged as the Jason Kidd of big men, a playmaker able to elevate his teammates from the low post. "In my 20 years in the NBA, Duncan is the best big to play the game," says former coach Jeff Van Gundy. "Shaq always had the benefit of a dominant perimeter player, but Duncan's never had that."

—Ian Thomsen, SI, June 4, 2007

TIM DUNCAN

▸ TWO-TIME NBA MVP
▸ THREE-TIME FINALS MVP

3

CHARLES BARKLEY

76ERS 1984–1992
SUNS 1992–1996
ROCKETS 1996–2000

" Barkley, says famed trainer Tim Grover, was "the most athletic person I ever worked with." Wide, physical and with springs in his sneakers, Barkley redefined his position. " —CHRIS MANNIX

▸ 1992–93 NBA MVP
▸ CAREER AVERAGES OF
22.1 POINTS, 11.7 REBOUNDS

THE SIXERS now march to the unpredictable drumbeat of one Charles Wade Barkley, who doesn't have a tactful bone in his wide body. For example, in case you're hazy on Barkley's value, here's how he assesses himself: "See, Maurice Cheeks is the best point guard in the league, but Magic Johnson, who's also a point guard, is the best basketball player. That's what I consider myself, a basketball player—a guy who doesn't have to have a position. There's Magic, Larry Bird, Michael Jordan, Clyde Drexler, maybe, and me. I put myself into that category." He's that rare player who can operate almost anywhere on the court—carving out position under the basket, or breaking the press with a behind-the-back dribble, or guarding a small forward, or checking a center who's eight inches taller than his own 6' 4¾".

—Jack McCallum, SI, January 11, 1988

Barkley was expressive on court and off.

PHOTOGRAPH BY JERRY WACHTER

4

KEVIN GARNETT

TIMBERWOLVES 1995–2007
CELTICS 2007–2013
NETS 2013–PRESENT

"A pioneer in more ways than one, KG showed a generation of players the intensity required to play championship defense." —LEE JENKINS

▸ 2003–04 NBA MVP
▸ CAREER AVERAGES OF 18.6 POINTS, 10.3 REBOUNDS

GARNETT'S MAIN contribution was at the defensive end, where he was Russellesque in shouting commands and guarding every corner of the court. The Celtics ranked No. 1 in overall field goal defense and three-point defense, a remarkable duality for a team that squeezes defenders around the ball. It's hard to remember a game in which Garnett wasn't guarding multiple positions, outworking opponents to tip a rebound to himself or running out to the three-point line to show on a pick-and-roll before sprinting back inside to block a shot. His tireless example spread throughout the team, inspiring everyone to display newfound defensive effort. "Kevin made it possible, let's just be honest," said Celtics coach Doc Rivers. "When your best player buys in defensively and then is as focused in shootarounds as he is, then everybody has to follow."

—Ian Thomsen, SI, June 9, 2008

Garnett is a 15-time All-Star.

PHOTOGRAPH BY WALTER IOOSS JR.

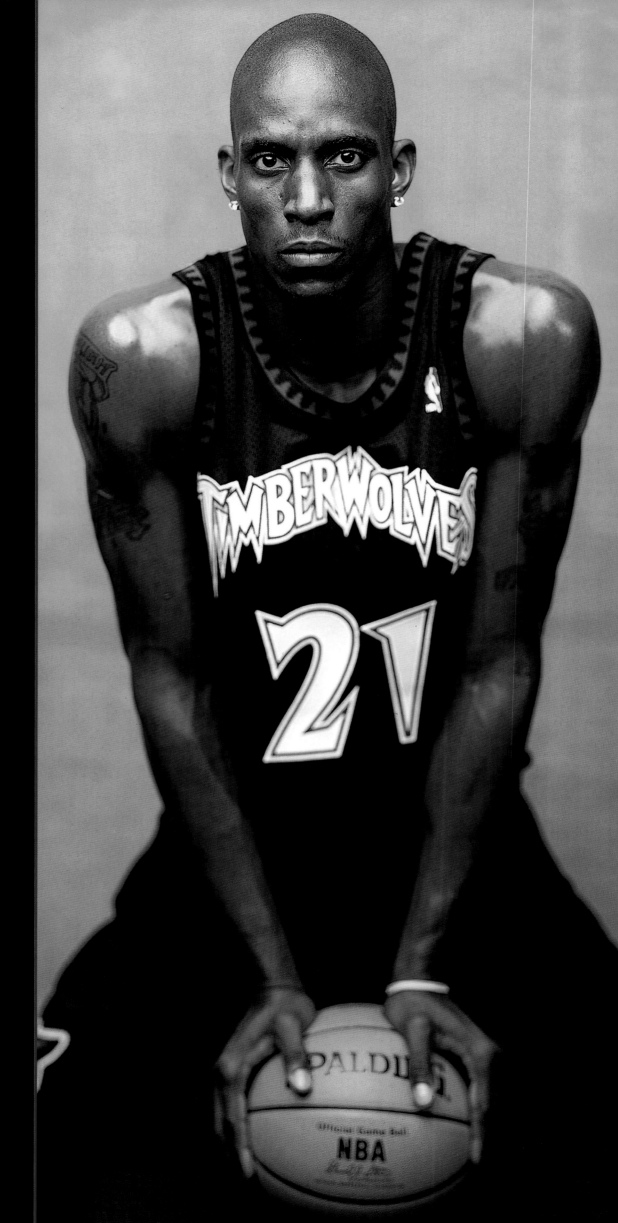

A KID SHALL LEAD THEM

Kevin Garnett, the first player in 20 years to go directly from high school to the NBA, changed the game, and it all began with a workout that turned Kevin McHale's head

BY LEIGH MONTVILLE

YOU THINK ABOUT IT NOW, and it's crazy. Four years ago nobody knew if this kid could play. Nobody. He has come from an uncharted nowhere to change the entire NBA. A high school kid. He is the highest-paid athlete in any team sport, $126 million over six years. He will be the highest-paid player in the NBA for the foreseeable future, thanks to the new labor agreement, which came out of the lockout that delayed this season for three months and two days.

He was the final reason for the lockout. He signed a contract for so much money that the people in charge scared themselves into action. "Where will all this end?" they asked. They risked the future of the league, shut down operations. Because of him. He is the kid who broke the NBA bank.

When Garnett was coming out of high school, his agent Eric Fleisher, to gauge the lottery teams' interest, set up a special workout. Helped by the fact that a bunch of general managers, coaches and scouts were in Chicago to attend a predraft NBA camp, Fleisher sent invitations to the 13 teams with the highest picks. He borrowed the University of Illinois–Chicago gym and brought in Detroit Pistons assistant John Hammond to run the drills. Fleisher invented the procedure as he went along. No one ever had done anything like this.

On the day of the workout, a weekday, Garnett followed his normal schedule. He took his sister to school, then took himself to school. He went to his classes, then to basketball practice, then to his SAT cram course. Finally he went to the NBA workout, at about the time he usually took a nap.

"A guy from the neighborhood, Billy T, drove me to the gym in this old, beat-up car, this Huffymobile, whatever it was," Garnett says. "Billy T was all excited. He kept yelling at me that this was my chance, what I'd been waiting for all of my life, that this was how I could climb out of the ghetto. It was all true. I knew it. I was so tired, though, I fell asleep on the way. I was just narked. I woke up and we were at the gym."

The general managers, coaches and scouts were sitting in the bleachers behind one basket. They formed a row of impassive famous faces. Garnett recognized Kevin McHale and Elgin Baylor and "that silver-haired guy who coached Miami before Pat Riley." (That guy would be Kevin Loughery.) There must have been 15, 20 famous people, all gathered to see him. The idea took his breath away. "A few of my boys had snuck in, too, but they were way at the top, keeping quiet so they wouldn't be thrown out," Garnett says. "Those were the only people in the gym."

"Do you want to stretch?" Hammond asked. Garnett pulled one foot back to touch his butt. He repeated the process with the other foot. That was all. He felt the same nervousness that he felt before big games.

The workout seemed confusing. The drills seemed to be meant for smaller men. Dribble the length of the court with the right hand. Take a jump shot. Dribble back with the left hand. Take another jump shot. Do it again. He'd spent most of his basketball time in the spot reserved for all high school big men, under the basket. Spin left. Spin right. O.K. Dribble? Crossover? Jumper from the key? From the baseline? He felt awkward. He was breathing hard when he finished.

"No one had said a word, not one of those guys from behind the basket," Garnett says. "I was just standing there when one of them—the first voice—said, 'Jump and touch the box [above the basket].' I jumped and touched the box. 'Can he touch the top of the box?' another voice said. I jumped and touched the top of the box. 'Again,' someone said. 'Left hand,' another one said. 'Right hand.' 'Again.' 'Try it with a running start.' Suddenly they all were yelling out things."

Garnett jumped and jumped and jumped some more. Somewhere in the middle of the jumping, he started shouting. Arrrrrrgh. He shouted with every jump. Arrrrrrgh and arrrrrrgh and arrrrrrgh. He jumped and shouted until the requests ended.

"When it was done, Kevin McHale came down to the floor and gave me a tip about my jump shot," Garnett says. "I'll always remember that. I thanked him, and then I walked back to the middle of the court while E [Fleisher] said goodbye to everyone. I lay down right in the middle of the court. I fell asleep for two hours. I was so tired." He awoke and his life had changed forever.

"I blew it," he told Fleisher, who had waited quietly.

"No, you didn't," the agent replied.

"I shouldn't have started shouting like that. They all think I'm a kid. Or uncontrollable. Or something. Why'd I shout? I blew it."

"You did fine," the agent said. "You did great." He had seen the looks on the famous faces. They were impassive no more.

"We had no idea we were going to take him in the first round," McHale, vice president of basketball operations for the Minnesota Timberwolves, says. "I didn't even want to go see him. I thought it was a waste of time. Then we went, and Flip Saunders [then Minnesota's general manager] and I were in the car afterward, and we just looked at each other. I said, 'Wow, we're going to pick a high school kid in the first round.' It was that obvious."

You think about it, and everything is timing, is it not? You have to have something to sell, and you have to have someone who wants to buy. There has to be a demand.

No one ever had better timing than this kid. ∎

5

DIRK NOWITZKI

MAVERICKS 1998–PRESENT

❝ Saddled early with Bird comparisons, he developed into one of the great half-court weapons ever. No player combined his size, shooting touch and unorthodox mid-post—often wrong foot—moves. Though never a great defender or rebounder, he was a great teammate and unselfish star. ❞ —CHRIS BALLARD

▸ 2006–07 NBA MVP
▸ CAREER AVERAGES OF 22.5 POINTS, 8.1 REBOUNDS

FOUR SECONDS remained in Game 6 of the NBA Finals, four seconds until Nowitzki reached the goal he set at 16, but he could wait no longer. Nowitzki bolted for the sideline, leaped over the scorer's table and began striding down the tunnel at AmericanAirlines Arena in Miami. He rushed into the visitors' locker room, into the showers, to a bench in the back. Without turning on a faucet, 13 failed seasons washed off his 7-foot frame, all of them down the drain. Here is a star who stayed for the struggle, who bore the burden and who proved that a title does not have to be won with a Big Three or a Fantastic Four. A true star rides in front and demands everyone fall in line. "You see around the league three or four big-name guys trying to get together," said Dallas guard DeShawn Stevenson. "Well, one was enough for us."

—Lee Jenkins, SI, June 20, 2011

Nowitzki was the 2010–11 NBA Finals MVP.

PHOTOGRAPHS BY JOHN W. MCDONOUGH (LEFT) AND BOB ROSATO

6

BOB PETTIT

HAWKS 1954–1965

"At 6' 9" and just 200 pounds, he was considered too slight to make it in the NBA. But there was nothing slight about Pettit's competitive heart, which was praised by Bill Russell, among others. The term "power forward" didn't exist in Pettit's day, but he is now recognized as the first." —JACK McCALLUM

▸ ALL-STAR IN EACH OF HIS 11 NBA SEASONS
▸ CAREER AVERAGES OF 26.4 POINTS, 16.2 REBOUNDS

ALL THE CHIPS are down in a world championship game; it is a time for greatness. Bob Pettit chose such a contest, against Boston in April, to demonstrate his, convincingly. He scored an amazing 50 points, single-handedly wresting the NBA title from the Celtics for St. Louis, and giving so much of himself to the effort that he was unable even to lift his head for photographers in the dressing room afterward. Bob's overpowering skill on attack has tended to obscure the fact that he is one of the best defensive players in basketball today. Pettit's daily Jekyll-Hyde transformation is a startling phenomenon. Off court, he is shy and mild to the point of meekness; when the whistle blows, he is a relentless bundle of aggression, irresistibly on the scent of victory.

—*Jeremiah Tax, SI, January 5, 1959*

Pettit was a two-time NBA MVP.

PHOTOGRAPH BY PHIL BATH

McHale grew from elite sixth man to starter.

PHOTOGRAPH BY MANNY MILLAN

7

KEVIN MCHALE

❝His body looked as if it had been assembled on a lab bench. But finely honed footwork allowed Kevin McHale to unleash an array of low-post moves, from hook to turnaround, that bamboozled even as you knew it was coming. ❞ —ALEXANDER WOLFF

▸ SEVEN-TIME ALL-STAR
▸ CAREER 55.4 FIELD GOAL PERCENTAGE

AFTER TAKING a pass from Magic for what looked to be a routine fast-break hoop, Kurt Rambis was lassoed around the neck in midflight by McHale, and McHale made no attempt to make Kurt's landing a happy one. Both benches emptied, and although no blows were landed, the point had been made.

—Anthony Cotton, SI, June 18, 1984

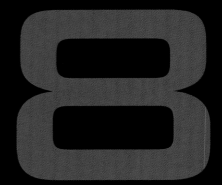

ELVIN HAYES

ROCKETS 1968–1972, 1981–1984
BULLETS 1972–1981

" Big E's turnaround on the block was one of the toughest moves to defend, and though he wasn't huge, he had a knack for rebounds: In 1970 he became the first man other than Wilt Chamberlain or Bill Russell to win a rebounding title in 12 years. " —MARK BECHTEL

▸ 12-TIME ALL-STAR
▸ CAREER AVERAGES OF 21.0 POINTS, 12.5 REBOUNDS

DURING HIS years with the Rockets, Hayes was variously considered a ball hog, a rotten apple, a dumbbell and a guaranteed loser. Each season Hayes would try to explain that as the lone big-name player on a poor team he was being assessed an unfair portion of the blame. As it turned out, all Hayes needed was a new team. He fit in easily with the Bullets, played excellently last season and has been even better this year, particularly in those areas only other players are likely to notice. Forward Mike Riordan points to Hayes's improvement at picking and passing. Hayes also has been a human Electrolux under both backboards. In 27 games this season he has ended up with more rebounds than points, a remarkable feat for a player who regularly scores more than 20.

—Peter Carry, SI, March 11, 1974

Hayes's Bullets won a championship in 1978.

DOLPH SCHAYES

NATIONALS/76ERS 1949–1964

> "One of the NBA's original stars, Schayes set himself apart with an unusually reliable two-handed set shot from the perimeter. He bridged the Syracuse Nationals' move to Philadelphia, where he finished his career as player-coach of the 76ers." —IAN THOMSEN

▸ 12-TIME ALL-STAR
▸ CAREER AVERAGES OF 18.5 POINTS, 12.1 REBOUNDS

"THE MOST important thing any athlete does is 'get up' mentally before the competition starts," Schayes says. "It's the difference between the ordinary, average performance and the extra effort that wins the game, the race, or whatever he's going to do. I start working on myself about an hour before game time. I keep repeating a few things to myself, over and over, before and during the game. It's only 48 minutes, I say, only 48 minutes I've got to deliver. Most of those people watching me have to deliver for eight hours every day on their jobs. I've got 48 minutes. That should be easy. They've paid to watch me and I want them to see my best. A lot of players in our league aren't really trying. Don't get me wrong, they give everything they've got—physically. But they just haven't learned how to get that extra something that comes from being 'up' mentally."

—*Jeremiah Tax, SI, January 14, 1957*

Schayes could score from inside or outside.

PHOTOGRAPH BY AP

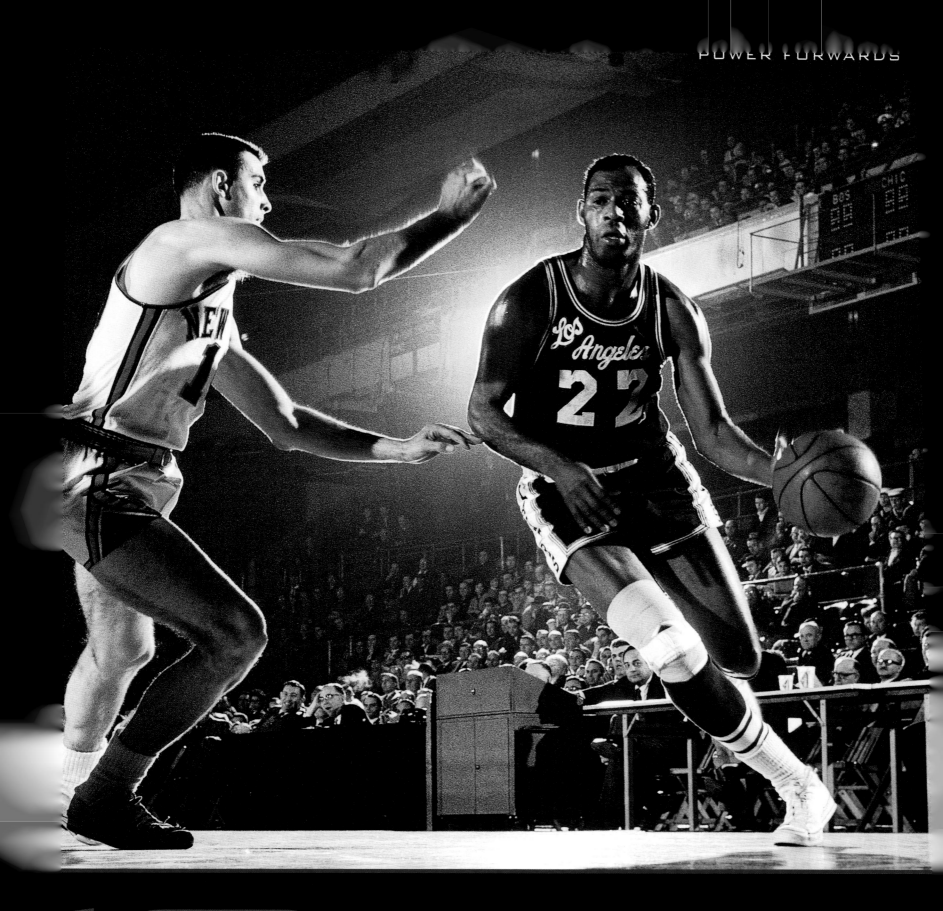

LAKERS 1958–1972

Baylor had the bulk to compete down low.

PHOTOGRAPH BY NEIL LEIFER

" I hold that his size (6' 5", 225 pounds) made the seriously underrated Baylor a 4-man in an era when a forward was just a "forward." " —JACK MCCALLUM

▸ 11-TIME ALL-STAR
▸ IN 1962–63 FINISHED IN TOP FIVE IN POINTS, REBOUNDS, ASSISTS AND FREE THROW PERCENTAGE

WHEN FRED SCHAUS, the Lakers' coach, was scouting, somebody asked him if Baylor was the finest ballplayer ever. "Yeah," Schaus said, "if there were money on the table, I'd take Elg over anybody." Somebody else said, really, if there were money involved, Baylor would win at any game. "Yeah," he said. "That too."

—Frank Deford, SI, October 24, 1966

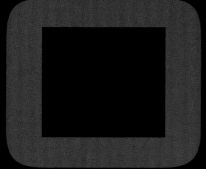

ELGIN BAYLOR

10

THE

BEST CENTERS

THE MOST ROBUST DEBATE FOR THE TOP SLOT AMONG PLAYER POSITIONS CAME AT CENTER, WHERE THREE PLAYERS FINISHED ONE-TWO-THREE ON EVERYONE'S BALLOT, AND EACH ONE OF THE TRIO RECEIVED AT LEAST ONE FIRST-PLACE VOTE.

THE TIME IN WHICH THESE TOP THREE PLAYED ALSO TELLS YOU SOMETHING ABOUT THE STATE OF CENTERS IN GENERAL. TWO OF THESE MEN, BILL RUSSELL AND WILT CHAMBERLAIN, BEGAN THEIR PRO CAREERS IN THE LATE 1950S, AND THE OTHER, KAREEM ABDUL-JABBAR, JOINED THE NBA IN 1969. THE ENTIRE LIST IS RIFE WITH OLD-TIMERS. IN EACH OF THE OTHER FOUR POSITIONAL RANKINGS, ACTIVE PLAYERS MAKE THE TOP 10. BUT AT CENTER, THE YOUNGEST RANKED PLAYER IS SHAQUILLE O'NEAL, WHO RETIRED IN 2011 AND SEEMED TO HAVE SEMIRETIRED A BIT BEFORE THAT—BEGINNING WITH THE "LEBRON'S BODYGUARD" PHASE IN CLEVELAND.

IT'S NO SURPRISE, REALLY. RATHER THAN OWN THE PAINT, MANY TEAMS PREFER TO KEEP THAT AREA UNCLOGGED SO THEIR POINT GUARDS AND WING PLAYERS CAN DRIVE TO THE HOOP. SEVEN-FOOTERS ARE AS LIKELY TO SPOT UP FOR THREE-POINTERS AS THEY ARE TO PLANT THEMSELVES DOWN LOW. IT MAY HELP AN OFFENSE FLOW, BUT WHEN THOSE BIG GUYS ARE WAY OUTSIDE, THEY SEEM SMALLER COMPARED TO THE GIANTS OF YESTERYEAR.

1

BILL RUSSELL

CELTICS 1956–1969

"It is because of Russell that the NBA's greatest players are judged by team championships rather than individual statistics. The greatest winner in American sports established the timeless standards for teamwork, defensive leadership and fast-break basketball." —IAN THOMSEN

▸ FIVE-TIME NBA MVP
▸ 11 NBA TITLES

"HE'S A FANTASTIC athlete," says teammate John Havlicek. "He could have been the decathlon champion. He could broad-jump 24 feet. He did the hurdles in 13.4. I've seen him in plays on a basketball court when he not only blocks a shot but controls the ball and feeds it to his forwards, and then he's up at the other end of the court trailing the fast break and if there's a rebound there he is, ready for it. He just might be the fastest man on the Celtics. Last year in the playoffs Archie Clark of the Lakers stole the ball three times and he must have had five steps on Russell and a free lane to the basket. Each time Russell caught him and blocked the shot. Think of that. Think of being on the other team. There's got to be a funny feeling, going for the basket when Russell's around."

—George Plimpton, SI, December 23, 1968

Russell was a player-coach for his final three seasons.

PHOTOGRAPHS BY WALTER IOOSS JR. (LEFT) AND LONG PHOTOGRAPHY INC.

4
HAKEEM OLAJUWON

ROCKETS 1984–2001
RAPTORS 2001–2002

"For a man who came to basketball relatively late, at age 15, Hakeem Olajuwon had a remarkable set of skills, with footwork any big man would envy and a host of moves and countermoves that earned their own name: Dream Shake." —MARK BECHTEL

▸ 1993–94 NBA MVP
▸ TWO-TIME NBA FINALS MVP

"TO MAKE the center position fun—that was my vision," Olajuwon says. "To add shakes and bakes and moves. If you're a center, you're thought to be mechanical. But when I faced up on a guy, I was no longer a center. I was a small forward." Defenders never knew which of the diverse skills, learned during his multisport upbringing in Nigeria, The Dream would call upon: light feet from soccer, power and craftiness from team handball, hand-eye coordination from table tennis, sudden levitation from high jumping and volleyball. "My game was to play the same as a little guy, a cat's game—but with big cats," says Olajuwon, who won a gold medal with the United States at the 1996 Olympics. (He became a U.S. citizen in '93.) "One or two hard dribbles in traffic. Quickness. And timing."

—Alexander Wolff, SI, July 2, 2007

Olajuwon could post up or face the basket.

PHOTOGRAPH BY MANNY MILLAN

THE STUFF OF DREAMS

Hakeem Olajuwon's best season might have been one in which he finished fifth in MVP voting but dominated the award winner in the playoffs on the way to a title

BY LEIGH MONTVILLE

THE VIDEOTAPED PICTURES GRAB Rudy Tomjanovich, pictures that leap off the oversized television screen in his office. He will be in the midst of dull work, trying to dissect the tendencies and weaknesses of some Houston Rockets opponent in this long playoff spring, when his attention will be drawn to his own team. Stop, rewind. He will watch Hakeem Olajuwon in action with a new and different eye.

Stop, rewind. Hakeem has the ball in that familiar spot, low, on the left side, back to the basket. He is spinning left, going to take that little eight-foot jump shot.

Stop, rewind. He is spinning right. The Dream Shake. He is going to fall out-of-bounds as he takes that even more familiar eight-footer that no one can handle. Stop, rewind. He has his man up in the air, and he is driving, one step, two steps, jam.

Stop, rewind. He is being double-teamed and passes out to one of his guards—to Clyde Drexler or Kenny Smith or Sam Cassell—for a carnival-easy three-point shot to win a Kewpie doll. Stop, rewind. The pass will be to a cutter for an easy basket. Stop, rewind.

Tomjanovich simply will stare at the lethal menu. His good fortune will overwhelm him. "Sometimes—often, really—I just look at the tape of Hakeem and say, 'God, what are the other coaches thinking?' " Rudy T says. "How do you stop that? What do you do?"

Stop, rewind.

The time has arrived for everyone to stare in amazement at this seven-foot gentleman from Lagos, Nigeria, to stare even harder than last year when he was the MVP in the NBA and led the Rockets to the NBA championship. That was the for-granted stuff. This is the surreal. He is one step away from winning the title this time pretty much by himself, taking an ordinary team to an extraordinary finish. This is his moment. This is his show.

"To my mind, he's the best player in the league, and he's been the best as long as I've been in it," says forward Mario Elie, a five-year veteran. "He's so good that sometimes you get caught up in just watching him."

If the championship of last year sometimes looked as if it were bought with inflated dollars—Michael Jordan had retired, the Rockets rolled down an easier path to the Finals when the No. 1–seeded Seattle SuperSonics were eliminated in the first round by the Denver Nuggets— this year's trip to the Finals against the Eastern Conference champion Orlando Magic did not come cheap. Lacking a proven power forward and usually playing no more than nine people, the Rockets have had to lean even more heavily on their superstar. Take away Olajuwon, and the big basketball news in Houston would be the interviews with potential lottery picks. Put him on the court, and the city goes borderline wacky, certainly wackier even than last year, people talking Rockets, Rockets, nothing but Rockets.

The credit that Olajuwon has never received, not even with a championship and an MVP award last year, has begun to arrive in a hurry. He is now doing the postseason stuff of Magic Johnson and Larry Bird and Jordan and Bill Russell. Maybe, hard though it may be to believe, he is doing even more. Did any of them have to perform with such a nondescript cast?

"The series he just played against San Antonio is going to be legendary," Tomjanovich says. "People will be talking about that series and how he played for many, many years."

He took apart Spurs center David Robinson in that series. That's what Olajuwon did. Robinson, who before the series was named the league MVP for this season (Olajuwon was fifth in the balloting), is Olajuwon's closest counterpart at the position. Tall, fluid, graceful, Robinson promised to be a mirror image, negating whatever good Olajuwon could accomplish. The problem was the basic premise: The reflection in the mirror was not nearly as sharp as the real object. Robinson never could handle Olajuwon. Olajuwon more than handled Robinson.

What are you going to do? The question Tomjanovich asked while viewing videotape was Robinson's nightly puzzle. Robinson thought he was playing pretty good defense. He said he knew that sounded odd, but he meant it.

Olajuwon's teammates think that the MVP voting should be reopened. "The MVP voting is closed," Olajuwon says. "Basketball is a team game anyway. The goal is to win the championship."

His best individual award this year might have arrived after Houston closed out San Antonio in Game 6. The door to the Rockets locker room opened. David Robinson entered. He was dressed in a bright and tailored blue suit, heading home and to summer vacation. He wanted, as losers traditionally do, to extend congratulations to the winners. He shook a few hands. He looked for Olajuwon.

"Where's Hakeem?" he asked Drexler.

"He's in the shower," Drexler replied.

"Well, tell him good luck."

"He really wants to see you. He's right there. In the shower."

"I don't know about that," Robinson said. "I don't know if I want to climb in the shower with the man."

"He really wants to see you," Drexler repeated.

The MVP of the NBA for 1995 shrugged mightily and went to the shower-room door in his bright blue suit. What could he do? He went inside to extend his congratulations. The man of the moment awaited. ∎

5

SHAQUILLE O'NEAL

MAGIC 1992–1996
LAKERS 1996–2004
HEAT 2004–2008
THREE TEAMS THROUGH 2011

" The calculus of Diesel's career demands that we remember the numbers he could've put up—he missed 5,317 free throws and more than 300 games. But he has a place in both the pantheon of greatest centers and most popular sports personalities. " —JACK McCALLUM

‣ 15-TIME ALL-STAR
‣ FOUR NBA TITLES

BECAUSE SHAQ'S influence on his team is so profound, because he has worked so hard at becoming a complete player and because he has played through so much pain, he bristles whenever it is suggested that his oversized body is the primary reason for his success—a suggestion that is made every night of the season.

"The truth is, I was created by you guys," the 7' 1", 345-pound O'Neal told the media last week. "When I was a young player having fun, doing movies and doing albums, you criticized me all the time. I'd hear, 'Shaq O'Neal is a great player, but he doesn't have a championship.' So, after taking criticism all my life, I know how to turn it into positive energy." Then he broke out into a huge smile. "So this is what you created, and I'm glad you did. Thank you, and I love you all."

—Jack McCallum, SI. June 17, 2002

Shaq's had a career field goal percentage of 58.2.

PHOTOGRAPHS BY JOHN BIEVER (LEFT) AND JOHN W. MCDONOUGH

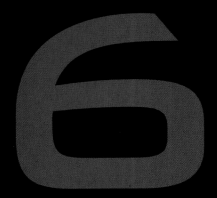

6

MOSES MALONE

ROCKETS 1976–1982
76ERS 1982–1986
EIGHT OTHER TEAMS

" No big man combined footwork, leverage and desire like Moses. He couldn't really jump, and no one accused him of a soft touch, but his motor was remarkable. His rebounding strategy, he once said, was, "If there are 100 shots in a game, then I go after all of them." " —CHRIS BALLARD

▸ THREE-TIME NBA MVP
▸ 13-TIME ALL-STAR

RICH KELLEY, the New Orleans center, who is a distant third in the league to Malone in offensive rebounding, says, "He has quickness, timing, all the things you would expect, but the main thing is his tenacity. Eighty percent of Malone's game is on the offensive board. It changes everything. You play the Rockets, it's something entirely different, because I'd say a third of their game is Moses on the offensive board, keeping the ball in play. And that's completely unique to any team. What goes through your mind is that you have to box him out every damn time, every time the ball goes up. It just wears on you, mind and body. The other good centers learn to cruise for a quarter. They pick their spots. Not Moses. By the end of every game against him, you're whipped."

—Frank Deford, SI, February 19, 1979

Malone was the 1983 NBA Finals MVP.

PHOTOGRAPH BY MANNY MILLAN

7

DAVID ROBINSON

" How much was the Admiral worth to the Spurs? San Antonio improved by 35 games in his first season. The versatile Robinson remains the last player in NBA history to post a quadruple double. " —MARK BECHTEL

▸ 1994–95 NBA MVP
▸ 1991–92 NBA DEFENSIVE PLAYER OF THE YEAR

ROBINSON scored 1320 on his SATs, majored in math at Annapolis, and uses words like golly and gosh. The moment the Admiral climbed aboard, all the talk about hoops being history in San Antonio ceased. "The term franchise player is overused," says owner Red McCombs. "But I'm not sure there would be a franchise here without David."

—*Jack McCallum, SI, December 15, 2003*

Robinson played on two title teams.

PHOTOGRAPH BY JOHN W. MCDONOUGH

GEORGE MIKAN

LAKERS 1948–1954,
1955–1956

" He turned basketball into a big man's game. The first dominant center forced the league to widen its lane and create a 24-second shot clock as Mikan launched the first NBA dynasty with the Minneapolis Lakers. " —IAN THOMSEN

‣ FIVE NBA TITLES
‣ CAREER AVERAGES OF 23.1 POINTS AND 13.4 REBOUNDS

BIG GEORGE played at 6' 10" and 245 pounds. He was quite probably the strongest man then playing the game. "He could raise that left elbow and move to the basket, and the bodies would just start to fly," says former teammate Swede Carlson. "I used to like to pass him the ball, cut out around him and then listen to the sound the guy guarding me made when he ran into George." But it was not so much his strength or the accuracy of his short hook shots that made him such a force—it was his indomitable will. Bud Grant, the longtime coach of the NFL's Minnesota Vikings, played for two seasons with Mikan and the old Lakers. He had this to say about his famous teammate: "I've seen and coached against some of the best—Walter Payton, to name one. But I'd have to say that George Mikan was the greatest competitor I've seen or been around in any sport."

—*Ron Fimrite, SI, November 6, 1989*

Mikan brought a power game into the paint.

PHOTOGRAPH BY AP

9
WILLIS REED

KNICKS 1964–1974

" Reed's heroic return for Game 7 of the 1970 Finals, after tearing a muscle in his thigh in Game 5, ranks as one of the greatest moments in NBA history. Knicks fans will remember his physical presence during New York's two championship runs. " —CHRIS MANNIX

▸ 1969–70 NBA MVP
▸ TWO-TIME NBA FINALS MVP

"REED PLAYS the pivotal role in the history of the Knicks. At the moment he was chosen in the 1964 draft the entire fortunes of the team began to change. Before that draft the Knicks had suffered from bad judgment, bad luck and a haughty attitude that was the child of self-delusion. For a time, for instance, the Knicks operated smugly with a general manager who lived in Denver. Ironically, the team that had Reed, who had averaged 26 points at Grambling, rated highest in the draft was the Los Angeles Lakers, a franchise that had been looking for a top center since George Mikan retired. But Lakers owner Bob Short demanded that his general manager, Lou Mohs, pick Walt Hazzard, the local (UCLA) whiz. So Reed, amazingly, was available to the Knicks and they took him, leading off the second round.

—Frank Deford, SI, October 23, 1967

The 6' 9" Reed averaged 18.7 points and 12.9 rebounds

10

BILL WALTON

BLAZERS 1974–1978
CLIPPERS 1979–1985
CELTICS 1985–1987

❝ "I'd play every minute I could even if there was no money at all," he once said. But because there were so many minutes he couldn't play due to injuries, that valedictory title with the Celtics in '86, to add to his crown with the Blazers in '77, seemed just. ❞ —ALEXANDER WOLFF

▸ 1977–78 NBA MVP
▸ 1985–86 NBA SIXTH MAN OF THE YEAR

THE BIG GUY was in full cry [in Game 6], ringing up his usual rather glorious numbers, such as 20 points, 23 rebounds, seven assists and eight blocked shots. "He changed everything we tried to do," Philadelphia's George McGinnis said. With one second left, McGinnis, driving to the right, pushed up one final funny shot put jumper, but this one bounced off also. After Walton leaped to knock the ball away, he whirled, ripped off his shirt and heaved it in the general direction of where he'd been swatting the Sixers' shots for a whole week: right into the heart of Blazermania. "If I had caught the shirt, I would have eaten it," said forward Maurice Lucas. "Bill's my hero." "Did I plan the shirt?" Walton laughed as people tried to shower his red hair and beard with champagne. "I only planned on winning," he said.

—Curry Kirkpatrick, SI, June 13, 1977

Foot injuries robbed Walton of three full seasons.

10 THE

BEST COACHES

THE SELECTION OF BASKETBALL'S TOP 10 COACHES HAS PRODUCED AN UNPRECEDENTED RESULT. IN THE PREVIOUS BOOKS IN THIS SERIES, FOR FOOTBALL AND BASEBALL, EVERY TOP COACH SELECTED BY THE PANEL WAS A CHAMPION (AND 18 OF THE 20 HAD WON MULTIPLE TITLES). BUT BASKETBALL GIVES US THE FIRST RINGLESS TOP 10 COACH: JERRY SLOAN.

SOME LENIENCY MAY HAVE BEEN SHOWN BECAUSE SLOAN COACHED IN THE AGE OF JORDAN, WHOSE BULLS TOPPLED THE JAZZ IN BOTH THEIR FINALS APPEARANCES. BUT IT HAS MORE TO DO WITH SLOAN'S EXTRAORDINARY STAYING POWER. SLOAN COACHED IN UTAH FOR 23 SEASONS AND HE PRODUCED ONE SCRAPPY, FUNDAMENTALLY SOUND TEAM AFTER ANOTHER.

IN 2002 SLOAN, SPEAKING ON THE SUBJECTS OF TITLES, TOLD SPORTS ILLUSTRATED, "A LOT OF GUYS WILL SHOW THEIR RINGS TO YOU WHO DIDN'T HAVE ANYTHING TO DO WITH WINNING A CHAMPIONSHIP. THERE'S SOMETHING TO BE SAID FOR COMING BACK AFTER YOU LOSE, FOR PUTTING YOURSELF ON THE LINE, FOR HAVING THE WILL TO TRY IT AGAIN AND AGAIN, FOR PUTTING EVERY OUNCE OF ENERGY INTO ACHIEVING SOMETHING AFTER YOU'VE FALLEN SHORT." CHAMPIONSHIPS ARE THE MOST OBVIOUS DEFINITION OF A WINNER, BUT SLOAN, THROUGH HIS EXAMPLE, PROVIDES ANOTHER.

1

PHIL JACKSON

BULLS 1989–1998
LAKERS 1999–2004, 2005–2011

"Yes, Phil Jackson was gifted with the best players, from Michael Jordan to Scottie Pippen, Kobe Bryant to Shaquille O'Neal. But the Zenmaster harnessed their egos and maximized their abilities." —LEE JENKINS

▸ 1,155–485 CAREER RECORD
▸ 11 NBA TITLES

EVEN THOUGH the Bulls had won 47 games in the '88–89 season, Doug Collins was dismissed and Jackson installed. And a strange feeling-out process began as Jackson and Jordan looked each other over. It was tense because the new coach was asking Jordan to integrate himself into this weird triangle offense that Bulls assistant Tex Winter had developed. Jackson was convinced that to win really big, the Bulls had to become less of a one-man team. Jordan didn't mind giving up a few of his points; he was just uncertain who among his teammates was capable of picking them up. But Jackson had all the leverage in any negotiation with his star player. Jackson knew how to win NBA championships; Jordan, at that point, did not. "More than anything," Jackson says, "Mike wanted us to find a way to win."

—Richard Hoffer, SI, May 27 ,1996

Jackson shared titles with both Bryant and Jordan.

2

RED AUERBACH

CELTICS 1950–1966
TWO TEAMS 1946–1950

" Coaching without assistants and refusing to scout, Auerbach was a staunch believer in a sharply executed game plan. Having Russell, Cousy and Havlicek probably helped. " —CHRIS MANNIX

▸ 938–479 CAREER RECORD
▸ NINE NBA TITLES

AUERBACH HAS little use for statistics. "I go by what I see," he says. "I'll be interested in statistics when they show me how they can measure intestinal fortitude, coming through in the clutch." When Auerbach recently asked his friend Allie Sherman, the coach of the New York Giants, why he had traded so-and-so, Sherman offered to show him movies that demonstrated the player was a half step slower. Auerbach wouldn't buy it. "We pay our boys on the basis of performance, not statistics. Too many points are gotten when they don't count, in what we call 'garbage-up time.' I can show you a guy with 16 points, 15 rebounds, 10 assists and he was ----. He threw the ball away, he wasn't running fast, he was showing me false hustle, he took bad shots, he messed up the good ones, his defense was bad, he did nothing in the clutch. When you can measure these, I'm interested."

—Gilbert Rogin, SI, April 5, 1965

Some Auerbach celebrations were more than just a cigar.

In Miami, Riley won titles as a coach and as a GM.

PHOTOGRAPH BY DAVID E. KLUTHO

3

LAKERS 1981–1990
KNICKS 1991–1995
HEAT 1995–2003, 2005–2008

" The man who gave the league its flashiest team, the Showtime Lakers, then turned around and showed he could grind it out too, taking the Knicks to the Finals and winning his final ring with the Heat. " —MARK BECHTEL

▸ **1,210–694 CAREER RECORD**
▸ **FIVE NBA TITLES**

PAT RILEY

WHEN HE came to Miami, Riley spoke of a champion's parade but vowed he wouldn't chase titles into his 60s. "That'll kill you," he said then. This April he said, "I want to win, deeply— win a championship; it's not any different. I never thought I would be a lifer. But here I am. So . . . play it out."

—S.L. Price, SI, May 1, 2006

4

CHUCK DALY

PISTONS 1983–1992
THREE OTHER TEAMS

" Forget all the wins and the Olympic gold, and the great respect he earned around the league. If he'd done nothing else, Daly might make this list for being the only coach to solve Michael Jordan with his famous Bad Boys teams and Jordan Rules. " —CHRIS BALLARD

▸ 638–437 CAREER RECORD
▸ TWO NBA TITLES

"CHUCK GAVE me the most important coaching lesson of my life," says Ron Rothstein of an incident that occurred when he was a Pistons assistant. "We're getting blown out in Dallas in the second quarter. We call a timeout, and I've got like six things written down to talk about. I mean, I'm going to blister some people, and I figure Chuck is too. We get in the huddle and he says nothing. Makes one substitution, sets up one play, sends them back out there, and we win the game. 'That was a great lesson out there,' I told him after the game. 'Less was more.'" Daly has never been a my-way-or-the-highway coach. Neither is he a "system" coach. He realizes that the best NBA teams are player-oriented. The players are the focus, not the coach. The players take care of most of the big problems. The coach is there to motivate, to prepare, to direct. But not to star.

—*Jack McCallum, SI, December 18, 1989*

Daly coached the original Dream Team.

PHOTOGRAPH BY LOU CAPOZZOLA

5
GREGG POPOVICH

SPURS 1996–PRESENT

"Gregg Popovich is a teacher (ask Tony Parker) and a tactician (see his championships), but the secret to Pop's success is his evenhandedness. For the last 18 years, Popovich coached the last man on the bench the same way he did Tim Duncan." —CHRIS MANNIX

▸ 967–443 CAREER RECORD
▸ FIVE NBA TITLES

POPOVICH WAS reading a book by Jacob Riis and was struck by a passage. "It was more meaningful than, 'There's no I in team' or 'Winners never quit' or crap like that," Popovich says. So he mounted a copy of Riis's *Stonecutter Credo* on the wall of the team's locker room. The framed placard reads: "When nothing seems to help, I go look at a stonecutter hammering away at his rock, perhaps a hundred times without as much as a crack showing in it. Yet at the hundred and first blow it will split in two, and I know it was not that blow that did it, but all that had gone before." Popovich then ordered framed copies of the quotation translated into the various languages his players spoke. It was a small touch, but one that reveals much about this decade's winningest NBA franchise.

—*L. Jon Wertheim, SI, March 9, 2009*

The intense Popovich runs a stable operation.

PHOTOGRAPH BY JOHN W. MCDONOUGH

THE REPUBLIC OF POP

When you combine military discipline with intellectual curiosity, you get the architect of a team that is both remarkably consistent and unusually adaptable

BY JACK McCALLUM

GREGG POPOVICH IS AS competitive as any coach in the NBA, but there are grace notes of humility in the man, the kind that stem from, say, going 2–22 in his first season at Pomona in 1980 and losing to Caltech, the program that would later gain national attention by dropping 310 straight conference games. Indeed, a couple of days after Caltech ended that streak with a 46-45 win over Occidental in February 2011, coach Oliver Eslinger entered his office to find a crate of Rock & Hammer wine from Pop's winery and a note that read, "Congratulations to you and the players for showing the true spirit of sport you display. I am thrilled for you, and as a former loser to Caltech, I wish you more wins."

It might be a leap to say (as do many around Pop) that he would be just as happy coaching in Division III—his approximately $6 million salary buys a lot of high-end vino—but it's obvious that his time at Pomona has stuck with him. It partly explains why in training camp Pop handed his players DVDs of a 2012 presidential debate or why he discusses Argentine politics and political conspiracies with guard Manu Ginóbili, somewhat the conspiracy theorist. "It is not sufficient to say merely that Gregg is smart," says his friend Steven Koblik, the former president of Reed College in Portland, author of such basketball staples as *Om Vi Teg* (a book about Sweden's response to the Holocaust that translates as *If We Remain Silent*) and Pop's academic adviser at Pomona. "He is also intellectually curious. Now, you combine that with basketball smarts and street smarts and add someone who's a very good judge of people, and that makes for a very unusual person."

Koblik, who is now the president of the Huntington Library in San Marino, Calif., one of the nation's largest research and rare-book libraries, visits Popovich a couple of times per season, and on his last trip he took Pop one of the four volumes of Robert Caro's biography of Lyndon Johnson. "He devoured it," said Koblik. "One of my roles in life is to make sure I read something that Pop will like and give it to him."

In his eighth year at Pomona, 1986–87, Pop took the sabbatical permitted to professors and interned with Larry Brown at Kansas. "It was obvious right away that he was the whole package," says Brown, now at SMU, his 13th head coaching post. "Pop has great character, great passion for the sport and great intelligence. Pretty much all you want." Brown didn't have a permanent spot for Popovich then, so Pop returned to Pomona and scheduled a game against the Jayhawks in Allen Fieldhouse just for the experience of it. His Sagehens lost 94–38 to the team that won the NCAA championship that season.

Popovich left the warm bosom of campus life for good in 1988, following Brown to become an assistant with the Spurs. The team's then owner, Red McCombs, let go Brown and his entire staff in '92, and two years of franchise unrest ensued before Popovich—who went to Golden State as Don Nelson's assistant—returned as general manager. Pop jettisoned coach Bob Hill, installed himself, heard thousands of boos, built a team based on defensive principles, drafted Tim Duncan, brought order to chaos, won a championship, closed the curtain and settled in for a long run as the pasha of the Republic of Pop.

It's not that the Spurs do anything magical. It's just that they do whatever they do consistently, from game to game, year to year, decade to decade. "The first thing I think about with them is that they're well drilled," says Kings assistant Jim Eyen. "You know you have college teams, Kansas and Duke, that play a certain way? The NBA version is the Spurs. They are as close to a program as you have in the league."

Handling people—more specifically, people within the Republic of Pop—is his strength, his Pop art. Pop's ability to lead comes from . . . who knows where? Some complex mosaic of East Chicago, the Academy, Pomona, all that fine wine, the cauldron of NBA competition, a dozen other places. He visits the subject of his leadership with reluctance but, once started, with zeal.

"The only reason the word *military* is used to describe what goes on around here is because I went to the Academy," says Pop. "But the correct word is discipline. And there are disciplined people in Google, in IBM and the McDonald's down the street.

"Yes, we're disciplined with what we do. But that's not enough. Relationships with people are what it's all about. You have to make players realize you care about them. And they have to care about each other and be interested in each other. Then they start to feel a responsibility toward each other. Then they want to do for each other.

"And I have always thought it helps if you can make it fun, and one of the ways you do that is let them think you're a little crazy, that you're interested in things outside of basketball. 'Are there weapons of mass destruction? Or aren't there? What, don't you read the papers?' You have to give the message that the world is wider than a basketball court."

Pop is getting antsy, worried that he's talking too much. The curtain is closing.

"As far as innovation goes . . ." one question begins.

"Oh, hell, I don't know anything about innovation," he says, rising. "Here is my innovation: I drafted Tim Duncan. O.K.? End of story."

And then he is off, back to the locker room, back where he can dispense blame and blessing in equal measure, back where the Republic of Pop functions best, nuanced and noisy but pretty much unheard in the outside world. ■

6

LARRY BROWN

TEN TEAMS 1972–2011

" Joke about the wanderlust all you want, but Larry Brown led nine teams to the playoffs, including the Bobcats—which alone should qualify him for this list. " —MARK BECHTEL

‣ 1,327–1,011 CAREER RECORD
‣ WON 2003–04 NBA TITLE WITH DETROIT

LARRY LED the ABA in assists his first three years as a pro, set the ABA assist record with 23 in a game. Then he became a coach, the keeper of a legacy, a branch of his sport's most legendary family tree. James Naismith, who invented the game, taught Phog Allen. Phog Allen taught Dean Smith. Dean Smith taught Larry. It was a source of deep pride, the only thing Larry ever came even close to saying in conceit: "My background," he'd say softly, ducking his head, "is probably better than anyone's." No coach was ever quicker than Larry at converting a collection of guys into a family. At UCLA he'd teach the freshmen at dinner how to start with the silverware on the outside. In the pros he took new players to look for apartments or cars and shoved restaurant tables together so his team could gather for a feast. No coach was ever quicker at spotting the smallest misstep, the slightest detour off the Right Way.

—Gary Smith, SI, April 23, 2001

Brown took Allen Iverson (right) to the Finals.

PHOTOGRAPHS BY JOHN BIEVER (LEFT) AND MANNY MILLAN

7

RED HOLZMAN

" When asked in 1967 to become the Knicks coach, scout Holzman first demurred. But he took the job and built a team that stressed pressure defense, unselfish offense and a cerebral approach to the game. " —JACK McCALLUM

▸ 696–604 CAREER RECORD
▸ TWO NBA TITLES

A GREAT coach is mature, able to understand his players. Red Holzman claimed that to get Dave DeBusschere to agree to anything you had to want the opposite of what you asked him. "Dave, we're not having shooting practice tomorrow," he would say. "Gee, Red, I don't think that's good for the team." "O.K., Dave, we'll shoot at three."

—*Bill Bradley, SI, October 31, 1977*

Holzman's Knicks made three Finals in a four-year span.

PHOTOGRAPH BY JOHN G. ZIMMERMAN

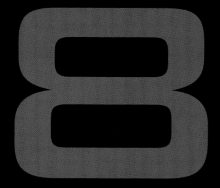

JOHN KUNDLA

LAKERS 1948–1959

> " A three-year $6,000 contract lured him from St. Thomas University to become the NBA's first dominant coach. Kundla transformed the Minneapolis Lakers into the league's original dynasty around the unprecedented low-post game of George Mikan. " —IAN THOMSEN

▸ 423–302 CAREER RECORD
▸ FIVE LEAGUE TITLES

KUNDLA'S FORMER players uniformly say that their coach's most valuable trait was a preternatural ability to cede power to the players without creating anarchy. "He was a great coach, one who really understood the players," says Mikan, who recently retired from his Minneapolis law practice and frequently joins Vern Mikkelsen and their old coach for breakfast. "John was very mild-mannered, but he'd let loose when we deserved it, and usually I was the first one he bawled out. The message he sent was that no one on the team was above criticism." "We had to be nice to John because he wasn't just the coach, he was also the traveling secretary, who reimbursed us for our expenses," jokes Mikkelsen. "John was a great X's-and-O's coach, and he was an absolute master at handling the egos. We had a lot of fun together, but when he had to, he ran a tight ship."

—L. Jon Wertheim, SI, November 3, 1997

Kundla rose to great heights with Mikan (99).

9

JERRY SLOAN

BULLS 1979-1982
JAZZ 1988-2011

" Perhaps the best coach never to win a championship, Sloan led Utah to the playoffs in 15 consecutive seasons. The pick-and-roll he ran for John Stockton and Karl Malone spawned a thousand imitators. " —LEE JENKINS

▸ 1,221–803 CAREER RECORD
▸ RECORD 1,809 CONSECUTIVE GAMES WITH ONE TEAM

THE MOST difficult challenge for an NBA franchise is to adjust to the loss of a superstar—or, in this case, two superstars. When, after the 2002–03 season, Stockton retired and Malone went to the Lakers, I was among those shocked that Sloan didn't follow. "Hell, no," Sloan snapped. "I'm looking forward to coaching these young guys."

—*Jack McCallum, SI, February 21, 2011*

Sloan's Jazz made it to the Finals twice.
PHOTOGRAPH BY JOHN W. MCDONOUGH

10

LENNY WILKENS

SONICS 1969–1972, 1977–1985
FIVE OTHER TEAMS

"A Hall of Famer as both coach and player, he turned around most of the losers he took charge of. And he led the Sonics to a title and U.S. Olympians to gold in 1996." —ALEXANDER WOLFF

▸ 1,332–1,155 CAREER RECORD
▸ WON 1978–79 NBA TITLE

SOMETHING EVEN more extraordinary than prolonged sunshine has been gracing Seattle lately. It could be some mystical force emanating from Slick Watts's headband. Or the figure from the past who has returned to lead the team out of the wilderness. Whatever it is, it began taking effect on Nov. 30. That was the day the Seattle SuperSonics stopped losing and started winning. Religiously. At that point they were 5–17, another candidate for Worst Team in History status. But on that Wednesday, the meek inherited the team. That is, smiling, beneficent Lenny Wilkens replaced howling, glowering Bob Hopkins as coach. And let anyone try to convince Wilkens he is not a genius. Under his leadership the Sonics are 12–3, including 5–2 on the road. "You always expect a little surge after a coaching change," says the modest Wilkens with a twinkle, "but this is too many wins to be a little surge." So it seems.

—John Papanek, SI, January 9, 1978

Wilkens's easygoing style fit his Seattle team perfectly.

PHOTOGRAPH BY PETER READ MILLER

10 THE

BEST SIXTH MEN

WHEREAS MOST OF THE STORY EXCERPTS IN THIS BOOK ARE UNAMBIGUOUS CELEBRATIONS, THE ONE IN THIS SECTION IS MORE UNEASY, A TALE OF ACCOMPLISHMENT TINGED BY DISAPPOINTMENT. IT IS THE STORY OF TONI KUKOC, WHO WENT FROM BEING A EUROPEAN SUPERSTAR TO A BENCH FIXTURE ON THE CHICAGO BULLS. WHILE HE EXCELLED AT HIS ROLE, HE WOULD RATHER HAVE BEEN ON THE COURT TO BEGIN THE GAME.

FOR SOME—INCLUDING KUKOC HIMSELF, EVENTUALLY—THE BENCH WAS INDEED A WAY STATION TO A STARTING ROLE. THE MOST NOTABLE EXAMPLES OF THIS ARE JOHN HAVLICEK AND KEVIN MCHALE. FOR SOME, THOUGH, IN THIS MIXED BAG OF A CATEGORY, THE BENCH POSITION WAS THEIR PEAK. CONSIDER VINNIE JOHNSON, WHO WAS AT HIS BEST IN HIS VALUED AND A DEFINED ROLE ON A TITLE TEAM.

COMPLICATING THE CATEGORY FURTHER ARE THE SIXTH MEN WHO PLAYED BIG MINUTES AND WERE OFTEN ON THE COURT WHEN GAMES WERE DECIDED AT THE END. THIS WAS TRUE OF THE INAUGURAL WINNER OF THE LEAGUE'S SIXTH MAN AWARD, BOBBY JONES IN 1982–83. THE NOMINAL STARTER AT POWER FORWARD ON THAT 76ERS TEAM WAS MARK IAVARONI, BUT "NO ONE EVER HAD TO TELL ME THAT BOBBY WAS BETTER THAN ME," IAVARONI SAID TO SI. "I KNEW IT MYSELF." SUCH RESPECT MAKES IT EASIER TO RIDE THE PINES AT THE OPENING TIP.

1

MANU GINÓBILI

SPURS 2002–PRESENT

" This was a tough choice since great sixth men are outstanding players who frequently start. But Ginóbili's off-the-bench dynamics have been a constant in San Antonio for a decade. " —JACK McCALLUM

▸ 2007–08 NBA SIXTH MAN OF THE YEAR
▸ FOUR NBA TITLES

EVEN AT THIS early stage of his career, the 6' 6" Ginóbili is different. He seems to be playing soccer on a basketball court. Rather than cutting and pounding and jackhammering, he swoops and pirouettes and floats. He does so much wrong, yet it often ends up being right. Coach Gregg Popovich doesn't know what to make of the kid, other than to love him. Ten years later Popovich will say that he never did coach Ginóbili, that if anything, "I had to learn to shut up and stop coaching, because if you put him too much in a cage, you lose his benefit."

Here was a player fueled not by stats or pride or fear—definitely not fear—but by pure intuition. That, and desire. Years later Kobe Bryant will say that there are only a few players in the league whose competitive fire he really respects. Ginóbili will be at the top of a short list. That guy, Bryant will say, "is a motherf-----."

—Chris Ballard, SI, June 10, 2013

Ginóbili has moved from bench to starter and back.

PHOTOGRAPH BY GREG NELSON

2

JOHN HAVLICEK

CELTICS 1962–1978

❝ It feels unfair to have Hondo on this team. Though known as a Sixth Man, he's also the Celtics' alltime scoring leader. A do-it-all player and the consummate winner, he's the guy everyone wants on his team. ❞ —CHRIS BALLARD

▸ MADE THREE OF HIS 13 ALL-STAR GAMES AS A SUB ▸ WON FIVE OF EIGHT NBA TITLES COMING OFF THE BENCH

"I STARTED TO shoot once against a very tall guy [in high school], and suddenly I knew I couldn't make the shot over him," Havlicek said. "So I just aimed for the backboard, rushed in, got the rebound and put it in. I took two shots to make one." Such quickness of body and mind have helped make Havlicek the superb substitute, even though he had come off the bench in only one game in college. He knew what coach Red Auerbach wanted: "My job was to come in there and get the team moving." He has been a key man in the fast break, since most breaks require three men. The two guards usually start the break, so the trick is to come up with the third man "to fill the lanes." Few cornermen can thunder out from underneath and catch up with their breaking teammates. Havlicek beats everybody downcourt.

—*Frank Deford, SI, May 9, 1966*

Even as a sub Havlicek averaged 20-plus points twice.

PHOTOGRAPH BY JAMES DRAKE

3

VINNIE JOHNSON

SONICS 1979–1981
PISTONS 1981–1991
SPURS 1991–1992

"Johnson—dubbed "the Microwave" for his ability to heat up quickly—was best known for the 14-footer he sank with less than a second on the clock to beat Portland in the series-clinching Game 5 of the 1990 Finals." —CHRIS MANNIX

▸ WON TWO NBA TITLES WITH PISTONS
▸ AVERAGED 14.1 POINTS IN PLAYOFFS IN 1988-89

VINNIE LEAVES a lot of defenders shaking their heads. He comes off the Pistons bench hotter than a microwaved sandwich. Detroit coach Chuck Daly calls it "a high-wire act." Get the ball, swing those long arms left, swing 'em right, dribble, lean, shoot that line-drive jumper. And he's not just an offensive player. "He comes after you," says Denver Nuggets guard Fat Lever, "and he's got the body to make you feel it. He's the little bear in a trench coat." Consider: Joe Dumars, who starts ahead of Vinnie, is rightly considered a tough, athletic, all-around player. But in 25 minutes per game, compared with Dumars's 31, Johnson has one less steal (60 to 61) and more rebounds (170 to 110). Any day in Detroit is apt to be V.J. Day.

—*Jack McCallum, SI, March 9, 1987*

Johnson was a bench player for all but one season.

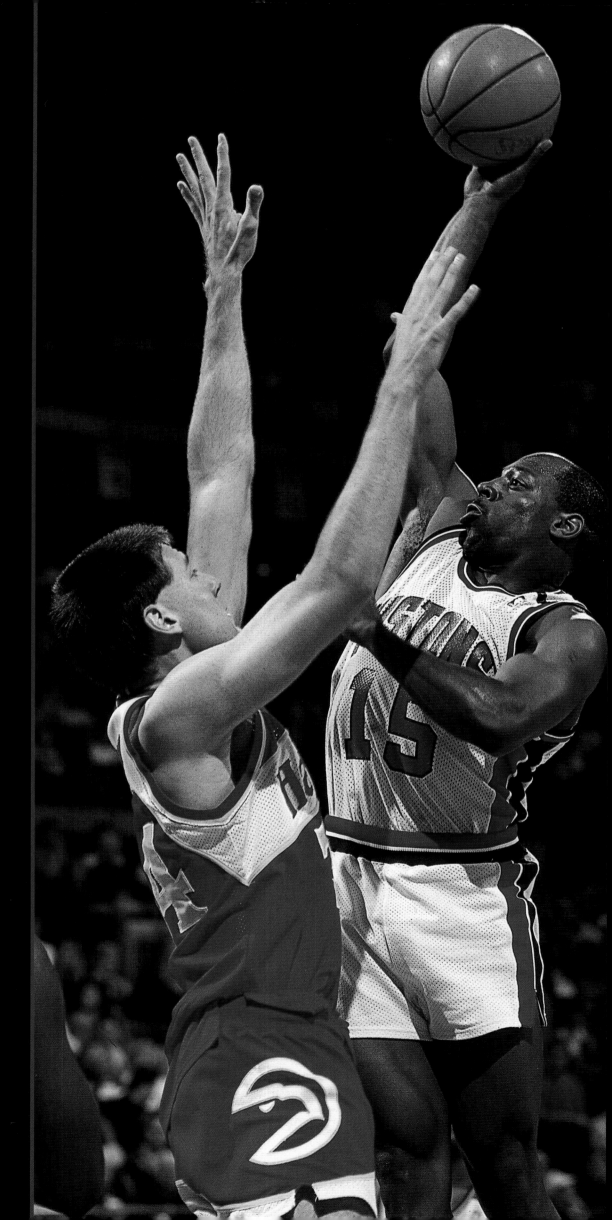

4

KEVIN McHALE

CELTICS 1980–1993

"Though he ranks among the NBA's greatest power forwards, the Celtics won two championships by bringing McHale off the bench over his first five seasons. His meticulous low-post game created diabolical mismatches against second-tier big men." —IAN THOMSEN

▸ TWO-TIME NBA SIXTH MAN OF THE YEAR
▸ NAMED ALL-STAR WHILE COMING OFF THE BENCH

BOSTON MAY HAVE been made even stronger by a spate of injuries that it sustained last month. Larry Bird's injury may have been significant on two counts. "When Bird went down they were forced to play Kevin McHale," says Philadelphia general manager Pat Williams. "Everyone in the league is scared to death of McHale anyway." As well they might be, because McHale is 6' 10" and extremely active, especially on defense. "When he's out there with Parish, there are so many long arms in your face you just can't get a shot up," adds Williams. And the Celtics learned something about themselves they might not otherwise have dared suspect. "People felt that without Bird the Celtics wouldn't be the Celtics," says Chicago coach Rod Thorn, "but they proved they are. Now they feel they're invincible."

—Bruce Newman, SI, April 19, 1982

McHale's long arms made his shots tough to block.

5

MICHAEL COOPER

LAKERS 1978–1990

> " Coop could play the 1, 2 or 3, but his greatest value was as a defender, coming off the bench to lock down whoever needed locking down. He was so tough on Larry Bird that he was dubbed Larry's Shadow. " —MARK BECHTEL

▸ NAMED 1986–87 DEFENSIVE PLAYER OF THE YEAR AS A SUB
▸ FIVE NBA TITLES

MICHAEL COOPER has become, quite simply, the best player off the bench in pro basketball. A third-round draft choice out of the University of New Mexico who was almost cut by the Los Angeles Lakers two seasons ago, Cooper earned a spot on the roster with his defense and then he went out last summer and got himself a jump shot. Now the second leading shooter among the league's guards (.541). Coupe de Ville, as he is called by his teammates, has become a virtual cult figure among Lakers fans, who breathlessly await each new Coop-a-Loop. That is an alley-oop, sky-slam play that Cooper has made his trademark this season. "We've been called a circus," Cooper says, "and while the fans come to watch the other guys, I show 'em my act. I'm just a sideshow right now, trying to get to the main tent."

—Bruce Newman, SI, February 8, 1982

Cooper was a weapon on both ends of the floor.

SIXTH MEN

6

DETLEF SCHREMPF

PACERS 1988–1993
SONICS 1993–1999
TWO OTHER TEAMS

─────────────────────────

" A forerunner to Dirk Nowitzki, Schrempf was a 6' 9" German import who could score, pass and rebound. For 10 consecutive years he topped 15 points per game. " —LEE JENKINS

─────────────────────────

▸ TWO-TIME NBA SIXTH MAN OF THE YEAR
▸ THREE-TIME ALL-STAR

Schrempf's strength was his versatility.

PHOTOGRAPH BY MANNY MILLAN

HE HAS bulked up 15 pounds, to 215, and [now] plays inside, but he still has the latitude to use his rare skills: the touch to hit the three-pointer, the power to rip a rebound and the speed to run the break. Most of Schrempf's family is in West Germany. It's a long way from Indiana, but winning is a major consolation.

—Hank Hersch, SI, December 25, 1989

7

BOBBY JONES

NUGGETS 1974–1978
76ERS 1978–1986

" After unfolding himself off the bench, Jones used his loping length to give Sixers teams of the early '80s a lift at both ends of the floor. No less an authority than Doctor J called him the best white dunker of all time. " —ALEXANDER WOLFF

▸ 1982–83 NBA SIXTH MAN OF THE YEAR
▸ FIVE-TIME ALL-STAR

PERHAPS THE Sixers' greatest strength is their bench. "We feel if we play the other team even with our starters, we will gain with our subs," says Julius Erving. Bobby Jones is in the John Havlicek mold as a sixth man and, having been a starter for all of his five-year career, relishes the role. "I get fewer minutes but they are more intense minutes," he says.

—John Papanek, SI, November 5, 1979

The gentlemanly Jones had tremendous hops.
PHOTOGRAPH BY ROBERT LEWIS/NBAE/GETTY IMAGES

The "MJ of Europe" played alongside the real thing.

PHOTOGRAPH BY DAVID E. KLUTHO

8

BULLS 1993–2000
THREE TEAMS THROUGH 2006

"One of the greater NBA What If questions is how good Kukoc could have been had he entered the league young and played on a team where he was the star." —CHRIS BALLARD

▸ 1995–96 NBA SIXTH MAN OF THE YEAR
▸ THREE NBA TITLES

CHICAGO HAS little use for the traditional concept of positions, because Michael Jordan, Scottie Pippen and Kukoc are all skilled enough to play the point and big enough to post up defenders. "Just a bunch of versatile guys playing different positions," Jordan says. "That's the way the game is going."

—*Phil Taylor, SI, January 29, 1996*

TONI
KUKOC

PINING FOR PLAYING TIME

The transition from European superstar to American bench player wasn't always a happy one for forward Toni Kukoc, even though it worked out superbly for the Bulls

BY MICHAEL FARBER

RENATA KUKOC FINISHES dressing, kisses four-year-old Marin and baby Stela, picks up a girlfriend, then starts negotiating her way from her northwestern suburb to the United Center on Chicago's West Side. The trip can take 35 minutes or it can take an hour, but if the timing is right and the traffic cooperative, Renata will settle into her end-court seat five or six minutes into the first quarter, sometimes at the precise moment her husband is stripping off his Chicago Bulls warmups.

Except for those nights when Dennis Rodman is serving a suspension for having split the uprights or something, Toni Kukoc is the sixth man for the NBA champion Bulls. Indeed, last season Kukoc won the NBA's Sixth Man Award, a prize that left him with a healthy ambivalence—as if someone had named him smartest kid in the dumb row or funniest sitcom on CBS. Kukoc received the Sixth Man Award at a ceremony in New York City during the playoffs. He was stuck in traffic, arrived late, offered his profuse and sincere thanks, then said if it were all the same, he would rather start. Kukoc may have felt somewhat like Abraham Lincoln, who when asked how he enjoyed being president, said, in effect, that if it weren't for the honor of the thing, he would just as soon have passed.

"That's the award I'm not supposed to care about," Kukoc says as he walks into the kitchen of his expansive home, brandishing the trophy. The Sixth Man Award has pride of place in the living room; it's the first thing visible from the front door. Kukoc is, in a measured way, truly flattered to have received it. But to put his impolitic response at the ceremony in context, you have to understand where Kukoc is coming from.

Europe. Kukoc has come from Europe. "He was the MJ of Europe," says Ivica Dukan, the Bulls' supervisor of European scouting and a former teammate of Kukoc's in their native Croatia. Now Kukoc plays with the MJ of the other six continents and—judging by the movie *Space Jam*—the galaxy as well. Like Bugs Bunny, Kukoc is a member of the Tune Squad, just one more role player in Michael Jordan's universe.

It has been almost four years since Kukoc left finger-rollin', zone-playin' Europe for the harder, richer life of the NBA, where the statue isn't Michelangelo's *David* but Michael outside the United Center. Kukoc has been a qualified success. His defense has improved from clueless to ordinary, he disappears on the road at times, and he still has trouble rebounding in traffic. But Kukoc has progressed enough that he is certainly one of the top 30 players in the league, one whose deadly shooting and inventive playmaking opponents respect, even fear. "If you put your big people on him, they can't handle him on the perimeter," says Milwaukee Bucks forward Vin Baker. "If you put your small people on him, he'll post them inside. He's a matchup nightmare."

"He's the X ingredient in our game," says Bulls coach Phil Jackson. "If he has a great game, we're going to be unbeatable."

For the privilege of being an NBA enigma, Kukoc, in 1993, bought out his contract with Benetton Treviso of Italy for about $3 million from his own pocket. Never mind the $4.4 million or so Chicago pays Kukoc each year; $3 million is still a princely sum to spend to be abused. Since Mike Ditka left Jim Harbaugh alone, has any Chicago athlete been yelled at as often as Kukoc? Jackson has zenned in on him; Jordan has hectored him; Scottie Pippen has goaded him. Kukoc has taken it well enough. But during his first two seasons in Chicago, after a poor game or an unsettling practice, Kukoc would storm into the house and say, "That's it, who needs it, we're going back to Europe."

"Our housekeeper, Zdravka, came to me in tears one time," Renata says. "She says, 'Are you really leaving? Toni says so.' I told her to leave him alone, that he would feel different tomorrow. Toni has packed and unpacked a hundred times in his mind."

Kukoc wouldn't still be trying to convert Euroball into NBA hard currency if he had been, say, some big kid from Duke. Trouble is, his reputation in Europe didn't so much precede him as retard him. Jordan declined to look at tapes Bulls general manager Jerry Krause supplied of the Croatian prodigy the Bulls drafted 29th overall in 1990, and when the GM asked Jordan to call and encourage Kukoc to come to Chicago, Jordan was quoted as saying, "I don't speak no Yugoslavian." Jordan and Pippen finally faced Kukoc when he was playing for Croatia at the '92 Olympics, and they not only had him for lunch, but they also looked as if they were having a grand time playing with their food.

Pippen in particular seemed offended by the extended courtship of Kukoc, not surprising when his own contract concerns were on the back burner. "This club went out of its way to find Toni, get Toni and pay him a lot of money," Jackson says. "At the same time [it] couldn't find a way to honor someone [Pippen] who had done the job [here] for years." This was business. (Pippen's salary is a paltry $2.375 million.) So, apparently, was Pippen's refusal to play the last 1.8 seconds of regulation in an Eastern Conference semifinal playoff game against the New York Knicks in 1994 after Jackson designed the last shot for Kukoc—a shot Kukoc sank to win the game.

If this were a perfect world Kukoc would be starting, playing 40 minutes, scoring 18 to 20 points per game, averaging seven assists and seven rebounds and "doing all kinds of things I used to over there." But this is the imperfect world of the World's Greatest Basketball Team. "I have a middle line," Kukoc says. "I am pretty much above that middle line, in between perfect and bottom." ∎

RICKY PIERCE

BUCKS 1984–1991
SONICS 1991–1994
SEVEN OTHER TEAMS

❝ A sixth man is basketball's version of an arsonist: Sneak in, light it up, disappear. Pierce did that as well as anyone, averaging more than 20 points a game twice while he was a sub. ❞ —JACK McCALLUM

▸ TWO-TIME NBA SIXTH MAN OF THE YEAR
▸ 1991 ALL-STAR WHILE A BENCH PLAYER

FOR THE first half of the first quarter, Ricky Pierce will sit, studying the play before him with practiced ease. His elbows rest on his knees; his hands hold a towel. After six or seven minutes have passed, coach Del Harris will summon Pierce and usher him into the game as Milwaukee's first substitute at big guard or, more often, small forward. "My job," he says, "is to come in and score." The 31-year-old Pierce is known as the Deuces by his teammates, as much for his ability to quickly pile up points in pairs as for his jersey number, 22. Last season Pierce averaged 23.0 points and 29 minutes a game, which gave him a projected scoring average of 38.1 points for a full 48 minutes; only Chicago's Michael Jordan (41.4) and Utah's Karl Malone (39.1) had higher projected scoring figures.

—Hank Hersch, SI, January 14, 1991

Pierce averaged a career-best 23.0 points in 1989–90.

Ramsey was the original sixth man.
PHOTOGRAPH BY FRED KAPLAN

10

FRANK RAMSEY

CELTICS 1954–1955, 1956–1964

" He never started for the Celtics, but Ramsey made the Hall of Fame for his contributions to seven championships. Red Auerbach invented the "sixth man" to define Ramsey's game-changing role off the bench. " —IAN THOMSEN

▸ JERSEY RETIRED BY CELTICS
▸ AVERAGED 23.2 POINTS IN 1958–59 PLAYOFFS

RAMSEY'S DEPARTURE is, in a way, more the end of an era than Bob Cousy's was [when he retired]. Ramsey is the last of the 6' 3" forwards. In the playoffs, 6' 3" forward Ramsey guarded 6' 11" forward Nate Thurmond. There will be no more of that.

—*Frank Deford, SI, May 4, 1964*

10 THE

BEST THREE-POINT SHOOTERS

ONE CATEGORY IN WHICH WE DID NOT POLL OUR PANELISTS WAS FREE THROW SHOOTING, BECAUSE IT DID NOT SEEM THERE WOULD BE A LOT TO IT. YOU LOOK AT THE LIST OF TOP ALLTIME SHOOTERS, YOU COPY THE LIST, MAYBE ADJUSTING FOR CLUTCH SHOTS OR HOW YOU FEEL ABOUT RICK BARRY SHOOTING UNDERHAND, AND THERE YOU HAVE IT.

THE VOTE FOR BEST THREE-POINT SHOOTERS DID NOT GO BY THE NUMBERS. LOOK AT THE LIST OF ALLTIME FIELD GOAL PERCENTAGE LEADERS AND YOU'LL SEE PLAYERS SUCH AS HUBERT DAVIS, TIM LEGLER AND JASON KAPONO WHO RECEIVED NARY A VOTE. FOR THOSE ROLE PLAYERS, THREE-POINT SHOOTING WAS THE REASON THEY LASTED IN THE NBA. THE PANEL IN MANY CASES FAVORED STARS FOR WHOM THEIR THREE-POINT ACCURACY WAS BUT ONE WEAPON IN THEIR ARSENAL. FOR NUMBERS TO MATTER, THEY HAD TO BE EXCEPTIONAL. STEVE KERR, WHO IS THE NBA CAREER LEADER IN THREE-POINT PERCENTAGE, RANKS FOURTH HERE.

THIS LIST HAPPENS TO BE HOME TO THE YOUNGEST PLAYER IN THE BOOK AT ANY CATEGORY, STEPHEN CURRY. IN HIS FIRST FIVE SEASONS HE SHOWED A VERSATILITY THAT LED SOME PANELISTS TO OVERLOOK THE BREVITY OF HIS EXPERIENCE. THE THREE-POINT LINE HAS ONLY BEEN IN THE NBA SINCE 1979–80. CURRY IS SHOWING WHAT A PLAYER CAN DO WITH IT.

1

RAY ALLEN

BUCKS 1996–2003
SONICS 2003–2007
CELTICS 2007–2012
HEAT 2012–PRESENT

" The accuracy of the NBA's alltime leader in threes made improved as Allen extended his career. His conditioning and a blink-quick trigger culminated in Allen's championship-saving three in Game 6 of the 2013 Finals. " —IAN THOMSEN

▸ 40.0 CAREER THREE-POINT PERCENTAGE
▸ LED NBA IN THREE-POINTERS MADE THREE TIMES

SEATED IN his folding chair while nodding toward a basket 35 feet away, Allen asked, "What's the chance of me making this right here?" One in three, someone said. "He won't hit the rim," shouted backup guard Antonio Daniels. Allen rocked back in the chair, lifting his right foot and then slamming it down for leverage as he released. The ball spun like a golfer's wedge shot before ricocheting off the edge of the backboard. Daniels retrieved the ball. "One in three," Allen repeated, and his next attempt hit the side of the rim. The third shot flew over the head of the momentarily distracted Daniels, who missed the result. "Did he make that?" Daniels said. Make it he did. A swish from a folding chair at 35 feet.

—Ian Thomsen, SI, May 16, 2005

Allen shot over Kobe Bryant in the 2010 NBA Finals.

PHOTOGRAPH BY BOB ROSATO

2

REGGIE MILLER

PACERS 1987–2005

" He had parking-lot range, a sublime release, a Havlicekian way of moving without the ball and a knack for the moment. Most three-point artists are complementary players, but for 18 years in Indianapolis, Miller was the main man. " —ALEXANDER WOLFF

▸ 39.5 CAREER THREE-POINT PERCENTAGE
▸ LED NBA IN THREE-POINTERS MADE TWICE

TO A LARGE degree the art of jump shooting remains a mystery. Miller admires several shooters—he names the Cavaliers' Mark Price, the Suns' Dan Majerle and Danny Ainge, the Nuggets' Dale Ellis and the Pistons' Joe Dumars—but doesn't see much stylistic resemblance among them. If he wanted to be a textbook shooter, Miller knows that he would have to keep his right elbow in, tucked close to his body. But his elbow flies out to the side. Like many great shooters, he is somewhat superstitious and subscribes to a pregame routine that does not change: He always puts on his compression shorts first, then his game shorts, then his jersey, then a T-shirt over the jersey. Then he takes an Advil because— endorsement alert!—"I know I'm going to be talking a lot, and I don't want to get a headache."

—Jack McCallum, SI, November 7, 1994

Miller was a vocal believer in his abilities.

PHOTOGRAPH BY MANNY MILLAN

3

LARRY BIRD

CELTICS 1979–1992

" With a high release and unflinching confidence that he could make threes from, well, anywhere, Bird was automatic from deep. Still is, really. In his mid-50s and with a debilitating back injury, Bird reportedly made 15 jumpers in a row at a Pacers workout. " —CHRIS MANNIX

▸ 37.6 CAREER THREE-POINT PERCENTAGE
▸ LED NBA IN THREE-POINTERS MADE TWICE

"THE ONE thing you have to avoid when you talk about Bird is statistics," says Red Auerbach. "It's his presence, the total way he commands attention on the court, that counts." Indeed, Bird reserves a spot in his personal hell for the guy who plays with one eye on the stat sheet. . . . Above all, it is Bird's ability to hit a shot under pressure that makes him great. Scott Wedman may beat him in H-O-R-S-E now and then, and Ainge took him for $35 in a game two weeks ago in Seattle, but turn on the TV lights and put 15,000 hostile fans in the seats and Bird has no peer. His winning 18-of-25 performance in the three-point field-goal contest on NBA All-Star Game weekend proved that. "When I found out Birdie could make 10 grand shooting baskets in one afternoon," said Kevin McHale, "I knew it was all over."

—Jack McCallum, SI, March 3, 1986

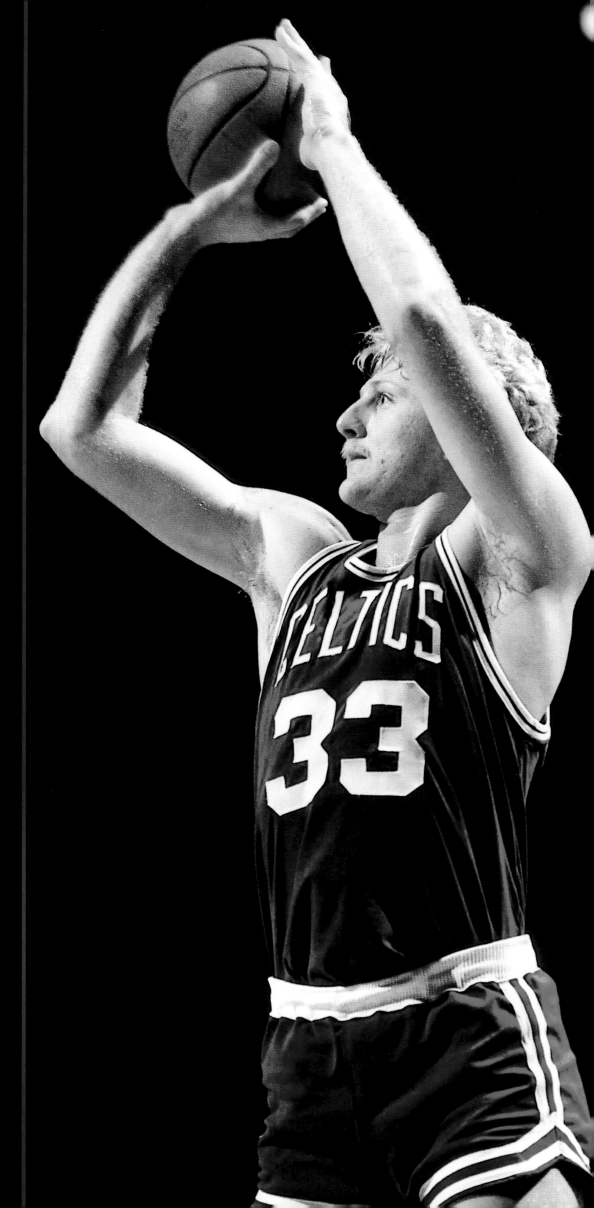

Bird was at his best when the pressure was highest.

STEVE KERR

BULLS 1993-1998
SPURS 1998-2001, 2002-2003
FOUR OTHER TEAMS

" The most accurate three-point sniper ever, Kerr won five NBA titles, and he did more than space the floor for Michael Jordan. His three-pointer in the closing seconds of Game 6 of the '97 Finals lifted Chicago over Utah. " —LEE JENKINS

▸ 45.4 CAREER THREE-POINT PERCENTAGE
▸ SHOT 52.4 PERCENT FROM THREE IN 1994-95

IN SAN ANTONIO, Spurs brake for goose bumps, not speed bumps, as when Steve Kerr steered onto his street after Game 6 of the Western Conference finals and slowed to see, in yard after yard, hand-lettered signs limned in porch light: CONGRATULATIONS, STEVE, and GO SPURS GO. His own yard lay beneath a riot of toilet paper, as if a shower of Charmin had fallen on the city. A day later, as all of San Antonio was abuzz about Kerr—and his four three-pointers that sent the Spurs into the NBA Finals against the Nets—he slipped into an Italian restaurant for dinner. As recognition registered, patrons began popping to their feet, table by table, until the entire room had risen in applause. "Pretty amazing," says Kerr, 37. "And all for 13 minutes of action."

—*Steve Rushin, SI, June 16, 2003*

Kerr came off the bench in all but 30 career games.

PHOTOGRAPH BY NATHANIEL S. BUTLER/NBAE/GETTY IMAGES

TOUGHER THAN YOU THINK

Steve Kerr may have a vanilla exterior, but he showed rare resiliency in overcoming much more than limited athleticism to become an alltime great outside shooter

BY MICHAEL SILVER

WITH HIS FRAIL-looking frame, freckled face and milky skin, Kerr can walk onto any playground in the country with no chance of being picked first. All over America, whenever quicker, stronger gym rats see Kerr in action, they must wonder, How can that guy be out there instead of me?

That's a question even Kerr concedes is valid. It is why, he says, "I don't have any fans my age. Almost all of my fans are either grandmothers who think I look like their grandsons or eight-year-old boys, who can relate to me."

Even so, Kerr has carved out a niche as one of the NBA's best long-range shooters. His signature shooting style—quick jump, arm and fingers extended, hair flying—is one born of a million practice shots. Charles Barkley said that if he had to pick one player to sink a game-winning shot, it would be Kerr. And Kerr's reaction? "I thought he was joking."

There were times in Kerr's career when he was in awe of his surroundings, and none more so than the latter part of the 1994–95 season, his second with the Bulls. After finding lukewarm success in stints with Phoenix, Cleveland and Orlando, Kerr had become a significant member of the Bulls immediately following Michael Jordan's retirement in October '93. But according to coach Phil Jackson, when Jordan returned to the team in March '95, "it was tough on Steve because our players had used our offensive system to get *their* shots, and now everything had changed. All of a sudden players were putting on the brakes and saying, 'Oh, well, we'd better watch Michael go one-on-one.' There was tension, and it boiled over the next year in training camp."

The Kerr-Jordan relationship was further strained in the off-season when the two players took opposing sides in the NBA players' union split during labor talks. The bitterness came to a head during a practice in which Kerr and Jordan were repeatedly pushing off while defending each other. Kerr, who hadn't been in a fight since elementary school, takes a hard shove from His Airness and suddenly started swinging. "I knew I had two choices," Kerr says. "Either let it go and be obedient to Michael forever, or fight and probably get my ass kicked. I picked a real winner for my adult fighting debut." He wound up with a black eye.

When Kerr arrived home, he found an apology from Jordan waiting on his answering machine, and the relationship quickly changed for the better. Previously Jordan rode Kerr for everything from a missed shot to a lack of aggressiveness. That stopped after their fight, and Kerr has become a Jordan favorite.

The two players have a lot in common, including the fact that their fathers were murdered.

Shortly before 3 a.m. on Jan. 18, 1984, during his freshman year at Arizona, Steve was awakened in his dorm room by a telephone call. Vake Simonian, a Presbyterian minister and a family friend, delivered the bad news: Steve's father, Dr. Malcolm Kerr, a noted Middle East scholar and the president of the American University in Beirut, Lebanon, had been assassinated. A group of unknown assailants gunned down Dr. Kerr, 52, as he stepped from a university elevator, an apparent act of anti-American terrorism. "I was an 18-year-old kid who had just left home, and it scared the hell out of me," Kerr says. "It's a lot different reading in the newspaper about someone dying than actually having it happen to you. It's an instant dose of perspective. It makes every day more precious when you realize it could all be gone in an instant."

Nevertheless he scored 15 points in a game two nights later. The tragedy steeled him for the challenges to come. During his sophomore and junior years Kerr developed into a solid starter. Then, as a member of the college all-star team representing the U.S. in the 1986 world championships in Madrid, he suffered torn anterior cruciate and medial collateral ligaments in his right knee, an injury that was initially diagnosed as career-ending. He sat out a year and returned in '87–88, helping Arizona to the first Final Four appearance in school history. The Suns made him a second-round pick in the draft.

Tonight in Chicago, the United Center is rocking for a rematch of last year's NBA Finals pitting the Bulls against the Seattle SuperSonics. Jordan, Dennis Rodman and Scottie Pippen of the Bulls and Gary Payton and Shawn Kemp of the Sonics have their moments, but the game doesn't pick up until the fourth quarter. With 9:57 to go Kerr nails a three-pointer to tie the game at 62, then makes two steals (one of which leads to a hoop) in 33 seconds. The game goes into overtime, and the Sonics take an 80–78 lead. With 2:59 remaining, Longley delivers a bounce pass into the paint to Kerr, who goes right to the basket fearlessly. He gets nailed by 6' 5" Nate McMillan, but the ball goes through the hoop. The free throw, of course, is good. His totals: 13 points on 5-of-6 shooting, with two assists and three steals. The Bulls win 89–87. As the buzzer sounds, Kerr and Jordan slap hands and revel in the moment.

It's one of those images those who grew up with Kerr would like to freeze and preserve for their own children, if only to show that dreams can come true. But Kerr is embarrassed by the corniness of his story. For him it's easier to file it away as a comedy than as a drama. "I don't think a day goes by where I don't think, How the hell did this ever happen?" he says. "It's like Walter Mitty, only it's the real thing. Or maybe Forrest Gump is more appropriate. He kept showing up in places out of nowhere, and it was like, How the hell did he get here?" ∎

5

STEVE NASH

SUNS 1996–1998, 2004–2012
MAVERICKS 1998–2004
LAKERS 2012–PRESENT

"Unlike a lot of guys with high three-point percentages, Nash has never been a spot-up shooter. He's always been a creator, and as a result, he's mastered one of the game's toughest shots, the three off the dribble." —MARK BECHTEL

▸ 42.8 CAREER THREE-POINT PERCENTAGE
▸ NBA TOP 10 IN THREE-POINT PERCENTAGE EIGHT TIMES

WHEN STEVE NASH is not pulling up beyond the arc, he can corkscrew his body to get off a reverse in the lane or launch a deadly fadeaway. . . . If a lead guard is deadly from the outside, opponents have to play up on him, and that increases his opportunities for what the Suns call "blow-bys." There are nights when [guards such as] Gilbert Arenas, Allen Iverson and Baron Davis are unstoppable, but opponents can always play off them and make them hit a few outside shots. Steve Nash, like the Detroit Pistons' playmaker, Chauncey Billups, must always be crowded. The Phoenix assistants joke that they want to rebound for Nash when he works on his jumper before and after practice. "You just stand under the basket, and it comes right to you," says assistant coach Alvin Gentry.

—*Jack McCallum, SI, January 30, 2006*

Long balls were but one part of Nash's repertoire.

PHOTOGRAPH BY JOHN W. MCDONOUGH

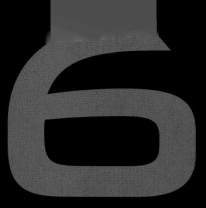

6

DALE ELLIS

SONICS 1986–1991, 1997–1999
FIVE OTHER TEAMS

" Ellis's long-range percentage, only 24th alltime, belies his contention that he's the "best shooter ever." (Honest, he said that.) But he is the player who turned the trey into a weapon, a guy who would pass up a fast-break layup for a long-range dagger. The longer the shot, the more accurate Ellis was. " —JACK MCCALLUM

- 40.3 CAREER THREE-POINT PERCENTAGE
- LEAGUE-BEST 46.4% FROM THREE IN 1997–98

ONE WAY Ellis gets good three-point looks is by spotting up in transition. "I love trailing on the fast break, where my teammate will take the ball to the middle and dish it out to me on the wing," Ellis says. "Sometimes I might even let the guy on the other wing run out ahead of me to draw the defense toward him." Conventional wisdom might dictate putting a rangy defender on a three-point specialist to keep him from getting a clear view of the rim, but the 6' 7" Ellis doesn't buy that approach. "I can get open a lot easier against taller, slower guys, either by going around them or running them off screens," Ellis says. "Smaller, quicker guys do a better job denying me the basketball, but I can shoot over them." Try to keep him from getting open? That's a long shot indeed.

—*Marty Burns, SI, January 26, 1998*

Ellis was mainly a post-up player in college.

PHOTOGRAPH BY JOHN W. MCDONOUGH

GLEN RICE

HEAT 1989–1995
FIVE TEAMS THROUGH 2004

" Though dogged by a selfish rep for most of his career, no one doubted Rice's stroke. The third-leading scorer on the Lakers' 1999–2000 title team, Rice's perimeter skills cleared gaping holes for Shaquille O'Neal and Kobe Bryant to operate. " —CHRIS MANNIX

▸ 40.0 CAREER THREE-POINT PERCENTAGE
▸ LEAGUE-BEST 47.0% FROM THREE IN 1996–97

WHEN THE SUN was setting and the other kids were leaving the courts, young Glen Rice would hang around, taking jump shots in the dying light, straining to see the rim as the sky grew darker. Gray would fade to black, and still Rice would shoot, thinking that if he could train his eyes to find the basket in the night, shooting in decent light would seem easy by comparison. It may not have been the most scientific theory, but Rice believed in it, and any shooter can tell you how important that kind of faith is. Shooting is a matter of the mind. Rice's mind has always been strong, his faith in that jump shot unwavering. "The only thing more consistent than Glen's jumper," says T.R. Dunn, an assistant coach for Rice's Hornets, "is his confidence in his jumper.

—*Phil Taylor, SI, February 24, 1997*

Rice's jumper made him a three-time All-Star.

PHOTOGRAPH BY JOHN W. MCDONOUGH

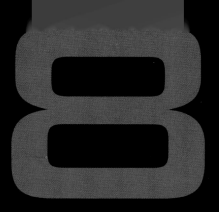

STEPHEN CURRY

WARRIORS 2009–PRESENT

" Weird to say of such a young player, but Steph may already be the best of all time. Unlike most spot-up shooters, he excels off the dribble, from deep distance and on the move. He can hit runners, fadeaways and fast-break threes. The accuracy of most volume shooters suffers; Steph nearly led the league in percentage in 2012–13 while breaking the alltime makes mark for a season. " —CHRIS BALLARD

- 44.0 CAREER THREE-POINT PERCENTAGE
- LED NBA IN THREE-POINTERS MADE TWICE

"IF THE Mike Millers and Danny Greens of the NBA are Floor Spacers, sentries arrayed around the arc to create room for their team's stars to operate, Curry is a different breed. He creates his own space, but he also thrives in the absence of it. Because Curry is the primary ballhandler, Golden State can essentially use him to create for other Spacers. For to leave Curry open behind the line, unattended and feet set, is to invite death-by-three-ball. "Oh, I'd love to be one of those spacer guys," Curry says. A good approximation of how this might look is a drill the Warriors guards do, in which they take threes at various spots around the arc until they miss two in a row. Curry's high? Seventy-six.

—*Chris Ballard, SI, May 13, 2013*

Curry can strike quickly from anywhere on the floor.

PHOTOGRAPH BY JOHN W. MCDONOUGH

PEJA
STOJAKOV

KINGS 1998–2006
FOUR TEAMS THROUGH 20

" Taller than most marksmen, Stojak
was almost impossible to contest, lea
him with open threes he rarely miss
He played for five teams, but he will
remembered for stretching the net
in Sacramento. " —LEE JENKIN

▸ 40.1 CAREER THREE-POI
PERCENTAGE
▸ LED NBA IN THREE-POINT
MADE IN 2003–04

FINDING FAULT with Peja Stojakovic
offensive game these days is
difficult, even for Kings assistant
coach Pete Carril, who describes
himself as "the crankiest, most
critical pain in the ass there is."
Timberwolves guard Fred Hoiberg
considers Stojakovic "number 1
by far" among NBA shooters. And
no less a deity than Larry Bird, to
whom the 6' 9" Stojakovic can
be compared in size and shooting
range, considers him "the best
shooter in the league by far." The
former Celtics great recently
marveled to *The Sacramento
Bee* about the consistency of
Stojakovic's shot. "When Peja lets
the ball go, it looks like it's going
in every time," said Bird. "The ball
hardly goes left or right. If he misse
it's always front or back rim. That'
the sign of a great shooter."

—Jack McCallum, SI, January 19, 2004

Stojakovic's form was unconventional but effec
PHOTOGRAPH BY ROBERT BECK

ROBERT HORRY

ROCKETS 1992–1996
SUNS 1996–1997
LAKERS 1997–2003
SPURS 2003–2008

" He had a way of finding himself on great teams and in huge situations. Whether "Big Shot Rob" made others better or vice versa, the master of the timely three wound up winning seven titles with three different clubs. " —ALEXANDER WOLFF

4.1 CAREER THREE-POINT PERCENTAGE
5.9 CAREER THREE POINT PERCENTAGE IN PLAYOFFS

ROBERT HORRY, the 6' 10", third-year forward, was clearly the Rocket who opened the most eyes during the playoffs. Horace Grant, the Magic power forward who had such a difficult time in the Finals against Horry, astutely compared Horry with Scottie Pippen, Grant's former Chicago teammate. Horry's astounding versatility was indeed reminiscent of Pippen's. He is both a dangerous three-point shooter and an excellent slasher and finisher around the basket. He also played defense, rebounded and handled the ball exceedingly well, and had it not been for the spectacular play of Hakeem Olajuwon, Horry would have received serious consideration for Finals MVP.

—Phil Taylor, SI, June 26, 1995

e Spurs were one of Horry's three title teams.

PHOTOGRAPH BY BOB ROSATO

1

WILT CHAMBERLAIN

WARRIORS 1959–1965
76ERS 1965–1968
LAKERS 1968–1973

"At 7' 1" and 275 pounds, Wilt the Stilt towered over opponents in the paint, treating every rebound like his birthright. The leading rebounder in NBA history, Chamberlain averaged more than 21 rebounds per game in 10 different seasons." —LEE JENKINS

▸ CAREER AVERAGE OF
  22.9 REBOUNDS
▸ 11 REBOUNDING TITLES

CHAMBERLAIN WAS magnificent [in Game 6 of the East finals]. He set a playoff record of 41 rebounds, many of them coming because he was trailing every Boston break when he should have been gasping for breath at the other end of the floor. "I've never moved so much in my life," he said later. "Not even the night I scored 100." That says more about the way Chamberlain played than all the testimonials. On offense there was no pressure on the 76ers to set up and wait for him to move into the pivot. On the contrary, by throwing the long lead pass repeatedly, Wilt was taking himself out of the offensive play, giving his teammates the scoring advantage. On defense he allowed them to play the aggressive game that the Celtics have used with Russell for a decade.

—*Frank Deford, SI, April 17, 1967*

Wilt rebounded well even after his scoring declined.

PHOTOGRAPH BY LONG PHOTOGRAPHY INC.

DENNIS RODMAN

PISTONS 1986–1993
BULLS 1995–1998
THREE OTHER TEAMS

❝ At 6' 7", the Worm pulled down boards with sheer desire and hustle. When his career was over, he had twice as many rebounds as field goal attempts—and five rings. ❞ —MARK BECHTEL

▸ CAREER AVERAGE OF 13.1 REBOUNDS
▸ SEVEN REBOUNDING TITLES

"WILT WAS JUST bigger and stronger than everyone," says TNT analyst Chuck Daly, who coached Rodman when they were both with the Pistons. "Russell was built more along the lines of Dennis, but he didn't have to go up against power forwards and centers as big as the ones Dennis has to face night after night. When you factor size into the equation, I don't know how you could say there's ever been a better rebounder." Rodman simultaneously has reduced rebounding to a science while elevating it to an art. After winning a battle for the ball, he will cradle it like a baby, or look at it quizzically as if seeing it for the first time, or whip it quickly to a teammate as though it were some disgusting object. "I rebound with a little flair, a little something extra," he says. "It's not for the crowd, it's just for me. Rebounding is how I express myself on the floor."

—*Phil Taylor, SI, March 4, 1996*

Rodman first gained fame for his relentless hustle.

CELTICS 1956–1969

Spring and reach helped Russell clean the glass.

PHOTOGRAPH BY WALTER IOOSS JR.

3

BILL RUSSELL

" The NBA was transformed by the Celtics' fast break, which revolved around the outlet passing of Russell, who never led his team in scoring but led in rebounding every year. Athleticism and ambition enabled him to outreach the bigger centers. " —IAN THOMSEN

▸ CAREER AVERAGE OF 22.5 REBOUNDS
▸ FIVE REBOUNDING TITLES

"I REMEMBER one time I posed for a gag picture with Swede Halbrook," Russell said. "He's 7 foot 3—more than five inches taller than I am. He held the ball as high as he could over his head and I stood next to him and reached up. My hands were on that ball. Don't think that's not a help in rebounding."

—Jeremiah Tax, SI, February 3, 1958

4
MOSES
MALONE

ROCKETS 1976–1982
76ERS 1982–1986
EIGHT OTHER TEAMS

" At his bogarting best Moses was the most gifted offensive rebounder of all time. " —ALEXANDER WOLFF

▸ CAREER AVERAGE OF
12.3 REBOUNDS
▸ SIX REBOUNDING TITLES

"IN THE FIVE seasons since [joining the Rockets], he has won two NBA rebounding titles, finished second twice and third once. The numbers this year: 14.8 rebounds, more than two a game better than anyone else. He's the reason the Rockets have become only the second team with a losing regular-season record (40–42) ever to reach the NBA Finals. "I love to rebound," Malone says, convincingly. "Scorers will have off nights. But the boards. They'll be there." After he grabs a rebound and kicks it out to a guard. Moses's slow gait downcourt, with his small hands swinging at his sides, seems to reflect a disdain for all that between-the-legs stuff. But when he gets his 6' 10", 235-pound frame to the paint, he's a study in perpetual motion, the hardest worker in the league. It's his weapon, his way of countering those who have always wanted to beat him by beating him up.

—Roy S. Johnson, SI, May 11, 1981

Malone averaged 5.1 offensive rebounds for his career.

PHOTOGRAPH BY ANDY HAYT

STOP JIVIN' ME, COACH

Moses Malone's pronouncement to Maryland coach Lefty Driesell made basketball history as the high schooler decided that he was bypassing college to play in the ABA

BY FRANK DEFORD

MOSES MALONE IS AN original. He not only cut a new path to glory, but he also performs as no one else ever has. He was the first basketball player to go directly from high school to the pros, and he is the first to make a name in the craft of offensive rebounding.

"Basically, I just goes to the rack," he says. *Rack* is a rather obscure colloquialism, meaning the rim of the basket, but the way Malone gives voice to it, the rack takes on the aspect of a specific territory, demarcated as surely as the lane or the crease or the mezzanine or the city limits: You'll know just where to find him.

Moses moves at a controlled lope until he reaches the rack, but once there he immediately goes into a series of purposeful darts and dashes. Curiously, what most attracts attention are his hands, which are disproportionately small. Malone is genetically inexplicable; his father is 5' 6", his mother 5' 2". Only his hands seem a result of that union. During a game they hang altogether loose, but they are never lazy. No doubt this is because, unlike other men his size, Moses cannot take his hands for granted. He says he can palm the ball, but he can't manhandle it, toy with it. "If Moses just had normal hands for a man his size, he'd have to be outlawed," says teammate Rick Barry.

When Moses was about 14 or so and began to appreciate how very good he was, he wrote out a message to himself and placed it in the family Bible, which was worn and dog-eared and had no cover, that Mrs. Malone's father had passed on to her. A great many people close to Moses know about this note. Apparently, it was a promise from Moses to himself that he would become the best high school player in the country by the time he finished his junior year. Then, that accomplished, it seems he sat down and wrote another note for the Bible, this one to the effect that he would become the first high school player to go directly into the pros.

For his last two seasons Petersburg was undefeated, state champs, 50–0. Meanwhile, in the classroom Malone was present and accounted for, but never involved or particularly proficient. A great part of his problem was psychological. Schoolwork was both alien and intimidating to him. "He'd say nothing, even if he knew something," says Pro Hayes, Malone's high school assistant coach. "He didn't want to risk being embarrassed." It is also true that Moses had bad teeth, and so he refrained from talking, keeping his head down when he had to speak.

Almost from the beginning Malone had decided to play for Lefty Driesell at Maryland. But he kept this decision to himself, for he en-joyed all the fuss, and he listened courteously to all the recruiters' lies and supplications. It was a game, and he became a cottage industry in Petersburg, with doltish recruiters getting conned out of all sorts of front money by hustlers who promised that they could deliver Moses.

In the end he signed a letter of intent with Maryland, and it was only a matter of days before he started matriculating at College Park that the Utah Stars showed up with a "multimillion-dollar contract." In fact, it guaranteed very little, being studded with one-year, one-way options. Malone made the Stars show the contract to Driesell, and as soon as the coach took one look at the document, he called in Donald Dell, the Washington lawyer and former Davis Cup captain who had made a formidable reputation representing tennis players, notably Arthur Ashe.

Dell was caught in a tricky situation. He had been summoned to help Malone by Driesell, who was obviously a rival of the Stars. Furthermore, it was one of the more Draconian of the NCAA rules that a kid who took on counsel to help him decide between pro and college ball was automatically deemed a pro. Dell had to gingerly position himself as no more than a friendly adviser.

He and one of his law partners, Lee Fentress, read the contract and then went into a room in their offices where Driesell, Maryland star John Lucas and Moses and his mother were assembled. "As soon as I entered the room," Dell says, "Moses dropped his head. At that time, that was his natural response to any stranger. I wanted to catch his attention, and so I walked right over to him, and even before I said hello. I said, 'You ever hear of slavery, Moses?' His head came up like that. He stared straight at me, and he listened to every word I said."

Dell explained the contract's loopholes, but because he was sure that Utah would be back, raising the ante, he told Malone that he was welcome to call him for advice. "But understand this, Moses," Dell told him. "The minute you sign one thing, one scrap of paper, forget it, because then I can't help you." The next day, from Petersburg, Malone called Dell constantly. "Eighteen calls—18." Dell says. "Every time Utah made a new move, Moses called me. I knew then that he was a hell of a lot smarter than he was given credit for."

Again Dell assembled all the principals in his offices. The Utah envoys were put on hold in one room while Dell and Fentress met with the Malones, Driesell and one of his assistants, Dave Pritchett. It was an emotional encounter, and as Lefty perceived that the kid's mind really was made up, he grew anguished and distraught. He talked about the promise in the Bible. "The Good Lord won't mind you waiting for a year or two," he said. Moses did not budge. Pritchett began to cry, and Driesell, despairing all the more, became melodramatic.

Suddenly, Malone looked up and glared at his friend. "Stop jivin' me, Coach," he snapped. Driesell froze. School was out. ∎

JERRY LUCAS

ROYALS 1963–1970
TWO TEAMS THROUGH 1974

❝ Lucas's career rebounding average ranks behind only Wilt Chamberlain's, Bill Russell's and Bob Pettit's. Lucas grabbed his boards the hard way, banging on the inside and outhustling opponents to loose balls. ❞ —CHRIS MANNIX

‣ CAREER AVERAGE OF
15.6 REBOUNDS
‣ AVERAGED 21.1 REBOUNDS
IN 1965–66

WHEREAS BILLIONS of others would simply see a hoop, Lucas saw the notches of a clock face on the top of the rim. He would first shoot 25 shots at nine o'clock, trying to slip the ball as close as possible to the inside left edge of the rim. Then he'd shoot for three o'clock, just inside the right edge, and so on, until he wearied of making shots. Whereupon he would miss them, at each spot on the dial in turn, all the while calibrating arc and velocity so he'd know precisely where to spring for the rebound. "In games I never blocked out," he says. "I wasn't going to waste my time on blocking out. I'd go up to tip the ball in before anybody knew it was missed." For hours a day in Sunset Park he would shoot to make and shoot to miss, with Swiss precision, countless times—only nothing was countless to Lucas. He counted everything.

—Alexander Wolff, SI, June 30, 2003

The 6' 8" Lucas boldly took on bigger players.
PHOTOGRAPH BY WALTER IOOSS JR.

—Alex Hannum with Frank DeFord, SI, November 25, 1968

THURMOND, AS even Rick Barry

10

KAREEM ABDUL-JABBAR

BUCKS 1969–1975
LAKERS 1975–1989

" The iconic image of the Goggled One would surely show him releasing his sky hook, but for the first 12 years of his career he averaged double figures in rebounding. He never put up the prodigious numbers of Chamberlain and Russell, but he played farther from the basket. " —JACK MCCALLUM

▸ CAREER AVERAGE OF 11.2 REBOUNDS
▸ NBA REBOUNDING LEADER IN 1975–76

IN GAME 1 against Boston, Celtics center Robert Parish beat him up and down the floor all night. Snickers about Abdul-Jabbar's advanced age began. In the Lakers' video session the following morning, Abdul-Jabbar stationed himself directly in front of the screen instead of in his normal spot in the back of the room. The next day, during a frantic two-hour practice, Abdul-Jabbar whipped himself mercilessly up and down the court. He approached each player with a quiet message before Game 2: "We may not win, but let's make it worthy of us." He scored 30 points with 17 rebounds. The last five games, he ran Parish into exhaustion, and once grabbed a rebound, dribbled the length of the court and swished a sky hook. "What you saw," says coach Pat Riley, "was passion."

—Gary Smith, SI, December 23, 1985

Abdul-Jabbar is third on the NBA career rebounds list.

10 THE

Best Clutch Performers

IN A STORY THAT MUSED ON THE IMPORTANCE OF THE FINAL SECONDS OF A GAME, MARIO ELIE, A PLAYER FOR SEVERAL TEAMS WHO HAD A HISTORY OF COMING UP BIG, EXPLAINED THE SECRET OF HIS SUCCESS. "I WANT THE SHOT," HE SAYS. "SOMETIMES IT'S NOT STRATEGY, NOT X'S AND O'S, THAT MAKES THE DIFFERENCE. IT'S WHETHER A PLAYER REALLY WANTS TO TAKE THE SHOT. THE ONLY WAY YOU'LL SUCCEED IS IF YOU'RE NOT AFRAID OF WHAT WILL HAPPEN IF YOU FAIL."

ELIE DID NOT MAKE OUR EXPERTS' TOP 10 LIST, BUT THE CONFIDENCE OF WHICH HE SPEAKS IS A RUNNING THREAD IN SEVERAL OF THE CLASSIC SI STORY PASSAGES THAT ACCOMPANY THE CHOICES. SOME OF THE PASSAGES DESCRIBE LAST MINUTE HEROICS, BUT OTHERS EXPLORE THE MIND-SET OF THE PLAYER WHO BELIEVES IT'S BEST FOR EVERYONE IF THEIR FATE IS IN HIS HANDS.

IN THE STORY IN WHICH ELIE WAS QUOTED, THE WRITER, PHIL TAYLOR, OPINED THAT THERE IS NO MORE VALUABLE COMMODITY IN BASKETBALL THAN A GREAT CLUTCH PLAYER. THE PROOF OF THAT: ROBERT HORRY WAS VOTED BY OUR PANEL INTO TWO TOP 10S, WHILE MULTIME ALL-STARS SUCH AS PATRICK EWING AND VINCE CARTER ARE BLANKED. HORRY DIDN'T EVEN START HALF HIS CAREER GAMES, BUT HE BECAME "BIG SHOT ROB" IN THE FINAL SECONDS, SO MANY TIMES DID HE TAKE, AND MAKE, THAT DECIDING PLAY.

1

MICHAEL JORDAN

BULLS 1984–1993, 1994–1998
WIZARDS 2001–2003

" The "Ehlo" shot in '89, the six first-quarter threes in the '92 Finals, the Last One against Bryon Russell and the Jazz in '98, six season and six Finals MVPs— need I go on?" —JACK McCALLUM

IN ONE BRIEF, devastating burst of brilliance at the end of Game 6, Jordan had secured another championship. After a John Stockton three-pointer with 41.9 seconds left had given Utah an 86–83 lead, Jordan almost immediately got the ball at the other end, drove past the Jazz's Bryon Russell and scored a layup, using up only 4.8 seconds. On the other end Jordan sneaked up behind Utah's Karl Malone and stripped the ball from him. Back upcourt, he faked Russell nearly out of his hightops to free himself for a 17-foot jumper that gave Chicago the lead with 5.2 seconds left. When Stockton missed a three-pointer, the Bulls were champions for the third straight year. Jordan's game-winning sequence, which capped a 45-point performance, may have surpassed the countless other memorable moments of his career, even Game 5 of last year's Finals, in which, despite being sick with a stomach virus, he scored 38 points to lead the Bulls to victory. "I didn't think he could top that," said coach Phil Jackson. "But he topped it here tonight."

—Phil Taylor, SI, June 22, 1998

At the ends of games, Jordan rose up.

PHOTOGRAPHS BY DAVID E. KLUTHO (LEFT) AND JOHN BIEVER

2

LARRY BIRD

CELTICS 1979–1992

"Astronomical self-confidence. He wanted the ball for the big shot, told the defender what he was about to do, then did it. One great moment in Bird clutch, from among many: Lifting a number 1 finger salute the moment he released the ball that won the 1988 three-point shootout, before it was anywhere near the basket and walking off. Of course it went in." —CHRIS BALLARD

BIRD, AT THE age of 29, at last seems comfortable with being Larry Bird. And just who is that? It's someone who plays with a recklessness and intensity that are as unfathomable as they are unfashionable. It's someone who, like Muhammad Ali, challenges himself by boasting. Last year in the fifth game of the Eastern Conference semifinal against Detroit, Bird stared at Isiah Thomas, who had just led a Pistons charge, and said, "Are you through?" "No," said Thomas. "Well, you're through now because it's my turn," said Bird. And it was. Bird took over the game, and the Celtics won 130–123. One comment from Red Auerbach says it all. "The best I've ever had in rising to the occasion were Bob Cousy, John Havlicek and Bill Russell. And Larry goes beyond them in that particular phase of the game. He wants the ball, and he knows what the hell to do with it."

—Jack McCallum, SI, March 3, 1986

Jack Ramsay called Bird the best clutch player ever.

PHOTOGRAPH BY ANDY HAYT

Magic was the Lakers' steadying hand.

PHOTOGRAPH BY MANNY MILLAN

3

MAGIC JOHNSON

" MVP center out hurt in the championship series? No problem. Just put the rookie point guard in the middle. In Game 6 of the 1980 NBA Finals, Magic set the tone for the rest of his career, scoring 42 and grabbing 15 boards in place of Kareem Abdul-Jabbar as the Lakers took the title. " —MARK BECHTEL

THE MOST successful NBA teams are those with an identity, and the Lakers have been consistent winners since 1979 largely because they knew who they were: They were Magic's team, pure and simple. Late in a game, there was no question about who would direct traffic and determine the best final shot.

—*Jack McCallum, SI, November 18, 1991*

4

BILL RUSSELL

CELTICS 1956–1969

" Russell's painful habit of throwing up before big games gave odd comfort to his Celtics teammates: Russell was 17–2 in elimination games while winning 11 championships in 13 NBA seasons. He dominated those games with defense and teamwork. " —IAN THOMSEN

LAKERS GUARD Frank Selvy released an easy jump shot. It was three inches too high and rolled off the rim. Los Angeles forward, Elgin Baylor, way up in the air and ready to tap the shot in, thought it was going in by itself. He pulled back his hand, giving Bill Russell a chance to snatch the rebound as time ran out. Russell hugged the ball and sank to the floor on one knee. He remained there—motionless—for 25 seconds, before walking slowly over to a rickety chair where the Boston trainer poured a pitcher of ice water across the back of his neck. Then he came back to lead the Celtics to a 110–107 overtime win. "There is still no one who can counteract the things Bill Russell can do to you," says Lakers coach Fred Schaus. "The Celts will be strong until they lose him." After scoring 30 points and getting 40 rebounds in the final game, during which Russell never stopped running, passing, or intimidating shooters, the end of his ordeal caused a tremendous emotional release. He got sick the moment he reached the locker room. Then he began to cry.

—Arlie W. Schardt, SI, April 30, 1962

Eleven championships proved Russell's case.

JERRY WEST

LAKERS 1960–1974

"If you surpass your regular season play in the postseason once or twice, you're a franchise icon. If you do it eight years in a row, as West did in the 1960s, you earn the name Mr. Clutch and they make you The Logo." —JACK McCALLUM

WILT, UNDER the basket, reached down in dismay for the ball and took it out-of-bounds. West looked up at the clock that had stopped at :03. The Lakers had no timeouts left. Wilt passed the ball in to West at the left of the lane. He used three dribbles, cutting to the right with the last one, for Willis Reed had suddenly loomed up before him. In fact West didn't shoot uncontested. Reed had a hand high, jumping with him, as he began his shot. West stepped, finally, about two feet beyond the free throw circle, 63 feet from the basket, and let fly with the ball. Chick Hearn, the Lakers announcer, whose game account is broadcast in The Forum, his voice droning in the background like some Himalayan chant, said: "An 80-foot jumper. [Pause.] Good." No one else was any more lucid or composed as the ball tumbled into the basket, just missing the back rim. New York's Dave DeBusschere, later to characterize it as "a disheartening hoop," was standing three feet from where the ball landed. He threw out his arms and collapsed backward in a heap.

—*Frank Deford, SI, May 11, 1970*

West's nickname was Mr. Clutch.

PHOTOGRAPH BY WALTER IOOSS JR.

6

KOBE BRYANT

LAKERS 1996–PRESENT

> " The numbers will tell you his overall "clutch" stats aren't elite, and this is true, but if you're an opposing coach, how many other players in history do you fear more than Kobe when it comes the last shot? His desire and skill, paired with his ability to always get off his shot, are scary. " —CHRIS BALLARD

SO WHERE does Kobe's legendary competitive drive come from? Pam Bryant played basketball as a girl, she used to hound boys on the court. Later, in family games, she never shied from contact. Once, when Kobe was 14 and he tried to dunk on her in a backyard game, she leveled him with a forearm. "She would drop you," says Kobe. "Oh, yeah, she was rough." Pam came from basketball talent. Her younger brother is Chubby Cox, a guard at Villanova and USF before a seven-game NBA stint with Washington in the early 1980s, and her nephews include John Cox, who is now a pro in France, and Sharif Butler, who played at TCU in the mid-'90s. It was Sharif, Kobe's older cousin, who relentlessly beat him at one-on-one. "He'd terrorize me," says Kobe. "I think that's part of what made Kobe who he is," says John Cox. "Losing those games to Sharif." This fire was Pam's gift to him, as Kobe sees it. "My mom's the feisty one," he says. "She has that killer in her."

—Chris Ballard, SI, May 14, 2012

Bryant's desire is what makes him dangerous.

PHOTOGRAPHS BY JOHN W. MCDONOUGH

Knicks fans know Miller's heroics well.

PHOTOGRAPH BY MANNY MILLAN

PACERS 1987–2005

REGGIE MILLER

" If you don't believe Reggie Miller is clutch, you should go ask Spike Lee. It says something that even though Miller played his entire career for Indiana, he delivered the most memorable Madison Square Garden performances of anyone this side of Willis Reed. " —MARK BECHTEL

MILLER MADE two three-pointers in 3.1 seconds to tie the score at 105–105. After the Knicks' John Starks missed two free throws, Miller won the game by hitting two foul shots with 7.5 seconds remaining. And he did it all while yapping at court jester Spike Lee and gloating in the faces of the stunned New York players.

—Gerry Callahan, SI, May 15, 1995

A CAN'T MISS PROPOSITION

Reggie Miller was at his best when the stakes were highest, as he showed when he scored 25 points in the fourth quarter of a playoff game against the Knicks

BY JACK McCALLUM

AME 5 CONFIRMED Reggie Miller's status as the league's premier practitioner of the ancient art of jump shooting. (During his rampage he also strengthened his reputation as the game's premier lip-flapper by going one-on-one with film director–Knicks superfan Spike Lee, who was sitting at courtside.) Except for the free throws and one 15-foot field goal, none of Miller's shots came from closer to the basket than 19 feet. One of his three-pointers was a what-the-hell heave from about 27 feet, but it was still a classic Miller jumper, arms extended above the head, elbow on the shooting arm slightly askew, eyes following the ball. (For the record, he did miss two of the 10 field goals he attempted in the period.)

Indiana trailed 70–58 at the end of the third quarter. Miller's first basket of the fourth quarter came 50 seconds into the period, when, as he ran leisurely on the wing of a controlled fast break, he stepped back behind a pick set unconsciously by teammate Kenny Williams and hit a three-pointer. "The key to that was that I had studied the Knicks' defense," said Miller. "Their strategy on fast breaks is to retreat to the paint and then to spread out. So, I trotted up slowly, saw [Knicks defender John] Starks back in the paint playing penetration, used Kenny as a screen and got off the three. Easy."

Miller's second basket came on an inbounds play at 10:23. Starks had been replaced by 6' 5" guard Hubert Davis, who was now assigned to cover Miller. "I was aware they had made a lineup change, of course, and I knew I could run circles around Hubert," said Miller. He found himself out on the right side all alone and took a pass from Williams for another three-pointer.

Miller's third field goal came at the 9:14 mark, when he drove right on 6' 2" Knicks reserve guard Greg Anthony, pulled up, pump-faked and swished a 15-footer.

Miller's fourth basket was a 20-footer from the left corner with no Knick within six feet of him. Starks, who was now back guarding Miller, got caught in a pile of bodies as Miller, using various picks, crossed from the right side to the left. The play clearly illustrated the fact that half of a shooter's battle is running an obstacle course as he attempts to get open. "Most teams' strategy in stopping Reggie is to beat him up before he gets the ball," says Pacers assistant coach George Irvine. Miller professes not to care. He says he has gotten stronger by working in the weight room (though you can't tell it by his pipestem arms) and enjoys the hand-to-hand combat that goes along with being a jump shooter.

That fourth field goal also showed Miller's relative disregard for the three-point line; he could have stepped back and taken a trey but did not. "I never want to be conscious of the line," he said. "I never get ticked off, like some guys do, if my foot's on the line and I get a two instead of a three. It's too difficult just to get open. My eyes are looking ahead of me, to the point where I'm going to get the pass and take my shot, so they can't be looking down at the floor."

The fifth shot was remarkable. Miller found himself directly in front of the basket, 27 feet away. He still had his dribble, and he saw teammate LaSalle Thompson heading toward him to set a possible screen, but he just squared up and let fly. The ball whistled through the net cleanly, as do most of Miller's field goals, "like somebody drops the ball straight down from the center of the arena," as Pacers president Donnie Walsh puts it. The three-pointer gave Indy a lead, at 75–72, that it never surrendered.

"Shooting is concentration and rhythm," said Miller, "and sometimes it is pure confidence. Sometimes things are going so right you feel you can will the ball into the basket."

Miller's sixth basket came on a three-pointer from the right side at the 6:59 mark. The play actually began with Miller setting a pick down on the baseline. "A lot of times I begin the play by being the screener," said Miller. "That's because if a shooter goes down and sets the screen, chances are the defense won't double on the guy he's setting the screen for because that means a shooter will be free."

Miller's seventh basket was a fortuitous bit of business that occurred when Pacers forward Dale Davis drove to the hoop on a fast break, nearly running over Starks and the other New York guard, Derek Harper, and awkwardly passed the ball out to a wide-open Miller. Standing just a few feet from the Knicks bench and their wildly gesticulating coach, Pat Riley, Miller drained his fifth and final three-pointer of the quarter. (Why Starks by this point was not stuck on Miller like flypaper is anyone's guess.)

After Miller released the shot, he kept his right arm extended in the air for a few seconds, a gesture that has infuriated opponents in the past. "I don't do it to taunt anyone," Miller said. "I do it because when my father taught me to shoot, he taught me to extend that arm and keep it up there real high. That's how you assure yourself that you're following through." That's probably true, but by now Miller is clearly aware of the taunting aspect too.

"I also keep my eyes on the ball after I let it go, whereas most players watch the basket," he said. "But if I watch the ball, I can see the rotation, the way it looks in the air, and maybe learn something for the next shot."

Miller's eighth and final field goal came at 3:24 and gave Indiana an 83–79 lead. Moving left to right, he took a pass from forward Derrick McKey and simply jumped over the 6' 5" Starks, who was now playing him tight, to release a 19-footer. Nothing but net. ∎

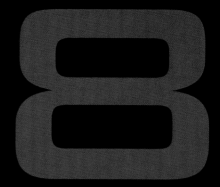

SAM JONES

CELTICS 1957–1969

❝ No Celtic came up more reliably clutch than the maestro of the bank shot. In playoff crucibles he shot down Philadelphia, New York and L.A. with late scores. ❞ —ALEXANDER WOLFF

THREE SECONDS LEFT in Game 7, 18 feet out and off-balance, Jones went up off his left foot. Don Nelson saw Jones's shot clear Wilt Chamberlain's hand, and then he turned for the rebound. The ball was high but short. John Havlicek thought: "Just make the rim anyway." The basket at that end was a different one this game, set "extremely tight," so Havlicek told himself "anything can happen if it gets to the rim." The shot hit the rim "absolutely exactly" in the middle of the ball. The ball jerked up again to the rear of the basket. In disbelief, almost behind Jones, Jerry West watched as the ball hit the back rim and then dove down into the cords. "The Lord's will," West said. Jones just stared, stunned. "I thought to shoot it with high arc and plenty of backspin," Jones explained carefully afterward, "so if it didn't go in Bill Russell would have a chance for the rebound." Russell, of course, was not in the game. "What the hell," Celtics guard Larry Siegfried said. "You make a shot like that, you're entitled to blow some smoke about arc and backspin and things like that."

—*Frank Deford, SI, May 12, 1969*

Jones helped the Celtics win 10 championships.

ROCKETS 1992–1996
SUNS 1996–1997
LAKERS 1997–2003
SPURS 2003–2008

Horry was the master of the three-point dagger.

ROBERT HORRY

" Right place, right time? Maybe. But opportunity does not always equal success, and it seemed like every time Horry found himself with an open shot in big moments, he made it. And he has seven championship rings to prove it. " —CHRIS MANNIX

WHO CAN forget the one against the Kings in Game 4 of the Lakers-Kings series in 2002? That time Horry nailed a walk-off three to give the Lakers a 100–99 victory and even the series at 2–2. In the timeout just before the shot, teammate Lindsey Hunter had said, "It's time for Big Game Rob to take over."

—Chris Ballard, SI Presents, June 29, 2005

10

ISIAH THOMAS

PISTONS 1981–1994

" Sixteen points in 94 seconds of a playoff game; 25 points in one quarter of a Finals game; back-to-back titles in which he made just about every improbable shot for the Pistons. Zeke embodied clutch. " —LEE JENKINS

ISIAH THOMAS'S studied, mature orchestration of the Pistons' NBA championship last week went a long way toward changing his image among basketball purists. Thomas kept the tempo at a controlled, even pace, which disrupted the fast-breaking Trail Blazers. And when he wasn't doing that, he was creating something from nothing, with long-distance jump shots, body-twisting drives and steals in the open floor. Six other NBA guards, including teammate Joe Dumars, were selected by the media ahead of Thomas on the three All-NBA teams this season. But by the time the Pistons had beaten the Blazers 92–90 in Game 5 to clinch their second straight championship in Portland, there was only one great guard still playing basketball—Isiah Lord Thomas III. As the Pistons left the locker room, teammate Bill Laimbeer cornered a reporter. "Isiah's one of those special guys, right?" said Laimbeer. "You know it now, right? You don't play like that unless you're something special, one of the true greats, right?"

—*Jack McCallum, SI, June 25, 1990*

Thomas defined himself with postseason heroics.

PHOTOGRAPH BY MANNY MILLAN

10

THE

Best Defenders

THESE RANKINGS GO A LONG WAY TOWARD JUSTIFYING ANOTHER ONE OF THE SELECTIONS IN THIS BOOK—THE CHOICE OF THE 1995–96 CHICAGO BULLS AS THE GREATEST SINGLE-SEASON TEAM EVER. THE FAMILIAR PIECE OF SUPPORTING EVIDENCE IS THAT THE TEAM WON 72 GAMES, BUT THIS SECTION IS A REMINDER THAT THEY DID THAT BECAUSE THEY HAD THREE TOP 10 DEFENDERS: MICHAEL JORDAN, SCOTTIE PIPPEN AND DENNIS RODMAN.

JORDAN'S SIGNATURE LOGO IS OF HIM SOARING THROUGH THE AIR TO DUNK, BUT AN EQUALLY APPROPRIATE, THOUGH MORE CLUTTERED, INSIGNIA WOULD HAVE HIM GETTING IN THE FACE OF AN ENEMY GUARD. "DEFENSE IS WHAT THEY USE TO CUT YOUR HEART OUT," AN OPPOSING COACH SAID OF THE BULLS THAT YEAR.

THIS LIST IS HEAVY WITH PLAYERS WHO HAVE WON TITLES. AMONG THE TOP 10 DEFENDERS ONLY DIKEMBE MUTOMBO IS RINGLESS. SEVEN OF THIS GROUP ARE MULTIPLE-TIME CHAMPIONS, AND HALF HAVE WON ONE FOR THE THUMB, AT LEAST. BILL RUSSELL HAS HIS 11, JORDAN AND PIPPEN WON SIX TOGETHER, RODMAN HAS FIVE TITLES (THREE WITH THE BULLS AND TWO WITH DETROIT), AND THEN THERE'S TIM DUNCAN, SITTING AT FIVE IN SAN ANTONIO. A COACH SELLING HIS TEAM ON DEFENSIVE EFFORT WOULD DO WELL TO POINT TO THAT TREND.

1

BILL RUSSELL

CELTICS 1956–1969

> " Quite simply, he changed the way the game was played by blocking shots to start fast breaks. " —JACK McCALLUM

▸ NAMED TO INAUGURAL ALL-DEFENSIVE TEAM IN 1968–69 ▸ PLAYED BEFORE BLOCKED SHOT STATISTICS WERE KEPT

"HIS FIRST GAME as a pro wasn't much, either," said Red Auerbach. "Harry Gallatin of the Knicks just ate him up. So the next time we played the Knicks I thought I'd play Russell at corner. But Russell came to me and said he wanted to try again against Gallatin. Well, what a job he did on Gallatin. Maybe the guy got one shot on him, maybe two. Russell destroyed him. That's a word you can use about him—he 'destroyed' players. You take Neil Johnston, a good set shot and a great sweeping hook shot, a big long-armed guy who played for Philly and was the leading scorer in the NBA the year before. Russell destroyed him. He destroyed him psychologically as well, so that he practically ran him out of organized basketball. He blocked so many shots that Johnston began throwing his hook farther and farther from the basket. It was ludicrous, and the guys along the bench began to laugh, maybe in relief that they didn't have to worry about such a guy themselves."

—George Plimpton, SI, December 23, 1968

Russell controlled the paint like no one else.

PHOTOGRAPH BY WALTER IOOSS JR.

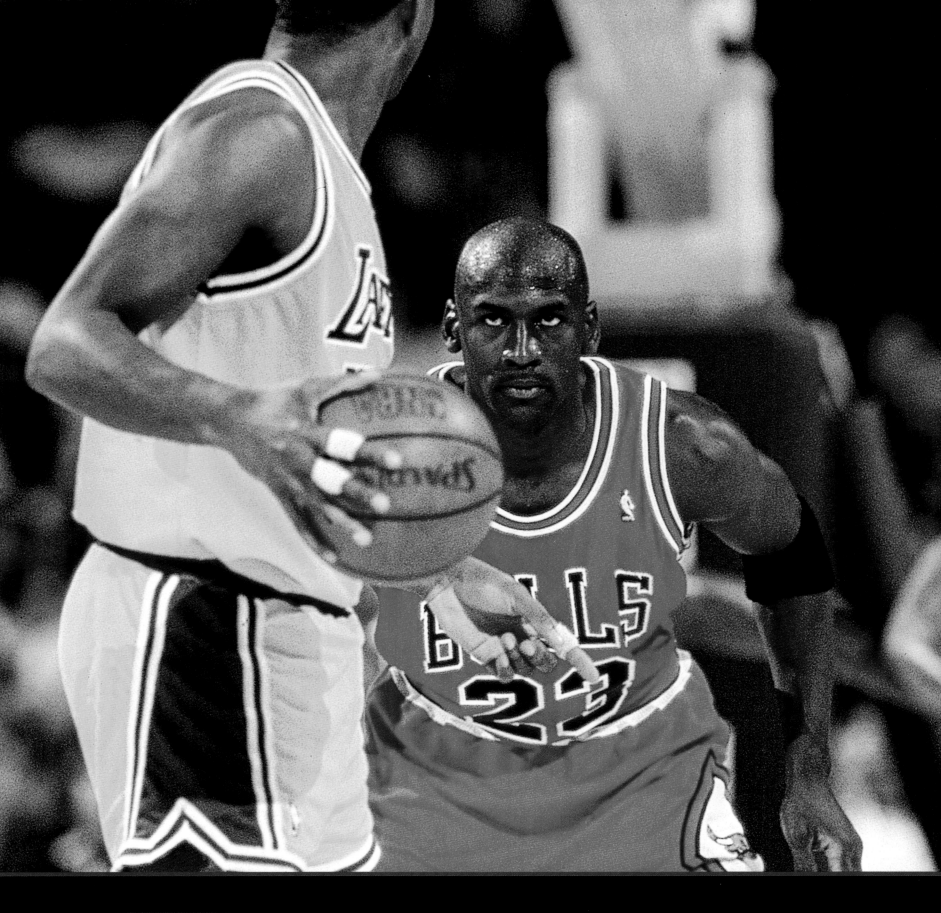

2

MICHAEL JORDAN

BULLS 1984–1993, 1994–1998
WIZARDS 2001–2003

"There were few sights scarier than being guarded by a pissed-off Michael Jordan (ask Ron Mercer). He terrorized opponents with his athleticism, instincts and his greatest weapon: his mental edge." —CHRIS BALLARD

▸ 1987–88 NBA DEFENSIVE PLAYER OF THE YEAR
▸ NINE ALL-DEFENSIVE TEAMS

THE BULLS have the rare defense that works from the outside in. Jordan, Scottie Pippen and Ron Harper form a long-armed outer shell protecting a vulnerable interior. "We're not afraid to come up the floor and extend our defense," says Bulls assistant coach John Paxson, "because we've got [the] guys to do it."

—Phil Taylor, SI, June 10, 1996

3

HAKEEM OLAJUWON

ROCKETS 1984–2002

" The same athleticism that made him so tough with the ball served him well as a defender. He was quick with his feet and his hands (he's eighth on the NBA career steals list), which combined with his size made getting past him impossible. " —MARK BECHTEL

▸ TWO-TIME NBA DEFENSIVE PLAYER OF THE YEAR
▸ NINE ALL-DEFENSIVE TEAMS

THE OLAJUWON-EWING battle is unlike the marquee matchups from NBA Finals of the recent past, such as the confrontations between Magic Johnson and Larry Bird. This time the two combatants play the same position and will spend most of the series matched against each other. It is the battle in the pivot that will probably swing the series. That's bad news for the Knicks, if recent history is any indication. Olajuwon is at the top of his game, and recently he has owned Patrick Ewing. In their two regular-season matchups Olajuwon averaged 33.0 points and 16.5 rebounds to Ewing's 12.0 and 9.5. The Rockets' 94–85 win in New York in December, in which Olajuwon scored 37 points and held Ewing to 12 (on 4-of-20 shooting), was one of the low points of the season for the Knicks. "He causes me problems with his quickness," Ewing admits in an understatement.

—Phil Taylor, SI, June 13, 1994

Olajuwon's Rockets topped the Knicks in 1994.

PHOTOGRAPH BY JOHN W. MCDONOUGH

4

DENNIS RODMAN

PISTONS 1986–1993
BULLS 1995–1998
THREE TEAMS THROUGH 2000

" What Rodman at 6' 7" lacked in size he made up for with some of the sharpest fundamentals in the game. A strong base held off bigger opponents, and flawless footwork kept him in front of quicker ones. " —CHRIS MANNIX

▸ TWO-TIME NBA DEFENSIVE PLAYER OF THE YEAR
▸ EIGHT ALL-DEFENSIVE TEAMS

RODMAN WAS at his most helpful in Game 2 at Chicago's United Center, when he grabbed 20 rebounds, including 11 offensive boards to tie the Finals record, but in Game 3, he did even more damage to the Sonics' psyche. Frank Brickowski, his main foil throughout the series, was ejected with 5:46 left in the fourth quarter after committing a flagrant foul against Rodman in what was almost a replay of his ejection in Game 1 . . . The Bulls have had held their opponents to less than 20 points in 27 of their 60 quarters—or 45% of the time. No NBA champion has come close to that percentage since the league went to its current four-round playoff format in 1983–84. The '90 Pistons were the closest, with 26.3% (21 times in 80 quarters). Those Pistons, not coincidentally, featured Rodman.

—*Phil Taylor, SI, June 17, 1996*

You could question Rodman's hairdo but not his hustle.

5

GARY PAYTON

SONICS 1990–2003
FOUR TEAMS THROUGH 2007

—

" With his jutted jaw, bobbing head and flapping lips, The Glove blanketed opponents and told them all about it. Payton set the standard for on-ball tenacity. " —LEE JENKINS

—

▸ 1995–96 NBA DEFENSIVE PLAYER OF THE YEAR
▸ NINE ALL-DEFENSIVE TEAMS

HE HAS BEEN called The Glove, because he covers opposing guards as snugly as one, but The Mouth would be more appropriate, and it will be until Payton shuts his, which Indiana Pacers guard and former Payton teammate Ricky Pierce once estimated would happen "about two months after he's dead." Payton is the NBA's preeminent trash talker, a mantle he has carried with some pride. To play against him is to risk being buried under an avalanche of verbiage so deep that according to another former teammate, Cleveland Cavaliers forward-center Michael Cage, "when you're done, you just want to go find a library or something, someplace totally silent." He once looked around a mostly empty Meadowlands Arena in New Jersey and told guard Kenny Anderson, who was then with the Nets, "at least nobody will see me take the ball from you."

—*Phil Taylor, SI, May 13, 1996*

Payton averaged 1.8 steals per game.

PHOTOGRAPH BY RICHARD MACKSON

Lean but long, Pippen could take on bigger players.

PHOTOGRAPH BY MANNY MILLAN

6

SCOTTIE PIPPEN

BULLS 1987–1998, 2003–2004
TWO OTHER TEAMS

"Jordan's wingman with wingspan was, according to a teammate of both, a better all-arounder. "[With] defense, offensive rebounds and defensive boards," Ron Harper said, "Pip made the game easier for us to play." " —ALEXANDER WOLFF

▸ 10 ALL-DEFENSIVE TEAMS
▸ CAREER AVERAGE OF 2.0 STEALS

NO ONE is more versatile than Pippen. "He's the best defender I've seen," Blazers coach Mike Dunleavy says. "Jordan, at his position, may have been as good as there was. But Scottie could guard more positions than Michael. Scottie can handle more sizes."

—S.L. Price, SI, December 13, 1999

Duncan can lock down while barely leaving his feet.

PHOTOGRAPH BY JOHN W. MCDONOUGH

7

TIM DUNCAN

SPURS 1997–PRESENT

"A brilliant defensive quarterback, he anchors every San Antonio rotation. Most teams can rotate effectively two or three times, max. With Duncan, the Spurs can go four, sometimes five times." —CHRIS BALLARD

▸ 14 ALL-DEFENSIVE TEAMS
▸ CAREER AVERAGE OF 2.2 BLOCKS

DUNCAN IS the unrequited love of assistant coaches the world over, a big man so completely rational in his play, that his greatness can be difficult to discern. There's nothing sexy about not leaving your feet on a shot fake, or showing-and-recovering on a screen. Unless, that is, you find studied excellence to be sexy.

—Chris Ballard, SI, June 20, 2013

WHATEVER YOU TRY WILL FAIL

Those who attempt to rattle Tim Duncan with taunts and tactics don't understand how deep his stoicism runs and how much he likes to use it as a weapon

BY S.L. PRICE

WHEN FRIENDS TRY to explain Tim Duncan, the first place they turn is the island. Duncan grew up in the U.S. Virgin Islands with his father, jack-of-all-tradesman Bill Duncan, and mother, Ione; two older sisters, Cheryl and Tricia; and Cheryl's husband, Ricky Lowery, who was as close to Tim as a brother. Bill Duncan all but doubled the size of their home single-handedly—every nail and truss, every shingle had to be pounded and fit just right, above code—and the house, like the man, was a rock. When Hurricane Hugo tore through in 1989, leveling trees, peeling the corrugated tin off the homes around them, the Duncans huddled in a small cinder-block bathroom while Bill sat out on a bed for five hours, eyeing the seams and just daring that roof to move. It didn't.

Self-reliance was valued in the Duncan home; self-importance was not. When Dave Odom, the coach at Wake Forest, called Tim in the fall of his senior year in high school to set up the boy's first interview with a big-time coach (the ACC! Division I!), Tim shrugged. "Yeah," he said, "you can come down if you want to."

On the day before Tim's 14th birthday, just weeks after the six-month power blackout caused by Hugo had fully lifted, Ione Duncan died of breast cancer. After Tim got the news from his father, who was at the hospital, he walked into Tricia's bedroom and told her. She began sobbing. She's sure that Tim must have cried too, but her lasting memory of that moment is of Tim walking out, silently planting himself in front of the TV and playing video games the rest of the morning. His birthday got lost in the grieving. By the time of the funeral he felt like an old man.

"I've been grown-up for a long time," he says. "I went through that with my mom, and I grew to where I understood life and death and everything in between."

Bill Duncan worried about his son's stoicism, wondered how Tim could keep so much inside without cracking. Tim, who was considered one of the top freestyle swimmers in his age group and is certain to this day that he would have been good enough to compete for the V.I. in the Olympics, quit the sport cold. He began playing more and more basketball with Lowery. Lowery, a former player at Division III Capital University, took one look at Tim's big hands and springy frame, saw how much the kid hated to lose and knew what he had to work with.

He put Tim through endless drills, dribbling on stones, up stairs, carrying Lowery on his back around the front yard. By the time Tim went to Wake Forest, he could score with his left hand as well as his right. Four years later, when Tim's number, 21, was retired after one of the great careers in college basketball history, Bill Duncan took a microphone on court and began talking about Ione and her death and how only he and Tim could know how proud she would be. Then he began to say the mantra again—*Good, better, best . . .*—and Tim's defenses kicked in. He walked up behind his father, "draped him," Odom recalls, "almost like a vine," and said, "That's enough, Dad."

The silent man makes everybody nervous. It's an old saw of negotiating that the less you say, the more your opponent reveals. Duncan lives this. There are players who babble and bait him, none more than Minnesota Timberwolves forward Kevin Garnett, whose athletic gifts as a 7-footer match (or even exceed) Duncan's. Yet Duncan never speaks on the court. "Emotion doesn't work for me," he says. "If I get too high or low, something always happens. If there's 10 seconds left and I hit a shot and I'm jumping up and down and high-fiving everybody on the side? It's a guaran-damn-tee that they're going to hit a shot and the game's going to be over. And I'm going to look like an ass."

But then there's the quality that separates Duncan from all the sweet-tempered giants who never panned out, the thing that makes him one of the greatest players ever: He enjoys what happens when he doesn't speak. It gives him control and, paired with his skill, frustrates his victims, shames them, beats them mentally as much as physically. Duncan isn't like Shaq, wearing out the opposition with his bulk. He's Garry Kasparov in hightops, a former psychology major who delights in the power of his silence. "You destroy people's psyches when you do that," he says. "You absolutely destroy them. They can't get inside your head. They're talking to you, and there's no response other than to make this shot, make this play, get this rebound and go the other way. People hate that."

When, during college, Duke center Greg Newton ripped Duncan for being "passive," "soft" and "babyish" after one game, reporters dutifully trotted to Duncan for a response, sure that he would rise to the bait. The insults were just too blatant. "He's a great player," Duncan said calmly, and Newton has been living down the comments ever since.

When Duncan distances himself from even his peers, it is as calculated as it is effective; it creates mystery. "People don't know anything about me," he says, "and it's good." Nearly any conversation with Duncan is on his terms. When Odom started pitching the 16-year-old Duncan on the merits of Wake Forest, he found himself competing with a football game on TV; holding his temper over such rudeness, Odom plopped himself down next to the screen so Duncan would be forced to glance at him during timeouts.

"[His aloofness] drives people nuts," says Duncan's wife Amy, "and the fact that he knows that gives him the power." ∎

8

LeBRoN JAMES

"No one since Jordan has carried such a burden on offense, then been asked to do the same thing on D. James can guard four positions and, peeved that he hasn't been named top defender, will likely take on some centers." —JACK McCALLUM

▸ SIX ALL-DEFENSIVE TEAMS
▸ MASTER OF THE
  CHASE-DOWN BLOCK

JAMES HAS become the coolest toy a coach could imagine. He can not only guard the Chris Paul, but he can also switch to power forward David West on a pick-and-roll. "Instead of a little guy like Mo Williams, now it's LeBron switched on to West, and he can bang him," says Cavs assistant Mike Malone. "You know how tough that is for a team?"

—Chris Ballard, SI, February 2, 2009

No shooter wants to see James closing in.

PHOTOGRAPH BY JOHN W. McDONOUGH

KEVIN GARNETT

TIMBERWOLVES 1995–2007
CELTICS 2007–2013
NETS 2013–PRESENT

" Garnett established his defensive leadership in Boston, where he won one championship and came within minutes of another by becoming his era's Bill Russell. Everyone who played with Garnett was forced to meet his high standard. " —IAN THOMSEN

‣ 2007–08 NBA DEFENSIVE PLAYER OF THE YEAR
‣ 12 ALL-DEFENSIVE TEAMS

"WHAT I DIDN'T understand before was KG's basketball knowledge and awareness," says Minnesota teammate Sam Cassell. "He's a guy who studies the tendencies of every single player in the league. Nothing gets past him. You don't see that in a young guy, a guy of 27." "It was Kevin's all-around game that impressed me, the things you don't see unless you play with somebody," says Latrell Sprewell. "He can post, he can shoot, he rebounds, he blocks shots, he passes, he runs the floor, he makes free throws. What player in the league does that? Tim [Duncan] rebounds and defends and blocks shots, but he can't do it out on the perimeter like Kevin." Says Cassell, "Kevin is the best player in this league by far. He can guard any player, big or small, slow or quick."

—Jack McCallum, SI, March 1, 2004

Garnett helped the Celtics top the Lakers in 2008.

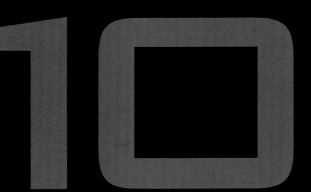

10

DIKEMBE MUTOMBO

NUGGETS 1991–1996
HAWKS 1996–2001
ROCKETS 2004–2009
THREE OTHER TEAMS

" It wasn't just the shot blocking that made Mutombo great, it was the way he owned the lane. Never at a loss for words, Mutombo best summed up his greatness: "I make a lot of coaches change their offense." " —MARK BECHTEL

▸ FOUR-TIME NBA DEFENSIVE
  PLAYER OF THE YEAR
▸ CAREER AVERAGE OF
  2.8 BLOCKS

AGAINST SEATTLE he set an NBA record of 31 blocks in a playoff series. Everything the Sonics took to the bucket went bye-bye. Mutombo single-handedly turned a jamming team into a jump-shooting team. A bad one. "Their game was from the paint, from the inside," he states. "To me, going for blocks was the only way we could win. I kept telling them, 'Don't come!' " Mutombo then bored into the craniums of the Jazz in the Western Conference semifinals, swatting away a new NBA playoff record of 38 shots. It's hard to say how many shots Mutombo altered in the playoffs, but as Golden State coach Don Nelson puts it, "There's nobody else in our league who has the intimidating presence he has in the hole. He's one of a kind."

—Rick Telander, SI, November 7, 1994

Mutombo led the NBA in blocks five times.

PHOTOGRAPH BY GREG NELSON

1

MICHAEL JORDAN

BULLS 1984–1993, 1994–1998
WIZARDS 2001–2003

"He brought the NBA from the world of sports to the world of entertainment with his tongue-wagging dunks, his 60-point outbursts and his must-see commercials. Before Air Jordan became the best player, he was the ultimate showman." —LEE JENKINS

MICHAEL JORDAN was born on Feb. 17, 1963, in Brooklyn, but Air Jordan was launched on Feb. 6, 1988, at Chicago Stadium. He bounded down a hardwood runway, took off from a thin white stripe and flew into our national consciousness, short shorts and splayed legs, one arm cocked by his ear and the other outstretched like a wing with a red wristband. If you were a child of the '80s, you claimed Michael Jordan was the best basketball player in the world, no matter where you lived. His picture was first up on the bedroom wall. You had to watch him as he took off, the way his tongue wagged and chain flapped and body sailed through the canned air. On Feb. 6, 1988, everybody watched. It was just a dunk contest, in the same way the Beatles' appearance on *The Ed Sullivan Show* in 1964 was just a performance. It accelerated the most successful advertising campaign in sports history and signaled a new era in the NBA, ruled by a new king.

—*Lee Jenkins, SI, February 18, 2013*

In games and contests, Jordan's dunks were electric.

PHOTOGRAPH BY JOHN W. MCDONOUGH

2

JULIUS ERVING

SQUIRES 1971–1973
NETS 1973–1976
76ERS 1976–1987

" Hang time is an elusive concept. Does it exist? Can players make themselves stay in the air longer? We never thought much about it until Dr. J arrived to the NBA with a surreal aerial game and, if that wasn't enough, a friendly personality and an all-world Afro. " —JACK McCALLUM

IT WAS the Summer of '76. The dawning of the NBA-ABA merger, when a Mr. J. Smiley of Detroit appeared at the Cobo Hall ticket window, whipped out his $200 Ford Motor Company payroll check and mumbled something to the effect of: "Gimme all you got for the Doctah!" That's just about all anyone needs to know to understand the effect Erving had upon pro basketball. The uniform, the team, the city didn't matter. "The Doc changed ball," Magic Johnson once said. "The Doc went past jumps, hooks, sets, went past everything and made the playground *official*"—but also with a certain grace and attitude, a basic, off-the-ball humanity that somehow made the game a better place. He would narrate *Peter and the Wolf* at the Philadelphia Zoo, read the Declaration of Independence at the city's Fourth of July celebration. Not to mention that he could jump through the roof and Ferris-wheel an absolutely indescribable slam every minute or so.

—*Curry Kirkpatrick, SI, May 4, 1987*

Erving brought ABA spirit to the NBA.

PHOTOGRAPHS BY JOHN D. HANLON (LEFT) AND HEINZ KLUETMEIER

3

PETE MARAVICH

HAWKS 1970–1974
JAZZ 1974–1979
CELTICS 1980

"His career was shortened by knee problems and he never went to an NBA Finals, but Maravich was among the game's most charismatic showmen. He loved to make acrobatic no-look passes in the open floor." —IAN THOMSEN

THE CURRENT Pistol Pete is an improved model. Rarely does he drive at breakneck speed into the corner or wildly fling the ball up from midcourt. Some of the original Maravich remains, but he does his between-the-legs, behind-the-back and over-the-shoulder passing and dribbling so fluidly that, along with his phenomenal quickness, they are now taken for granted. Still, in the last year he has proved that there are two things he does superlatively: handle the ball and shoot on the move. "I was criticized for everything I did when I came into the league," Maravich says. "They kept harping, 'Why do you dribble into traffic?' I enjoy going into traffic; that's my game. I can create that way. That's what me and a lot of young guys are into—revolutionizing basketball. The two-handed set shot used to be a big thing, but nobody's seen anyone take one in five years. We're working on things like passing and dribbling now. Take the chest pass. Five years from now you may never see another one of them."

—Peter Carry, SI, November 12, 1973

Maravich's game was daring and fast-paced.

PHOTOGRAPH BY HEINZ KLUETMEIER

4

MAGIC JOHNSON

LAKERS 1979–1991, 1995–1996

" The engine driving the Lakers' Showtime offense, Magic was a one-man fast break. Playing a freewheeling style Magic—along with some guy named Bird—dragged the NBA out of the tape-delayed postseason era to unprecedented popularity. " —CHRIS MANNIX

MAGIC SURELY has the most expressive face in the history of sports. As he steamed toward the basket, his eyes would widen and his mouth would round into an O as he looked off his defender, selling the pass to, say, Byron Scott on the right side and then suddenly zipping it over his shoulder to James Worthy on the left. The fast break is about making decisions in the wink of an eye, and Magic, like vintage Cousy, made excellent ones while earning thousands of style points in the process. Until he slowed down a bit in recent seasons, he was the consummate playground player— the high dribble, the spin moves, the outside shot that looked like an afterthought. But even in his most electrifying moments he was, in contrast to Michael Jordan, never a particularly acrobatic player. Like Larry Bird, that other noted relic, he never had a classic jump shot. Magic was never just like Jordan, never just like Bird. He was somewhere in between, and thus attracted fans from both camps.

—*Jack McCallum, SI, November 18, 1991*

The joy Magic took from the game was evident.

PHOTOGRAPH BY PETER READ MILLER

5

LeBron James

CAVALIERS 2003–2010, 2014–
HEAT 2010–2014

" Blessed with the speed and playmaking of a guard and the size and strength of a power forward, James is electric. The evolution of his game—the improved jump shot, the presence in the post—has made him arguably the toughest player to guard, ever. " —CHRIS MANNIX

THERE WAS a moment during a Cavaliers-Warriors game when it looked as if Golden State center Andris Biedrins, who is no small man at 6' 11" and 245 pounds, had been sucked out of an airplane hold, so forcefully was he sent flying backward. Biedrins was attempting to protect the rim when Cleveland forward LeBron James came charging down the lane in that straight-line, parting-the-waters manner of his. Gamely, Biedrins took to the air to try to block the shot, and then, *whoomp!* next thing you knew he was hurtling onto his backside. As for the 6' 8" James, he remained both on-balance and on-course, as if he'd merely hit a patch of turbulence on his solo commuter flight—nonstop from basket to basket, departing 15 times nightly— before rattling in a layup. Minutes later he took off again, only this time he toppled *two* Warriors, then threw down a one-handed dunk of surpassing violence.

—Chris Ballard, SI, February 2, 2009

James's speed and strength make him an athletic marvel.
PHOTOGRAPH BY DAVID LIAM KYLE/NBAE/GETTY IMAGES (LEFT)
AND HEINZ KLUETMEIER

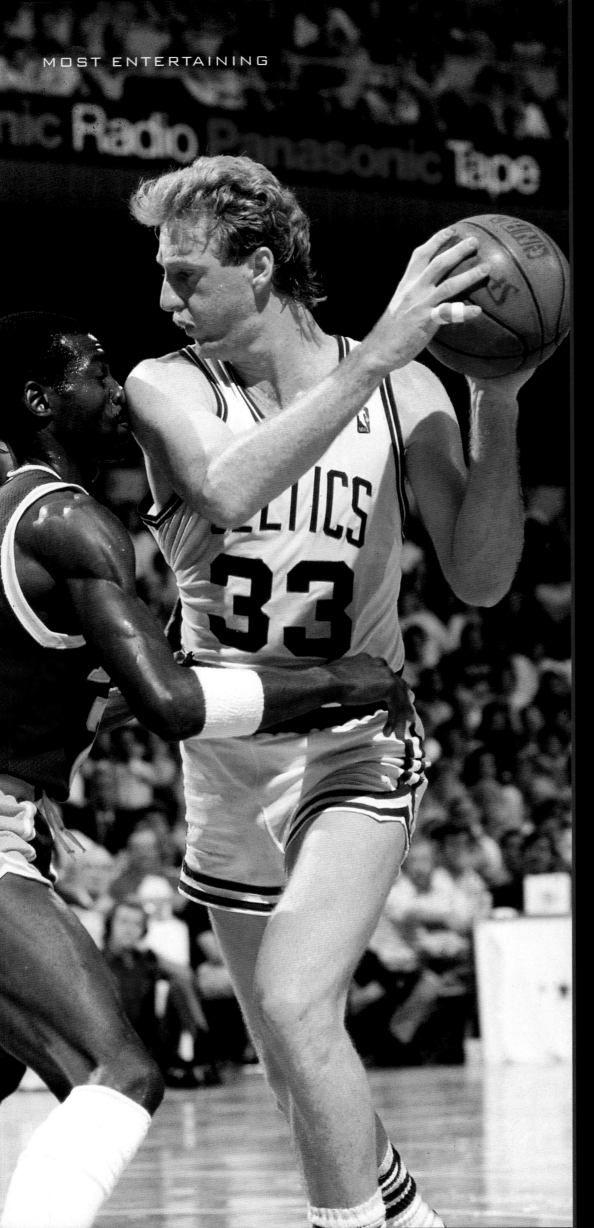

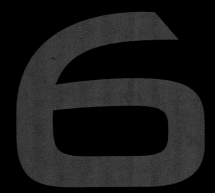

6

LARRY BIRD

CELTICS 1979–1992

❝ Sure, he didn't dunk much, but true basketball fans appreciated all the little things Bird did. Most of all, it was competitive spirit. Few, if any, wanted it more. ❞ —CHRIS BALLARD

"WINNING THE championship—I've never felt that way any other time," Bird says. "I remember the first time we won, against Houston [in 1981]. We were way ahead and so I came out with three minutes left, and my heart was pounding so, I thought it would jump out of my chest. You know what you feel? You just want everything to stop and to stay like that forever." And that, in his way, is what Larry Bird does for us. He not only slows the world down, but he turns it back. "I've studied it," says Bob Woolf, Bird's lawyer, "and I think, above all, there's just an innocence with him. I think Larry takes anyone who knows him—or sees him playing—back to grammar school. Remember back then? We dived after the ball. We looked after our friends. I think with Larry we believe he'll save the team. We believe he'll save us somehow. So you follow him." Look for the open man. Fill the lane. Box out. The game is a mile a minute. The world is a mile a minute. Even the memories are a mile a minute these days. But somehow, with Larry Bird, you can see it all before you. So slow. So dreamy. You just want everything to stop and stay like that forever.

—Frank Deford, SI, March 21, 1988

Bird was a hard-nosed throwback.

PHOTOGRAPH BY MANNY MILLAN

7

ALLEN IVERSON

" He could whoosh right by you, break your ankles with a crossover (remember, Mr. Jordan?) and sometimes elevate over you. You could knock him down, but you had to catch him first, and, anyway, he always got right back up. The Answer wasn't fun to guard, but he sure was fun to watch. " —JACK McCALLUM

THE 76ERS' determination was embodied by the six feet of scar tissue that is Allen Iverson. The battered and bruised Iverson was the most compelling character in this drama, stealing every scene whether in victory or defeat. It was the pencil-legged Iverson who commanded attention with his tireless, mile-a-minute pace and unwavering look of defiance.

—Phil Taylor, SI, June 18, 2001

Iverson played with scrappy emotion.
PHOTOGRAPH BY MANNY MILLAN

8

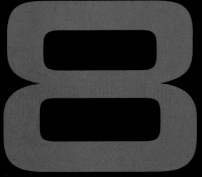

Barkley was exuberant on court and off.

PHOTOGRAPH BY JOHN W. MCDONOUGH

" What a gift to fans. The game's greatest personality resided in the body of one of its greatest athletes. He'd throw down a 360 dunk over a center one minute, spout wry commentary two hours later and then throw someone through a nightclub window in the wee hours of the next morning. " —CHRIS BALLARD

BARKLEY SIGNED anything, anywhere even while waiting at stoplights all over town. He signed cards, napkins, dollar bills, kids' drawings and even a pair of panties (pulled out of a purse by a 35-year-old woman). When one woman introduced him to foreign friends as "the biggest —— in the U.S.A.," Barkley took it with a smile.

—Rick Reilly, SI, November 9, 1992

CHARLES BARKLEY

DID HE JUST SAY THAT?

Charles Barkley has always talked like he doesn't care what anyone thinks, and that's why he is the star of the most enjoyable studio show in sports

BY JACK MCCALLUM

N MOST EVENINGS Charles Barkley is what you might call "Sprewell late" to the TNT studio—later than the pooh-bahs might like but comfortably in time for tip-off. But when he walks in on this unusually cold February night, it's as if the electricity is suddenly turned on in the building; his smorgasbord of insults signals the official beginning of the evening. "I finally decided on the right diet for you, T.K.," Barkley says to producer Tim Kiely. "The Illusion Diet. You got no chance of ever getting thin, so what you gotta do is start hanging around with fat people, give the *illusion* that you're skinnier." Barkley discovers that his broadcasting buddy, Ernie Johnson, the underrated glue of the show, is not feeling well. He feigns concern. "Get me a jar of Vaseline, Ernie," says Barkley, "and I'll stick my finger up your butt to find out what's wrong." Barkley's cellphone rings. He checks caller ID. "It's my son," he says, just before saying hello to Tiger Woods.

The TNT studio show is so absurdly good that the reasons for its success shouldn't be dissected. It can be compared, one supposes, with Fox's NFL pregame show, but the easy affability of Barkley, Johnson and Kenny Smith seems less forced than the testosterone-laced assault sent out on autumn Sunday afternoons. As in most good things that appear to come easily, there is much work involved in pulling off this show, but by and large that work is not done by Barkley. Johnson is usually in his office by nine on the morning of a show and stays at least an hour after the broadcast, and Smith spends much preshow time in the control room watching action around the league. Barkley, after he arrives, invariably checks out *The West Wing* or scours one of the 21 monitors for something other than hoops, but his TV instincts are unerring. When he catches a glimpse of the horrible gray-and-white-checked sport coat worn by Houston Rockets commentator Calvin Murphy, Barkley leaps to his feet. "What the f--- is Calvin wearing tonight?" he says. "Lord save the man." He dashes out of the room to make sure his producers put up a shot of Murphy during the show.

Except for special gags—twin manicurists visiting Barkley on his 39th birthday, Mike Fratello delivering soup to Johnson, a taped challenge to Barkley from the members of the U.S. women's curling team because Charles had referred to their sport as "dusting"—nothing in the *Halftime Report* is scripted.

For all the free-form talk, the show ultimately works because the men come across as three guys who love watching hoops together. Smith, a former point guard, provides the limited X's and O's component.

Barkley's reactions are immediate and visceral. As he gets ready to go on, he catches a glimpse of Vince Carter passing the ball to Keon Clark instead of taking a potentially game-winning shot. "Do you believe this motherf------ pussy!" he hollers. He stands up and charges out of the control room. "Hey, Kenny. Kenny! You see this s---?"

The show over, Barkley spots a production assistant, a young woman who has a new boyfriend. "What's up for you tonight, honey?" Barkley says. "You making a booty call?" She blushes and punches him on the arm. The best thing about Barkley is not that he makes X-rated comments to a colleague like Johnson, it's that he takes the time to make a P.A. feel like an R-rated part of the team.

Around noon the next day Barkley is in a cab heading for a small airport in Atlanta, where he will board a private jet for Miami. Twice a season TNT sends its prize threesome to broadcast a game live. Johnson, Smith and various production people are already on the ground in Miami, having taken a 10 a.m. commercial flight. Barkley pays about $500,000 a year to a charter service and usually flies by private jet.

From the time Barkley arrives, at about 2 p.m. for an 8 p.m. tip-off between the Miami Heat and the New York Knicks, he is Concern Numero Uno for TNT's various production and public-relations people. *Get Charles out of the hotel gym. Get Charles into the shower. Get Charles to the lobby. Get Charles into the limo.* By the time Barkley enters the arena, at about 7:15, Smith and Johnson have been there for an hour, meeting with coaches and getting game notes together, little things like learning names of players. ("Who is *that*?" Barkley will ask later when Heat reserve center Vladimir Stepania enters the game.) *Get Charles hooked up next to Ernie and Kenny. Whew!*

The game is mediocre; the TNT threesome is terrific. At one point Barkley brings the conversation back to curling. "I'm still trying to get my grandmother off her old behind and into the Olympics," he says. "Why not? She can dust." The worse the game, the better Barkley is. He can talk about almost anything, criticize almost anybody, "straddle that line without going over it," as Turner Sports president Mark Lazarus puts it.

The fascinating question is how Barkley acquired what Johnson calls "diplomatic immunity," carte blanche to speak his mind. "I think it's because his softer side is well-known," says Johnson.

Barkley thinks it's because he's consistent. "You know I'm going to praise you if you do good, and I'm gonna criticize you if you do bad," he says.

Barkley has beaucoup postgame invitations and finally lands at a South Beach club called Crobar, where he falls off the wagon with a thud, drinking a concoction—blessedly unnamed since no one else in Western civilization has ever ordered it—of Merlot, ginger ale and ice. Even as an imbiber, Charles is an original. ∎

SQUIRES 1973–1974
SPURS 1974–1985
BULLS 1985–1986

GEORGE GERVIN

"One thing he could do was finger roll. From anywhere. Another was score in bunches, including 33 points in a quarter (and 63 in that game) to win the 1978 scoring title. "He's the one player I would pay to see," said Jerry West. Yep." —MARK BECHTEL

LOCAL PUBLICITY merchants had the idea of nicknaming Gervin's 18-month-old son, George Jr., Ice Cube and a still-to-be-born child Icicle. Though this gimmick produced some ink, at home it didn't wash. "My boy is just G Junior to me," says Gervin, "although if the new baby is a girl, I may have to call her Snowflake."

—Curry Kirkpatrick, SI, March 6, 1978

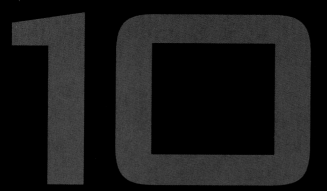

10

EARL MONROE

BULLETS 1967–1971
KNICKS 1971–1980

" Dervishing, double-pumping, almost mummer-strutting, Earl the Pearl had a spin-dribble style never seen before or duplicated since. When he turned his back on an opponent, he would win over the crowd. " —ALEXANDER WOLFF

HE IS SOVEREIGN in the all-pro Baker League, the toughest summer wheel in the country. The Baker floats to various locations, but no matter where it goes Monroe's fans follow it. The hub of the action is at 12th and Columbia in Philadelphia, in the gym that stands behind the Hope Baptist Church on the corner. Everyone is there to watch Earl Monroe go into his magic act. The faithful arrive early. Monroe, as has become his custom, arrives fashionably late, usually around the end of the first quarter. His presence is signaled by a knowing murmur that swells to a tremorous rattle. The fans cannot see Monroe, but they can feel him, and as he nears the court the buzz increases. "Magic's here, Magic's here," it goes, sweeping the gym. Monroe has been called more nicknames than any other athlete—and not one of them is a phony alliterative or geographical title invented by a p.r. man. He is called Pearl as much as he is Earl. And Magic too, a lot. Also he is Doctor, Slick and Batman, and underground he is Black Jesus or The Savior.

—Frank Deford, SI, November 4, 1968

Monroe was the original "Magic."

PHOTOGRAPH BY LANE STEWART

10 THE

BEST GAMES

NOT TO IMPLY THAT THERE'S ANY KIND OF CONSPIRACY, BUT THERE ARE SOME CURIOUSLY STRONG PARALLELS BETWEEN THE GREATEST BASKETBALL GAME EVER PLAYED AND ITS COUNTERPART IN BASEBALL, AS VOTED BY SI'S PANELS. THE GAMES TOOK PLACE LESS THAN EIGHT MONTHS APART—WHICH, WHEN YOU CONSIDER THE LONG HISTORY OF THE NBA AND THE TWICE-AS-LONG HISTORY OF MLB, IS A LONG SHOT. MOREOVER, THE EVENTS HAPPENED LESS THAN THREE MILES FROM EACH OTHER, IN FENWAY PARK AND BOSTON GARDEN. THIS IS IN ITSELF NOT ALL THAT CRAZY, GIVEN BOSTON'S RICH HISTORY AS A SPORTS TOWN.

BUT THERE'S MORE: BOTH HAPPENED NOT IN A GAME 7, IN WHICH YOU WOULD EXPECT ALLTIME DRAMA, BUT EARLIER (A GAME 6 AND A GAME 5). EVEN MORE CURIOUS, THE MOST MEMORABLE NAME IN BOTH GAMES WAS A PLAYER WHOSE TEAM LOST THE SERIES.

CARLTON FISK AND HIS RED SOX AT LEAST WON THEIR GAME 6 BEFORE TUMBLING TO THE REDS. THE SAME CANNOT BE SAID FOR THE TEAM OF GARFIELD HEARD, WHOSE TURNAROUND JUMPER WITH ONE SECOND LEFT ONLY EARNED HIS SUNS A TIE IN THE SECOND OVERTIME OF A GAME THEY WOULD DROP TO THE CELTICS IN THE NEXT EXTRA PERIOD. IT'S ALL COINCIDENCE, FOR WHAT ELSE COULD IT BE? BUT LIKE THE GREAT GAMES THEMSLVES, IT RAISES THE QUESTION: WHAT ARE THE ODDS?

215

VISITOR   PERIOD   HOME

PENALTY   TIME

5:00

NO
SMOKING

1

1976
NBA FINALS
GAME 5

CELTICS 128, SUNS 126

"There were three overtimes, two officiating controversies, a court-storming, a technical foul incurred on purpose, and The Shot Heard Round the World by the Suns' Gar Heard. But all of that was just a prologue to the Celtics' unforgettable win." —LEE JENKINS

▸ SERIES HAD BEEN TIED 2-2
▸ CELTICS ALSO WON GAME 6 TO TAKE THE TITLE

JOHN HAVLICEK put down his shoulder, drove past a wary Ricky Sobers and banged one in off the backboard from 15 feet out—111–110. Instant hysteria. The fans took over the floor. The problem was that there was still one second to play. In the ensuing confusion, Suns guard Paul Westphal came up with an ingenious idea. The Suns were to get the ball at the endline with one second and no chance at all. So when the floor had been cleared, Westphal called a timeout, which was illegal since Phoenix had no timeouts left. Celtics guard JoJo White therefore got to shoot a technical, which put Boston up 112–110. But the Suns had the ball at midcourt. They got it in to Garfield Heard who launched a jumper that brushed the ceiling and swished.

—Barry McDermott, SI, June 14, 1976

After a third overtime, fans could celebrate for real.

PHOTOGRAPHS BY MANNY MILLAN

@MIAMIHEAT   @MIAMIHEAT

2

2013 NBA FINALS GAME 6

HEAT 103, SPURS 100

" An unmistakable sign of a good game: League officials start setting up for a postgame trophy presentation and then have to quickly tear it down. That's what happened here, thanks to Ray Allen's dagger three that snatched the title from the Spurs. " —MARK BECHTEL

▸ SPURS WERE UP 3–2 IN SERIES
▸ HEAT WON GAME 7 95–88

WITH 28 SECONDS left in what was already an incredible sporting event, Miami trailed 94–89. The Spurs' Tony Parker had just scored five straight points, including a deep fadeaway three-pointer that seemed destined for two decades of highlight shows. LeBron James was struggling, Dwyane Wade was hobbling and Chris Bosh was serving as Tim Duncan's throw pillow. This was not what they planned. But they are discovering that sports, at their best, are not about carefully orchestrated celebrations, but those unplanned moments when you find yourself. This was the kind of game that made spectators feel like participants and participants marvel like spectators. "Best game I've ever seen," said Bosh. James said it was "by far the best game I've ever been a part of."

—Michael Rosenberg, SI.com, June 19, 2013

James (left) had 16 fourth-quarter points.

2
2013
NBA FINALS
GAME 6

FROM SPORTS ILLUSTRATED
DECEMBER 23, 2013

ANATOMY OF A MIRACLE

From the time the yellow celebration ropes went up to when Ray Allen knocked down his corner three, these closing seconds were filled with memorable moments

BY LEE JENKINS

THE BEST SHOTS REMAIN airborne forever, in driveways and alleys, at parks and YMCAs, amateur imitations of Magic Johnson's junior skyhook over the Celtics, Michael Jordan's stepback versus the Jazz. They live in dusty old gyms like the one at Santa Monica High, where on a warm November morning, a 64-year-old former professor and Air Force intelligence officer strides across the key to the right corner. He glances down at the strip of hardwood separating the three-point line from the sideline and marvels at how narrow it is. Someone shooting from that corner would have only three feet to leap and land—not much room for a man who is, say, 6' 5" and wears size-15 sneakers. "This son of a gun sprints all the way back here, turns his body, gets his balance, takes his time and sets up perfectly," the professor says. "He can't rush it. He has to follow through. And he does it all because he's done it a million times before. He's waited his whole life for this shot." Then Gregg Popovich pantomimes the stroke that broke his heart.

Miami had won the series in seven games, but it was the sixth that ate at Popovich: The Spurs, 28.2 seconds away from clinching their fifth title in 14 seasons, blew a five-point lead and lost 103–100 in overtime. Popovich presented the footage to players on the first day of training camp. The Spurs weren't hiding the wound. They were exposing it so it could heal. "I didn't want anybody going into the season thinking, Oh, gosh, we got screwed, the basketball gods took one away from us," Popovich says. "That's bulls---. There's a healthier way to move on. It wasn't just one shot. It was 29 seconds."

:28 Losing the Finals, players will tell you, is a little like being in a car accident. "Everything slows down," says Miami center Chris Bosh, "and you see things you don't usually see, hear things you don't usually hear. It's kind of terrifying." Trailing 94–89, the Heat huddled around coach Erik Spoelstra during a timeout. "I thought it was over," Bosh says. "I was having flashbacks." AmericanAirlines Arena looked the same to him as it did late in Game 6 of the 2011 Finals against the Mavericks. Security guards surrounding the floor, bent at the waist, holding yellow ropes in anticipation of another team's celebration.

:27 Spoelstra sent out a lineup with five three-point shooters, leaving Bosh on the bench. Popovich countered by removing center Tim Duncan. As forward Mike Miller prepared to inbound near the Heat bench, Miami's Ray Allen ran across the key, screening Manu Ginóbili and Danny Green to free LeBron James at the top of the circle. James caught the inbounds pass, but Green recovered and contested James's three-point attempt. The shot, as hard and straight as a four-seam fastball, smacked off the bottom right corner of the backboard square. My God, Popovich thought to himself. The game might be over.

:25 If James had shot a standard brick, San Antonio forward Kawhi Leonard would have grabbed the rebound. But the shot was so wild Leonard couldn't corral it, and the ball rocketed off his hand and straight in the air. The closest Heat player was guard Dwyane Wade, stuck behind Leonard. Wade jumped off his right leg, the one with the bone bruises in the knee that require daily treatment. "Kawhi has those claws—his hands are claws—and you're just doing anything you can to get a fingertip on the ball," Wade says. "I got just enough."

:24 Green was the Finals' breakout star, but here he made a costly mistake. Instead of shadowing James on the left wing, he assumed San Antonio would come away with the loose ball and he drifted downcourt. "Most important rebound of the game and we have a player who's backing up," Popovich says. "All he had to do was pick up LeBron."

:23 Wade's rebound tip bounced off Allen to Miller, who shoveled it back to James.

:22 "I was angry at the fans who left," Allen says. "This is it. This is Game 6. We don't win and it's summer." He saw the ropes, encircling the floor, as a metaphor for his rage. "When you get to the end of your rope," Allen says, "tie a knot."

:21 With Green scrambling back, James elevated on the left wing and buried an open three. "Suddenly the energy in the building totally changed," says Heat general manager Andy Elisburg.

:20 Popovich used his final timeout. Spoelstra told his players which Spurs to foul and what play he would likely call after the ensuing free throws. James nibbled his right thumbnail. Allen swigged a bottle of water. "There was a play we'd worked on all season, but we didn't use more than once or twice," Spoelstra says. The mere mention of it induces an eye roll from Bosh. "We practiced it a million times," he says. "We never ran it."

:19 Duncan extricated his feet from the ropes along the sideline and inbounded to Leonard, who was promptly fouled. Leonard missed the first free throw, made the second: 95–92.

:18 All season the Spurs had taken Duncan out when leading by three late in games because they switch defenders on every pick-and-roll to blanket the three-point line. At 37, he is the slowest of the starters—and therefore the likeliest to be late on a switch. Duncan, who had 30 points and 16 rebounds, was replaced by Boris Diaw. Bosh, however, was back in for the Heat.

:16 Allen jogged down the right side. But he was nothing more than a decoy to space the floor for James.

:15 Miami point guard Mario Chalmers continued to the left elbow. "Some people thought we should foul," Popovich says, though Chalmers shot 79.5% from the line last season. "O.K., so you're three points up and you foul, now it's a one-point game and a free throw shooting contest. And we're one of the worst free throw shooting teams in the league. All we need is a rebound and it's over. I wouldn't give that up for a free throw contest."

:13 Bosh screened point guard Tony Parker on the left wing to clear James at the three-point line, and since San Antonio was switching everything, Diaw picked up James. But San Antonio committed another uncharacteristic error. Instead of switching back onto Bosh, Parker joined Diaw and lunged at James. "It was my job to screen Tony," Bosh

says. "When he went under me, I was like, Oh, s---. I thought about screening him again, but I didn't want to pick up the foul." Bosh didn't yet recognize the opportunity Parker had handed him.

:11 James fired, Diaw in his face, Parker in his shorts. Bosh had nowhere to go but the rim.

:09 James missed—albeit with a lighter touch this time—and the ball caromed off the left side of the rim. Ginóbili, guarding Allen in the right corner, abandoned him to track the rebound. He got one hand on the ball. Bosh got two. Bosh held the ball only for a second, and in that second he noticed something. Ginóbili, the man assigned to the best three-point shooter in NBA history, was falling down.

:08 As a young player in Milwaukee, Allen invented a drill in which he lies in the key, springs to his feet and backpedals to the corner. A coach throws him a pass. He has to catch and shoot without stepping on the three-point line or the sideline. In Allen's first training session with the Heat, he performed the drill. "It was the first time I ever saw anybody do that," Spoelstra says. "He told me he does it for offensive rebounding purposes. He said, 'You never know when you'll be in a situation where you have to find the three-point line without looking down.' "

:07 Bosh backhanded the ball to Allen. "I wish I'd waited a bit longer," Bosh says, but John Stockton couldn't have made a better pass. Allen caught it at his rib cage with his right hand, and as he gathered, he took two final steps back over the three-point line. He didn't look down. The next day the NBA's Tim Frank asked Allen if he knew his size-15s were over the line. "I hoped," he said.

:05 With Ginóbili down, a cavalry of four Spurs charged at Allen, led by Parker. But he wasn't rushing. According to an ESPN *Sport Science* segment, Allen's average shot release takes .73 of a second. This time he waited a leisurely .83. Norris Cole knew first. "I was on the bench, in the opposite corner, so I had the best view of it," says Miami's backup point guard. "That's why I jumped so high." He tracked the flight of the ball, traveling at a 40-degree angle, and leaped three feet in the air. "Rebound Bosh!" announcer Mike Breen said. "Back out to Allen! *His* three-pointer! *Bang!*"

A viewing party at the AT&T Center in San Antonio fell silent. In Miami a security guard, holding the yellow rope behind Allen, pumped a fist. "There was a collective violence in the building," Elisburg says. "It was like an explosion."

At dinner, hours later, Bosh's heart was still racing. "We could play out that scenario a million times and maybe we win twice," he said.

On a trip to Toronto this season Allen ran into Frank, and he was reminded of the notorious yellow ropes. "I know you guys were just doing what you had to do," Allen said. In a way, he's grateful for those ropes. They added a little more thread to a 29-second tapestry that will live in montages and driveways forever. The extra twine helped produce the unbreakable knot. ∎

Bosh (left) rebounded and fed Allen (right) for the tying three-pointer.

3

1987
EAST FINALS
GAME 5

CELTICS 108, PISTONS 107

" The Pistons were five seconds away from seizing command of the series when Isiah Thomas's inbound pass was stolen by Larry Bird. " —IAN THOMSEN

▸ BIRD HAD 36 POINTS, 12 REBOUNDS, NINE ASSISTS
▸ CELTICS WON SERIES 4–3

CHUCK DALY was waving frantically and screaming for a timeout. Thomas didn't see him. He lobbed a soft pass to Bill Laimbeer, who was just a few feet away. The next few seconds will stand among the most dramatic in Celtics history. They'll be shown endlessly, frame by frame, Zapruder-like. And every time we'll see Bird have the presence of mind to get into defensive position rather than hang his head after a blocked shot. The Pistons celebrated. Bird calculated. He rushed to Laimbeer, intending only to foul him but, instead, snatched a pass. He saw that there was time for a better shot than a frantic, low-percentage jumper. He spotted Dennis Johnson—"his jersey," actually—cutting toward the basket, zipped the ball to DJ, who ducked under Joe Dumars's outstretched arms and put up a difficult righthanded layup from the left side.

—Jack McCallum, SI, June 8, 1987

Bird and Johnson made the winning connection.

5

1962
WILT'S 100
POINT GAME

WARRIORS 169, KNICKS 147

" If playoff performances and subtle stat categories defined Russell, this was quintessential Wilt: a throwaway regular-season game in Hershey, Pa., in which he put up a gaudy, bragworthy number. Remember: He doesn't hit 100 without making 28 of 32 free throws. " —ALEXANDER WOLFF

▸ CHAMBERLAIN SHOT 36 OF 63 FROM THE FIELD
▸ HIS CAREER FREE THROW PERCENTAGE WAS 51.1

MANY PUNDITS did not think the 100-point explosion was that big a deal. This was due partly to the NBA's low standing in the sports pantheon, to Wilt's status as the game's preeminent villain and partly to veiled racism. *The Boston Globe*'s Harold Kaese churlishly wrote that the scoring outburst "came as no surprise to this writer" and predicted that "within 10 years 100-point games will be common for pro players." Al Attles, Chamberlain's teammate that night, thinks the mark has resonated [over time because of] the serendipperous century mark itself: "I told Wilt, 'Big fella, I am really happy you didn't score one more basket. One hundred points sounds a lot better than 102.' "

—*Dick Friedman, SI, February 27, 2012*

Wilt's 100 points were neither televised nor filmed.

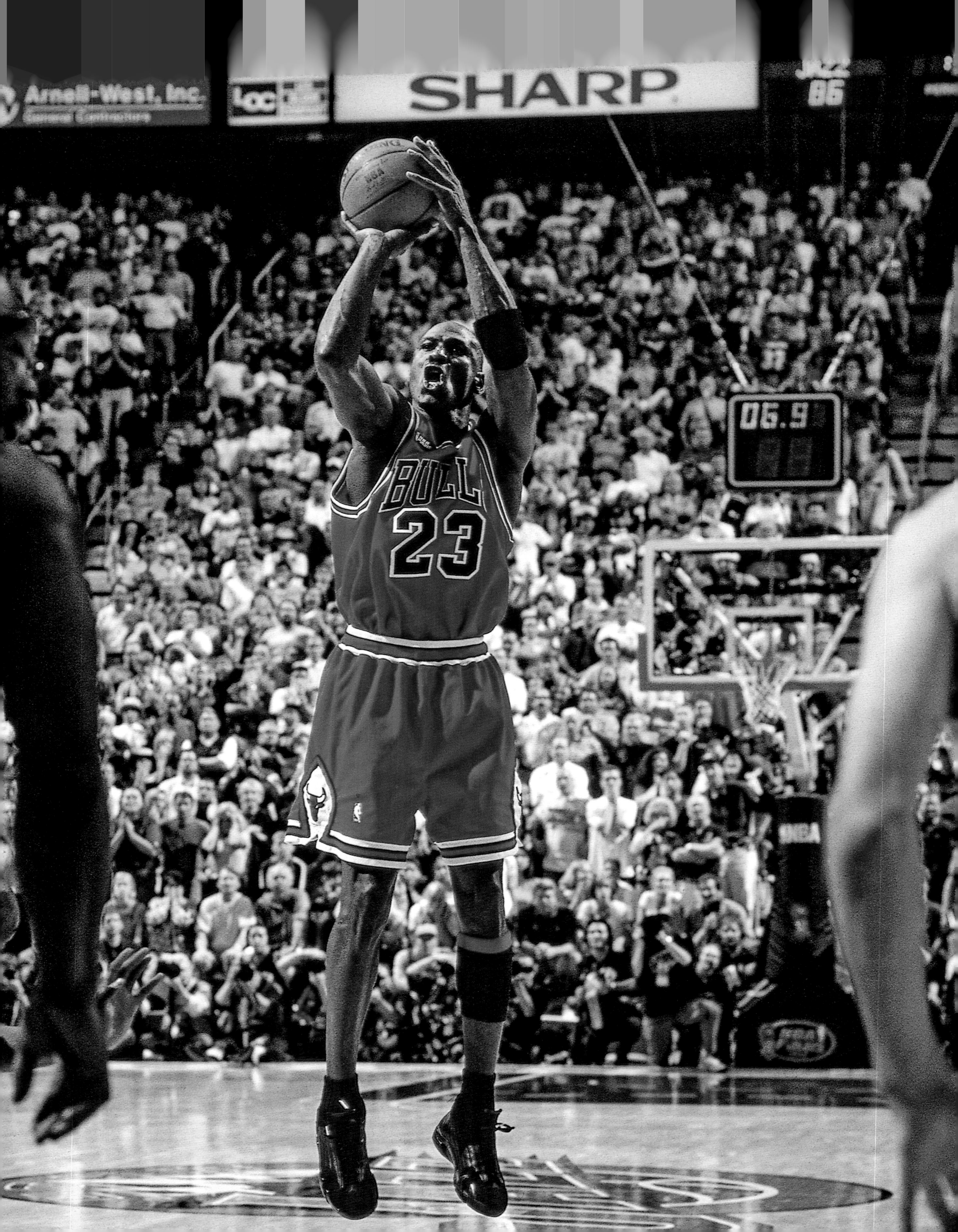
Arnell-West, Inc.
SHARP
JAZZ
86
06.9
BULL
23

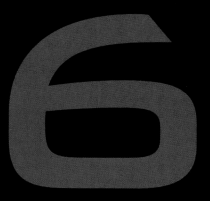

1998
NBA Finals
Game 6

BULLS 87, JAZZ 86

" Perhaps you recall what happened? It involved Michael Jordan, Bryon Russell and either one of the great moves, or great push-offs, of all time. The context: the Jazz and Bulls tied for the best regular season record. It was an away game for Chicago. Pippen got injured early. Jordan stripped Malone to lead to the final bucket. Fittingly, the most-watched NBA game ever. " —CHRIS BALLARD

- JORDAN SCORED 45 POINTS
- THIS WAS HIS FINAL GAME
  AS A BULL

BILL BRADLEY wrote that the athlete had an obligation to live out the full arc of a career, and probably this should be true for most athletes, even the best ones. But Jordan is a special case, the athlete for our time, and to see him tarnished at all, even occasionally to see age overtake him, is only to be so cruelly reminded how temporal and fragile we all are, how elusive and brief is perfection. For all his majesty, for that perfectly celestial final minute against the Jazz, still, we also saw the first leaf of autumn in these playoffs. No more, thank you. Besides, what actor had a better exit than the one Michael Jordan wrote for himself in Salt Lake City?

—Frank Deford, SI, June 22, 1998

The shot gave Jordan his sixth title.

PHOTOGRAPHS BY JOHN BIEVER (LEFT) AND WALTER IOOSS JR.

7

1957
NBA FINALS
GAME 7

CELTICS 125, HAWKS 123

"Of course you didn't see it, and I only have a vague memory of watching it on TV. But the Celts beat the St. Louis Hawks in double-overtime, Tommy Heinsohn scored 37 points, Bill Russell ran the length of the court to block a shot from behind, Bob Cousy and Bill Sharman combined to shoot 5 for 40. In short, LOTS happened." —JACK McCALLUM

▸ 38 LEAD CHANGES
▸ CELTICS' FIRST NBA TITLE

TWO SECONDS—the Boston Garden one deafening shriek of sound, guards restraining spectators from the edges of the floor, 13,000 sets of nerves on the raw edge. Alex Hannum threw a perfect strike the length of the court in a planned maneuver to hit the backboard for a rebound by a teammate. The ball bounced off—into the arms of Bob Pettit. Just exactly perfect. Pettit misses this kind of a shot about as frequently as destiny touches a comparative unknown like Hannum. Pettit took his shot. It rolled around the rim, and rolled out. Both Hawks owner Ben Kerner and Boston owner Walter Brown had waited 11 years for a winning team. It is no play with words to say that they both had just that.

—Jeremiah Tax, SI, April 22, 1957

The Celtics began a string of winning 11 of 13 titles.

8

1988
EAST SEMIS
GAME 7

CELTICS 118, HAWKS 116

" The divergent styles of Larry Bird and Dominique Wilkins were best expressed in one epic back-and-forth. Being a Celtic, Bird got the better that day. "Look in his eyes," Dominique would say, "and you see a killer." " —ALEXANDER WOLFF

- ▸ WILKINS SCORED 47 POINTS
- ▸ BIRD'S 34 POINTS INCLUDED 20 IN THE FOURTH QUARTER

THE HAWKS had an answer for everything in Wilkins, who would score 16 points in the fourth quarter, thereby silencing forever the critics who said he played with one hand on the trigger and the other on his throat. "A lot of games you wonder what more you could have done," said Wilkins, "but not today. I can honestly say I did everything I could. We all did." Obviously that goes for Boston too. However, as is so often the case, one man did just a little bit more. "Sometimes after Larry plays a game like this it makes me think ahead," said Kevin McHale, who had 33 points. "I'll be retired in Minnesota and Larry will be retired somewhere in Indiana, and we probably won't see each other much. But a lot of nights I'll just lie there and remember games like this, and what it was like to play with him."

—Jack McCallum, SI, May 30, 1988

Wilkins's greatest game wasn't enough against Bird.

PHOTOGRAPH BY DAVID E. KLUTHO

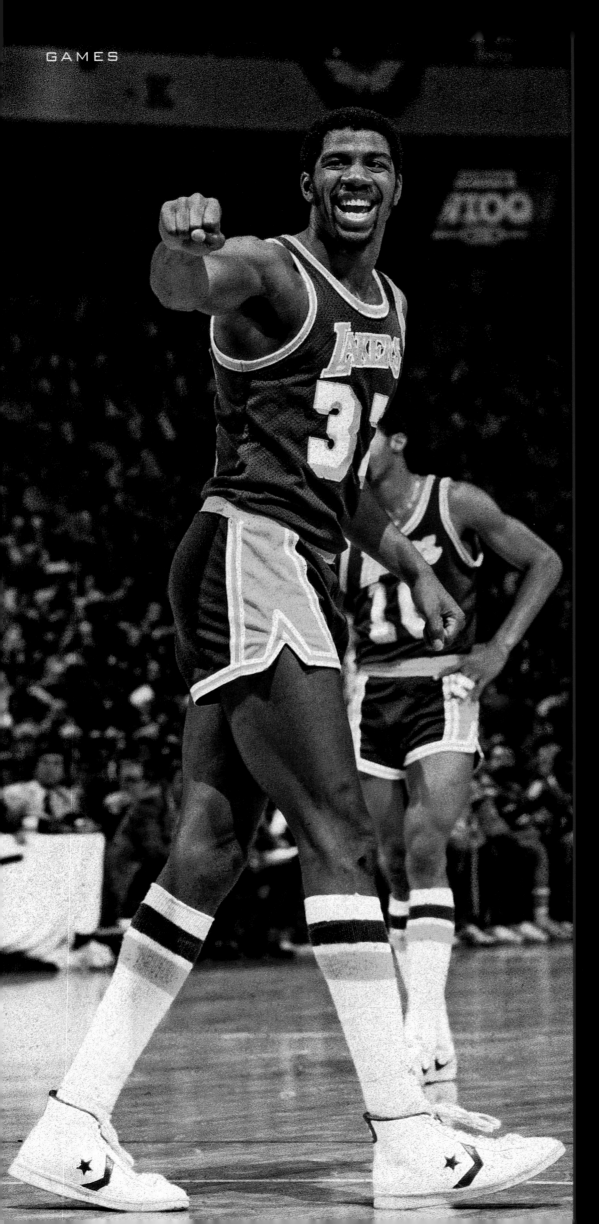

1980
NBA FINALS
GAME 6

LAKERS 123, 76ERS 107

"With Kareem Abdul-Jabbar out with an ankle injury, rookie Magic Johnson put up one of the great stats lines in Finals history: 42 points, 15 rebounds and seven assists." —CHRIS MANNIX

▸ MAGIC PLAYED 47 MINUTES
▸ HE WAS NAMED FINALS MVP

EARVIN (MAGIC) JOHNSON sort of waddled onto the court at Philadelphia's Spectrum and set himself in the center jump circle, fidgeting there for nearly a minute before anyone else was in position, trying to decide how to jump. "I didn't know whether to stand with my right foot forward or my left," he would say later. "Didn't know when I should jump or where I should tap it if I got to it." All the thinking and foot shuffling, the very idea of playing center for the first time since high school, made Magic Johnson giggle. Caldwell Jones, who jumps center for the 76ers, watched as Johnson got ready. Magic grinned as they shook hands. The 76ers knew, of course, that Kareem Abdul-Jabbar was home in Los Angeles. But the Sixers never expected to see a 20-year-old, 6' 9" rookie point guard lining up to jump center. Giggling.

—John Papanek, SI, May 26, 1980

Magic dominated and smiled while doing it.

PHOTOGRAPH BY MANNY MILLAN

10

1986 JORDAN'S 63-POINT GAME

CELTICS 135, BULLS 131

Jordan missed 64 regular season games that year.

❝On fresh legs after being sidelined for most of the season, Jordan exploded past the eventual champion Celtics before losing 135–131 in double overtime. "It's just God disguised as Michael Jordan," said Larry Bird.❞ —IAN THOMSEN

▸ MOST POINTS SCORED BY A PLAYER IN A PLAYOFF GAME
▸ JORDAN SHOT 22 FOR 41

JORDAN HAD to be a loser that day. And those Celtics had to be the winners, even in the face of the greatest individual postseason performance ever, to instruct Jordan in the most essential of hoop truths: that, in the end, a full team will beat any single player, no matter how good.

—*Alexander Wolff, SI, February 18, 2013*

10

THE

Best Single-Season Te

THE NBA IMPOSED ITS CURRENT SALARY CAP IN 1984, AND IT HAS BECOME STRICTER OVER TIME. NOW, NOT ONLY IS THERE A SALARY CAP, BUT A LUXURY TAX. IT IS ONE POSSIBLE EXPLANATION FOR WHY, IN OUR LIST OF THE BEST SINGLE-SEASON TEAMS, SO MANY CAME FROM THE PAST, AND NONE FROM THE LAST 18 YEARS.

ONE OF OUR TOP TEAMS IS THE 1982–83 SIXERS, AND THEIR ASSEMBLAGE WAS ONE OF THE CAP'S PRECIPITATING EVENTS. THE SIXERS HAD GONE TO THE FINALS THE PREVIOUS YEAR, AND YET THEY WERE ABLE TO ACQUIRE THE REIGNING NBA MVP, MOSES MALONE, AND SIGN HIM TO A RICH CONTRACT. IMAGINE THAT HAPPENING NOW— IF, SAY, THE HEAT, AFTER LOSING IN THE 2014 FINALS, SIGNED KEVIN DURANT, WHILE KEEPING ALL ITS ESSENTIAL PARTS. CAN'T HAPPEN. MUCH FROM THE PAST HAS BEEN RENDERED IMPOSSIBLE, SUCH AS KEEPING A CREW OF HALL OF FAMERS TOGETHER FOR YEARS, AS THE CELTICS DID IN THE 1950S AND '60S.

ONE OF THE MORE RECENT TEAMS ON THE LIST IS THE 1991–92 BULLS. DANNY AINGE, AFTER HIS TRAIL BLAZERS LOST TO THOSE BULLS IN THE FINALS, TOLD SI HE DIDN'T THINK THEIR TEAM WAS ALL THAT GREAT. "LET'S JUST SAY THEY'RE A VERY GOOD TEAM WITH ONE GREAT PLAYER," AINGE SNIFFED. THE QUOTE UNFAIRLY SLIGHTS SCOTTIE PIPPEN, BUT AINGE DID HAVE A POINT: THESE DAYS, ONE OR TWO GREAT PLAYERS CAN GO A LONG WAY.

1

1995–96
BULLS

72–10 REGULAR SEASON

"In Michael Jordan's first full season after his foray into baseball, he and Scottie Pippen led the Bulls to a league-record 72 wins. They were never threatened in the playoffs while welcoming the defense and rebounding of Dennis Rodman." —IAN THOMSEN

▸ OPENED SEASON 41–3
▸ BEAT SONICS 4–2 IN FINALS

SINCE NOVEMBER, it has been one long party for the Bulls. Everything seems to have gone right for Chicago in 1995–96, and the Finals were no exception. When Ron Harper suddenly came up with a sore left knee during warmups before Game 3, Phil Jackson inserted sixth man Toni Kukoc into the starting lineup, and he proceeded to hit three quick jump shots, including a three-pointer, to help stake the Bulls to their big first-quarter lead. Center Luc Longley provided surprising scoring punch with a playoff career-high 19 points. Pippen, who had 21 points in both of the first two games, added balance in Game 3 with a near triple double (12 points, nine assists and eight rebounds).

"That's the kind of team we have," Rodman said after Game 3. "Nothing gets to us, nothing makes us lose our cool. Not even me."

—Phil Taylor, SI, June 17, 1996

This season began the second of Chicago's threepeats.

1971–72
LAKERS

69–13 REGULAR SEASON

" Jerry West, Gail Goodrich and Wilt Chamberlain overcame the loss of Elgin Baylor early in the season and won a record 33 games in a row (the previous mark had been 20 straight) en route to the title. " —LEE JENKINS

▸ RECORD 16 CONSECUTIVE ROAD WINS
▸ BEAT KNICKS 4–1 IN FINALS

CHAMBERLAIN, who brilliantly led Los Angeles to the brink of success, had complained mildly of soreness in his right wrist after the Lakers' third win. Team physician Robert K. Kerlan announced that there was no fracture, but the sprain was severe—so severe that it was "very, very doubtful" Wilt would play the next game. He played. Did he play! Wearing the padded hand wraps interior linemen use, Chamberlain played his best game of a super series. He scored 24 points. He had 29 rebounds. On defense, he harassed Knicks shooters far outside, yet still scrambled back to block inside shots. In the end, he shut up those critics who for years claimed that he was a quitter, that he could not win important games. He was, padded hands down, the most valuable player as Los Angeles took its first championship by winning the fifth game 114–100.

—*Peter Carry, SI, May 15, 1972*

The L.A. Lakers had only been Finals runners-up until 1971–72.

3

1985-86
CELTICS

" Larry Bird and Kevin McHale in their primes, Bill Walton as a sixth man, ball movement that could be enshrined: But for six losses at the buzzer or in overtime, these Celtics would have won 73. " —ALEXANDER WOLFF

▸ 40-1 HOME RECORD
▸ BEAT ROCKETS 4-2
  IN FINALS

Former MVP Walton teamed with 1985–86 MVP Bird.

PHOTOGRAPH BY STEVE LIPOFSKY/BASKETBALLPHOTO.COM

OF ALL the things the Celtics have done this season, perhaps the most extraordinary has been to win every home game except for a 121–103 loss to Portland on Dec. 6. It seems appropriate that the only team to beat them at home goes by the name of Trail Blazers.

—Alexander Wolff, SI, June 9, 1986

GREEN, PLUS A TOUCH OF RED

With a rejuvenated Bill Walton coming off the bench and a driven Larry Bird leading the charge, the Celtics captured their third championship of the 1980s

BY JACK McCALLUM

AY THIS FOR THE HOUSTON Rockets: They are the team of tomorrow. But throughout this NBA season, with a single exception, there had been nothing but grim todays for visitors to the Boston Garden parquet. Game 6 of the championship series was no different. Systematically but passionately, the Boston Celtics destroyed the Rockets by a score of 114–97 to earn their 16th NBA championship. Hang another banner, sew a few more stitches of tradition into that big green quilt that drapes the NBA. And know that this Celtics team, which finished the season 47–1 at the Garden and 82–18 overall, can take its place alongside any that has gone before.

This particular Celtics championship long ago seemed ordained. It was "predestined," forward Kevin McHale said after the game—but at what moment?

Perhaps it was back in the preseason when Celtics president Red Auerbach traded a disenchanted Cedric Maxwell for an enchanted Bill Walton, who arrived in Boston via time machine. The fire burned in Walton's eyes and the passes flicked off his fingertips, just as they had done in 1977 when he brought a championship to Portland. The Celtics' jigsaw had been missing a giant piece—a center to spell Robert Parish—and Walton nestled snugly into place.

Or perhaps it was back on Feb. 16 when the Celtics beat the defending champion L.A. Lakers 105–99 at the Forum to complete a sweep of their two-game season series. Boston attacked the Lakers' soft underbelly of complacency—the same target Celtic opponents will be aiming at next season—and after that game the Celtics may as well have begun scouting the horizon for other challengers.

Or perhaps it was one week earlier in Dallas, on All-Star Weekend. Larry Bird had just won the NBA's first three-point-shot contest and he was ecstatic. "I'm the three-point king! I'm the three-point king!" Bird shouted over and over. Why was a superstar so excited about winning a contest that included Leon Wood and Kyle Macy, for heaven's sake? It spoke volumes about Bird's motivation this season. This was the year he wanted to stuff all the awards in the pocket of his blue jeans and tote them back home to Indiana. That's exactly what he did. He won his third straight MVP award for his play during the regular season, and after Game 6 he was voted the series MVP. Who says you can't have it all?

For Game 6, there was ample reason for Bird's intensity, which he said was as high as it had ever been for any game. The Celtics had returned to Boston from Houston Friday afternoon with scores to settle. One was with Ralph Sampson, who in Game 5 had picked a fight with Celtics reserve guard Jerry Sichting and been ejected. At 9:40 of the second period Sampson and Sichting, who at 6' 1" is 15 inches shorter than Sampson, became entangled during a Rockets possession. They bumped. Sichting didn't back down. Sampson gave him an elbow. Sichting said, "I'll get you for that." Sampson suddenly turned and threw a frightening right hand, then another, at Sichting. Dennis Johnson came running over—"to pull Jerry away," he said—and Sampson took a swing that landed near Johnson's left eye. Stick, as Sampson is called by his teammates, had suddenly become Stick And Move.

Both benches emptied. Akeem Olajuwon and Johnson squared off. Despite the fact that he had worn a DANCE FOR DISARMAMENT T-shirt to practice the day before, Walton tackled Sampson, who grew progressively enraged as the battle wore on.

The game brought out the worst in almost everyone, except for easygoing Celtics coach K.C. Jones, whose first words to the press were "*Oy vey*." Sichting said of Sampson's attack that he didn't know whether "it was a punch or a mosquito bite. My three-year-old son hits harder." Bird roasted both the officiating and the Houston fans and said he couldn't believe Sampson had picked on Sichting, because "my girlfriend could beat him up."

At their practice Saturday, the day before Game 6, the Celtics basically beat each other up. "I had to call it off before they killed each other," said Jones. McHale, normally Mr. Quip, left practice quickly, his dark, hollow eyes staring straight ahead. Bird said, "I'm ready to go. And if I'm ready to go, usually the other guys are too."

Certainly the Beantown fans were ready to go. In Game 6, Sampson was booed every time he touched the ball in the first half. One moron, standing next to a policeman, hung Sampson in effigy from the upper deck. Whether he felt pressured or not, Sampson played poorly, stiffly, uncertainly. He failed to get to the free throw line and finished with eight points on 4-for-12 shooting from the floor. Said Sampson later, "I wasn't tough psychologically." Or any other way.

But the Celtics played as if possessed. There was one brief sequence late in the first period when the NBA's future, in the person of Olajuwon, flashed before the Celtics' eyes. On three consecutive possessions Olajuwon came from behind Walton to make steals that led to Rockets baskets, two of them slam dunks by Akeem. Never had Walton, who will be 34 in November, looked older. But inevitably, inexorably, he had his moment. Right after Bird's three-pointer in the fourth period, Walton turned up the Garden decibel level to its highest point when he made a 15-foot jump shot. The Rockets called timeout, Walton raised his fist and the crowd went crazy. It was the moment he had come for, the apotheosis of his long, strange trip, as his friends, the Grateful Dead, might put it. ∎

4

1966–67 76ERS

Billy Cunningham (32) aided the 76ers' deep frontcourt.

PHOTOGRAPH BY WALTER IOOSS JR.

" New coach Alex Hannum designed a more egalitarian offense. The result: 11 fewer attempts per game for Wilt Chamberlain, but the Big Dipper averaged nearly eight assists and the Sixers set a record for wins. " —MARK BECHTEL

▸ BROKE CELTICS' STREAK OF EIGHT CONSECUTIVE TITLES ▸ BEAT WARRIORS 4–2 IN FINALS

THE MAN who had scored thousands of points but had never won a championship had taken exactly six shots that night. The losers had Rick Barry, who had taken 41. "Sometimes," Wilt said, for the ears of the people back in Philly, "it is actually easier to play against a team that has one man do most of the shooting."

—*Frank Deford, SI, May 8, 1967*

5

1982–83
76ERS

65–17 REGULAR SEASON

" They had a Little Mo (Maurice Cheeks) and a Big Mo (Malone), a Doctor (Julius Erving) and a Boston Strangler (Andrew Toney). They had flash, dash, sass and a near perfect run through the postseason that ended with a sweep of the Magic-Kareem Lakers. " —JACK McCALLUM

▸ 12–1 IN PLAYOFFS
▸ THREE PLAYERS NAMED FIRST TEAM ALL-DEFENSIVE

"WE USED to be a pretty team that looked good winning games," Erving said. "Now we win games without looking that good. Bodies are flying all over the place out there." Moses Malone has changed the Sixers' emphasis from finesse to the physical. As the games wore on and the other players wore out, Malone just kept getting stronger. "Let's not play make-believe," coach Billy Cunningham said. "When you talk about defending against Moses Malone, you have to give something up." First the Lakers gave up the outside shot to the Sixers, trying to double-team him. Then they gave up the pretense that they could match him with Kareem Abdul-Jabbar, choosing instead to alternate forwards Kurt Rambis and Mark Landsberger against him. "There are a lot of forces in nature you don't stop," Rambis said. "And he's one of them."

Bruce Newman, SI, June 13, 1983

Malone was the NBA regular-season and Finals MVP.

6

1986–87
LAKERS

65–17 REGULAR SEASON

"After absorbing a five-game whipping from Houston in the '86 conference finals, coach Pat Riley shifted the primary offensive responsibilities from Kareem to Magic." —CHRIS MANNIX

▸ 15–3 IN PLAYOFFS
▸ BEAT CELTICS 4–2 IN FINALS

"THERE'S NO question this is the best team I've played on," said Magic Johnson, a member of the 1980, '82 and '85 championship Lakers. "It's fast, it can shoot and rebound, it has inside people, it has everything. I've never played on a team that had everything before." Nor has a team often played with an individual who does everything to the degree that Magic did this season. Can the game be played any better than Magic played it in the third quarter on Sunday? After scoring only four first-half points, Magic was on the ropes and the Lakers were right there with him. But then he took over. Of the 30 Lakers points in the third quarter, Johnson scored 12 and assisted on eight others. He also grabbed four rebounds and was all over the place defensively, double-teaming down low and planting his body in every passing lane. The Celtics scored only 12 points in the period, and almost before they knew it, it was over. One sudden, explosive charge—that's Lakerball.

—*Jack McCallum, SI, June 22, 1987*

By Riley's design, Abdul-Jabbar ceded to Johnson.

PHOTOGRAPH BY MANNY MILLAN

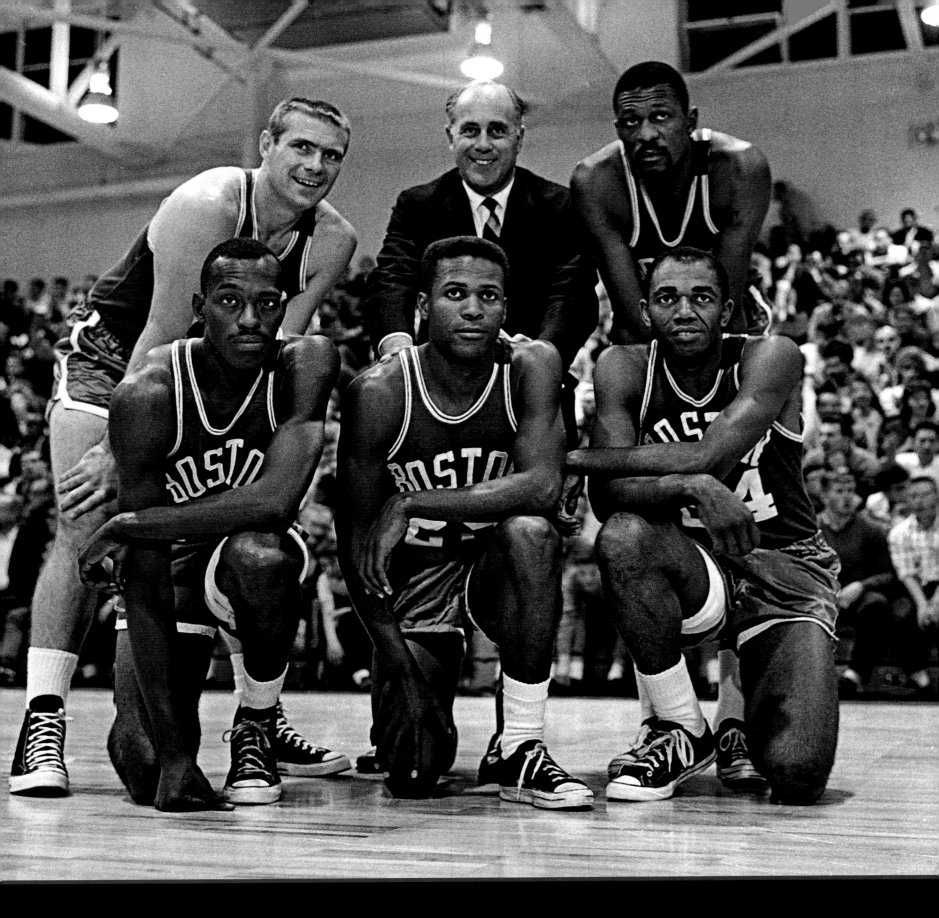

"Title season No. 8 and the classic Celtics at their best: Russell and John Havlicek and Sam Jones and K.C .Jones and Tom Heinsohn. The basketball IQ was off the charts. (John Thompson was a reserve.) Five players are now in the Hall of Fame." —CHRIS BALLARD

IT IS NOW wholly reasonable for the NBA to disseminate news of its playoffs by sending out fill-in-the-blanks postcards: "Greetings from Boston and__! Led by Bill Russell, this year the Celtics won four games to__. It was their__straight championship. Losing coach__said this Boston team was the 'greatest ever.' "

—Frank Deford, SI, May 3, 1965

1964-65
CELTICS

▸ "HAVLICEK STOLE THE BALL!"
▸ BEAT LAKERS 4-1 IN FINALS

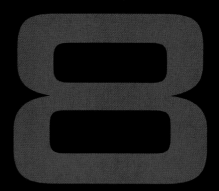

8

1969–70
KNICKS

60-22 REGULAR SEASON

" One of the most artful passing teams won an impassioned Finals Game 7 behind Willis Reed. Walt Frazier, Dave DeBusschere and Bill Bradley became New York legends. **"** —IAN THOMSEN

> BEAT LAKERS 4–3 IN FINALS
> REED WAS NBA MVP

WHAT REED has accomplished in these playoffs has been magnificent—particularly since he has been hobbled with a chronically sore left knee. No man has had to face, in succession, the quality of opponents he has—Wes Unseld, last year's MVP; Lew Alcindor, next year's MVP; and Wilt Chamberlain, MVP two years ago. The team's success depends on its outside shooting. After the first Finals game Jerry West could only shake his head in awe. "They just raise up and shoot," he said. "They're such a very, very intelligent team. Reed is so active, and they recognize this, and use him so well in their offense. And they just all can hit. They work for an open 15-foot shot, and if this man isn't open, he passes to another man for a 15-foot shot, and if he isn't open, they keep passing it until they find a man who is open for a 15-foot shot. And if he happens to miss, then they just go to the bench and find another man who can make a 15-foot shot."

—Frank Deford , SI. May 11, 1970

The 1969–70 Knicks-Lakers Finals remains a classic.

PHOTOGRAPH BY WALTER IOOSS JR.

This was the Bulls' second title team.

PHOTOGRAPH BY MANNY MILLAN

9

67–15 REGULAR SEASON

" Having evolved from scorer to superstar, the breadth of Michael Jordan's greatness was on display this season. He won his sixth straight scoring title and third MVP. " —CHRIS MANNIX

‣ TIED FOR FIFTH MOST WINS IN A SEASON
‣ BEAT BLAZERS 4–2 IN FINALS

1991–92 Bulls

WHENEVER Chicago had to win a game, it won it. Technically, Game 6 was not a must win because the Bulls held a 3–2 lead. But to have the series extended was a fate-tempting uncertainty that even this cocky group did not want to risk. Besides, with Olympic training camp beginning, Jordan's tee times were in peril.

—*Jack McCallum, SI. June 22, 1992*

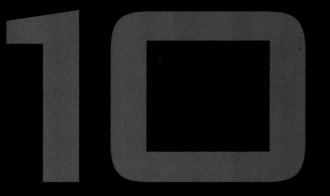

1988–89 PISTONS

63–19 REGULAR SEASON

"Despised but respected, the Bad Boys of Isiah Thomas and Bill Laimbeer, Dennis Rodman and Rick Mahorn lost just two playoff games, both to Michael Jordan's Bulls. A year later, the Pistons repeated as champions." —LEE JENKINS

▸ 15–2 IN PLAYOFFS
▸ BEAT LAKERS 4–0 IN FINALS

THE LAKERS were repeatedly caught flat-footed as Detroit's guards went rocketing past them for open jumpers or layups. The collision defenses usually employed in a championship series are supposed to make the lane a forbidding place for little men, but 6' 1" point guard Isiah Thomas and Joe Dumars, who is 6' 3", spent so much time motoring up the middle of the Lakers' defense that they looked like commuters headed home from the Ford plant near the Southfield Freeway. Several Detroit players said they were startled when they realized the Lakers weren't going to switch aggressively while running through Detroit's labyrinth of screens, a tactic Chicago had used successfully against the Pistons guards in the Eastern Conference finals. "You'd come off a screen and be open," Vinnie Johnson, Detroit's third guard, said of the Lakers defense, "so you'd go, 'Oh,' and just take it in for a layup."

—Bruce Newman, SI, June 19, 1989

Dumars and the guards powered Detroit's offense.

PHOTOGRAPH BY MANNY MILLAN

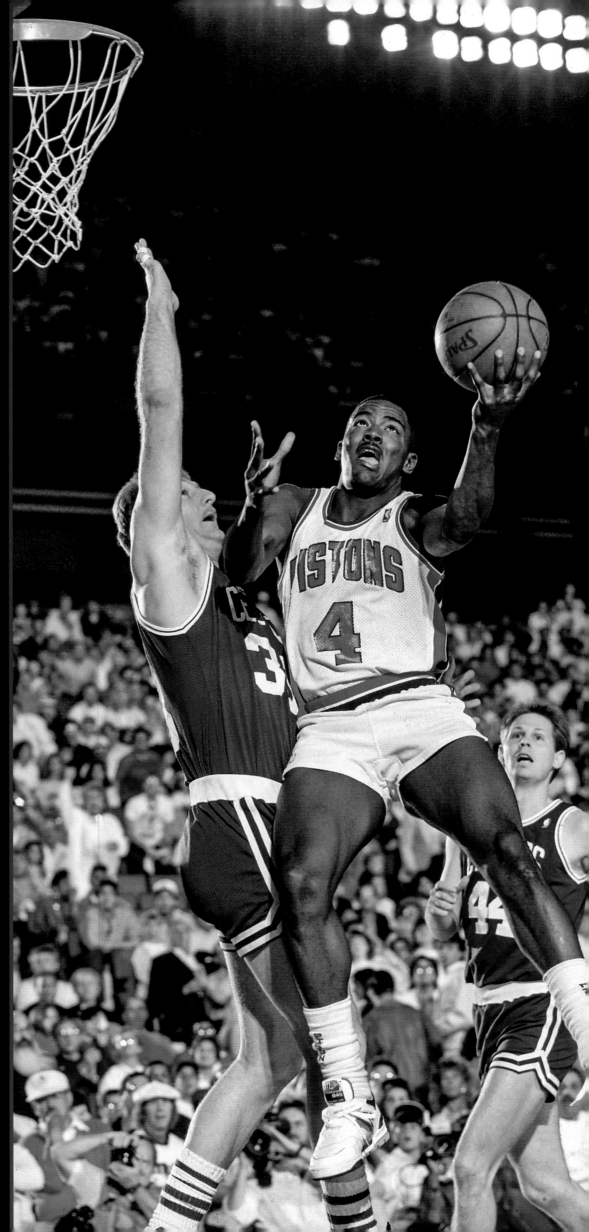

BEST FRANCHISES

THIS BOOK'S MOST SURPRISING OMISSION COMES IN THE FRANCHISES CATEGORY. BASKETBALL IS A KNOWN AS AN URBAN GAME, AND THE KNICKS PLAY IN AMERICA'S BIGGEST CITY, AND IN "THE WORLD'S MOST FAMOUS ARENA." THEY ARE THE TEAM THAT CONSPIRACY THEORISTS BELIEVE WAS PROPPED UP BY THE LEAGUE WITH A COLD ENVELOPE IN THE PATRICK EWING DRAFT LOTTERY BOWL. YET IN OUR ACCOUNTING, THE KNICKS FINISHED 11TH.

THE KNICKS WERE GREAT IN THE WALT FRAZIER ERA, BUT OTHER THAN THAT IT'S BEEN ROUGH—ESPECIALLY LATELY. EWING'S GOOD KNICKS TEAMS ARE REMEMBERED AS FOILS FOR REGGIE MILLER AND FOR JOHN STARKS'S HEAVES. THEN CAME STEPHON MARBURY, PRESIDENT AND COACH ISIAH THOMAS, EDDY CURRY, STEVE FRANCIS, ZACH RANDOLPH, J.R. SMITH AND HIS COMPULSION TO UNTIE PLAYERS' SHOELACES, AND MORE. IN FACT, THE KNICKS' MISGUIDED MOVES HAVE THE MAKINGS OF A COMPELLING TOP 10 LIST.

ONE THING FOR SURE: YOU CAN'T ACCUSE THE KNICKS OF NOT TRYING. THE BIG-NAME HIRES THEY'VE THROWN AT THIS MESS INCLUDE FOUR OF SI'S ALLTIME TOP COACHES: PAT RILEY, LENNY WILKENS AND LARRY BROWN ON THE BENCH, AND NOW PHIL JACKSON AS PRESIDENT. SURELY THEY WOULD MAKE A RUN AT RED AUERBACH IF HE WERE AROUND. OF COURSE, RED MIGHT RUN THE OTHER WAY.

1

THE CELTICS

FOUNDED 1946

" Boston has won the most titles of any franchise, and its stretch of 11 championships in 13 seasons is a run that will never be duplicated. From Bill Russell to Larry Bird, the Celtics jersey has been worn by some of the game's most iconic figures. " —CHRIS MANNIX

- 17 CHAMPIONSHIPS
- 51 PLAYOFF APPEARANCES

IT'S EASIER to compare the current Celtics with the franchise's 1974 and '76 championship teams [than it is the Bird-era teams]: Kevin Garnett is Dave Cowens, a relentless, two-way board banger with an outside touch. Paul Pierce is a better offensive version of Havlicek (though not as good all-around). Ray Allen is Jo Jo White in his silky smoothness. Even Boston's earliest NBA champions are a better fit: Garnett is Bill Russell. Pierce is Tommy Heinsohn, cocky and offensive-minded. Allen is Bill Sharman, fluid and fundamental, drop-dead accurate from the free throw line. (Rajon Rondo, however, is not Bob Cousy.) Such comparisons are, in the end, weaker than dishwater. But they are inevitable, for it is almost impossible to find a fan who will talk about the Celtics of the present without referencing the Celtics of the past. That's how it is and how it will remain.

—Jack McCallum, SI, June 30, 2008

History is everpresent at a Celtics game.

Nicholson and Magic brought glamour to Lakers games.

PHOTOGRAPH BY BRIAN LANKER

THE LAKERS

"Whether shivering in the North or baking in the West, the franchise has always found centers (Mikan, Wilt, Kareem, Shaq), guards (Magic, West, Kobe), forwards (Baylor, Worthy), coaches (Kundla, Sharman, Riley, Jackson) and championships." —JACK MCCALLUM

▸ 16 CHAMPIONSHIPS
▸ 60 PLAYOFF APPEARANCES

GEORGE MIKAN to Kareem Abdul-Jabbar to Shaquille O'Neal define an evolution of big men playing on a glamour franchise. Few teams have a tradition this rich, beginning with one of the pro game's pioneers, carrying through basketball's most complete center and culminating in a one-man multimedia empire.

—*Richard Hoffer, SI, November 11, 1996*

FROM SPORTS ILLUSTRATED
NOVEMBER 3, 1986

CUCKOO FOR HIS TEAM

The Lakers have the most celebrity-studded stands in the NBA, and no fan is more prominent than Jack Nicholson, whose passion for the purple and gold is no act

BY RICK REILLY

T'S ONE OF THE SIX BIGGIES—SKIING AND sex, art and acting, books and basketball—in his life, and nobody indulges his passions quite like Jack Nicholson. He allows almost nothing to come between himself and his two $125-a-night seats at the Forum, three seats down from the visiting coach. And when the Lakers are on the road he's often there with them, front and center, wearing one of his 25 pairs of designer sunglasses. If he can't get to the game, the Lakers make him a tape, with Chick Hearn's broadcast voiced over, and express-mail it to him. Nicholson even has season tickets for the L.A. Clippers just so he can have a front-row seat when the Lakers play them.

He is the most famous, most visible, most audacious fan in NBA history. And he is so ribaldly rabid about his team that he has ventured into the Boston Garden, the very tabernacle of the Celtics faith, waving towels, giving the choke sign, gesturing obscenely to the crowd—and every year he makes it out alive. Two years ago, somebody outside the Garden was selling T-shirts printed with a garden-variety vulgarity and Nicholson's name: BLEEP BLEEP, JACK. Delighted, Nicholson bought them all. "I loved 'em," he says. "All my friends got one."

How can you hate a guy who buys up all your insults?

As obsessive as he is about his Lakers, Nicholson is not your typical Lakers celeb. For one thing, he waits until after the national anthem to slip, sometimes unnoticed, into his seat. At halftime he slides down a back hallway with his cohorts—John McEnroe and Tatum O'Neal, record mogul Lou Adler (the one with the odd hat collection), Adler's son Nicky, *Chinatown* writer Robert Towne and a few others. In the glitzorama at Lakers games Nicholson is odd in that he doesn't go to the locker room afterward to slap tall backs. He was in the locker room only once—last year—after the team won the world championship in Boston. The players liked that.

"You can come in here some nights, and there's 1,000 celebrities in here," says former Lakers forward Mitch Kupchak, now an assistant GM for the club. "You can hardly sit down."

Nicholson is at so many games that some people have just stopped noticing him. While John Travolta is having the baby tomatoes in peyote sauce at Mortons, Nicholson is at the Forum watching Phoenix slog along. Says Laker Kurt Rambis, "That's my idea of a true fan."

If you sit with him, bring a hard hat. Once, in 1980, when the Bullets were playing at the Forum, Washington coach Dick Motta screamed at an official and then walked toward the scorer's table. What happened after that is disputed legend.

"He grabbed my leg!" Motta says. "I said, 'You touch me again and you won't need a frontal lobotomy.' He said, 'You're breaking the rules. There's your (coaching) box.' I told him, 'If you want to coach, you can buy me a team and I'll make you an assistant coach.' And you know, he almost took me up on it."

Nicholson has a different version: "He was up screaming and out of his box and I was standing in his way and he said, 'Hey, sit down!' And I said, '*You* sit down!' He said, 'This is my job, man!' And I said, 'I pay money for these seats!' Then he went out on the court, and I followed him out there. I told him it would take somebody bigger than him to sit me down—or something really intelligent like that. . . . Ever since then, he's been scared to death. You watch him, he don't even coach 'em in the Forum. He just sits in his little seat and never gets up." That's a *cold* cut; Motta is 4 for 18 at the Forum since then.

"I figure if we can make a plus-two or plus-three difference, that's enough," says Nicholson, and, in his years of Lakers rooting, he has learned a few tricks of the trade:

1) Save your loudest decibel yelling for drowning out the visiting coach just as he's trying to give crucial instructions. This works with everybody but Kevin Loughery, who now stands directly in front of Nicholson when he shouts instructions to the players.

2) Disguise your voice to make a referee think that insults are coming from the visiting bench. "We've got a couple T's out of that," Nicholson says.

3) Make your taunts original, so they'll listen. For instance, whenever Oscar Robertson was in the game against the Lakers, Nicholson would holler, "Put Oscar Robertson in!"

The Lakers, of course, are as used to seeing Nicholson around as they are to seeing Hearn. One time, in the middle of a fast break, Kareem Abdul-Jabbar hollered at Nicholson out of the side of his mouth, "Nice socks." They were lime green. With a black suit.

If basketball is thrilled with Nicholson's company, Nicholson is equally thrilled with basketball's. "I think he appreciates what we do," says Kareem. "The way one artist appreciates another's work."

Ask Nicholson why he follows the NBA, and he usually gives it the "Well, it's the game they play at night." But if they played it at sunrise in Bakersfield, he would be there. "These guys make plays that are phenomenal," he says. "The more you know about the game the more you enjoy it. That's why I call it the classical music of sport."

Nicholson also once said of basketball, "When you miss a play, it's a matter of microseconds. Little moments of truth. A game of the immediate." Ever dogged in his pursuit of the truth, Nicholson has dedicated himself to missing precious little of it.

One night during halftime warmups, Larry Bird dribbled over to Nicholson and said, "Hey, Jack, when you gonna get an *honest* job?"

Nicholson just grinned back like he had a hole in his sock. ∎

3

THE
SPURS

FOUNDED 1967

" Some call them boring. Others call them the model modern franchise. This is where the idea of basketball "culture" comes from: a system that is greater than any one player (unless his name is Tim), an unparalleled history of modern success, a cultish front office fraternity that churns out GMs and head coaches. We raise a glass of cabernet to you, Mr. Popovich. " —CHRIS BALLARD

▸ FIVE CHAMPIONSHIPS
▸ 42 PLAYOFF APPEARANCES

EVEN THE PATRIOTS admire the Spurs' combination of stability and humility, high character and high achievement. "To have sustained excellence over a decade is extremely difficult, and the Spurs have done it as well as anyone," says New England vice president of player personnel Scott Pioli, who has exchanged ideas about the right way to run a franchise with San Antonio general manager R.C. Buford. "What is really impressive is their player development, the fact that they've brought in so many international players and integrated them into a system." Says Jack Ramsey, an ESPN analyst and longtime coach who won a championship in 1977 with the Portland Trail Blazers, "If you're in the basketball business, the Spurs are who you want to be."

—Jack McCallum, SI, June 25, 2007

The Spurs emphasize a system over individuality.

PHOTOGRAPH BY AL TIELEMANS

4

THE BULLS

FOUNDED 1966

> " Only the Celtics and the Lakers have won more championships; the Bulls earned theirs in each of their last full seasons with Michael Jordan. On the heels of the 1992 Dream Team, the Bulls became the NBA's first global franchise. " —IAN THOMSEN

▸ SIX CHAMPIONSHIPS
▸ 33 PLAYOFF APPEARANCES

SOMEDAY SOON Jordan will [retire]. "It's going to be quick," says Phil Jackson. "And it's going to be painful." What then? Will the Bulls go back to what they were the season before Jordan—attendance of 6,365 a night, one fourth of the games televised, two photographers on the apron instead of 40? What in the world will they do at Chicago's Lakeview High, where, nine times a day, they use the Bulls' theme music to get kids to class fast? Who will be the big hero in Toronto, where the Raptors' mascot stomped on a Jordan jersey and was roundly booed for it? What will fans do for a team in Denver, where the crowd for the Chicago game this season wore four times as many Bulls jerseys as Nuggets jerseys? What will they write about at *The Philadelphia Daily News*, which recently put out a 52-page section to commemorate the career of an athlete who never played for a Philly team?

—*Rick Reilly, SI, May 11, 1998*

Jordan and Scottie Pippen were a dynamic duo.

PHOTOGRAPHS BY WALTER IOOSS JR. (LEFT) AND JOHN BIEVER

THE 76ERS

FOUNDED 1946

" Equal parts flash (Julius Erving, Allen Iverson), muscle (Dolph Schayes, Moses Malone) and grit (supersubs Billy Cunningham and Bobby Jones) have made the Sixers (and Syracuse Nationals before that) one of the league's most consistent winners. " —MARK BECHTEL

▸ THREE CHAMPIONSHIPS
▸ 47 PLAYOFF APPEARANCES

WHEN THE Sixers faced the Lakers in the 1980 NBA Finals, Erving was still looking for his first league title and a measure of redemption from the final series the 76ers had lost to Portland three years earlier. The Sixers made him the poster boy for their bizarre ad campaign following that season; "We Owe You One" was the theme. By 1983, the Doctor's hair was flecked with gray. In the NBA Finals that year, with the lead down to a single point late in the fourth quarter and with the shot clock showing only six seconds, Erving looked over the Lakers' defense from the top of the free throw circle and saw no openings. Erving brought the ball up over his head for that awkward looking jumper of his, and then he fired. When it went through the net the Lakers were finished, and so was Erving's long wait for a championship ring.

—*Bruce Newman, SI, May 4, 1987*

Malone (center) keyed the 1982–83 title run.

PHOTOGRAPH BY MANNY MILLAN

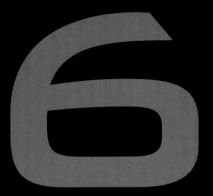

THE PISTONS

FOUNDED 1941

"After a long period of struggle, they embraced their Bad Boy side, ending an era of coastal domination (Boston/L.A.) and becoming the ideal team for blue-collar Detroit." —MARK BECHTEL

▸ THREE CHAMPIONSHIPS
▸ 40 PLAYOFF APPEARANCES

AS THE BLAZERS started to take the court, Bill Laimbeer noticed that the home team was about to break through the Pistons' line. Uh-oh. Picking up the ball, Laimbeer lowered his shoulder and roared straight ahead into the path of the Blazers' Terry Porter. "I was going to knock Porter on his ass, but he got away," Laimbeer says. "Ran right around us. So I aimed for Wayne Cooper, but he saw me, ducked and veered off down the side." Unfortunately for Michael Lloyd, a 150-pound local newspaper photographer who was backpedaling trying to capture the Blazers' dramatic entrance, he didn't see Laimbeer and couldn't duck or veer. *Boom! Shooosh! Splat!* Luckily, the photographer wasn't hurt badly. When the Pistons recovered from their laughter, the tone was set for the rest of the series. That night Laimbeer drew five charging calls on the home team and fouled out Buck Williams. The Blazers were never the same.

—Curry Kirkpatrick, SI, November 5, 1990

Laimbeer (far left) and Rick Mahorn were truly Bad.

FOUNDED 1974

Stockton and Malone played 18 seasons together.

PHOTOGRAPH BY NORM PERDUE/NBAE/GETTY IMAGES

7

" The NBA West may have had a rep as being "soft" during Utah's heyday, but in John Stockton, Karl Malone and Jerry Sloan, the Jazz got more over a longer stretch than any rival out of their polestars—backcourt, frontcourt, and on the bench. " —ALEXANDER WOLFF

THE ESSENCE of Malone and Stockton was evident in a tangle of bodies on the floor in Portland's Rose Garden. It wasn't a hang-from-the-rim dunk; it wasn't a three-pointer at the buzzer. It was simply 80 years worth of Hall of Fame bodies sprawled across the floor in reckless pursuit of a loose ball.

—Ian Thomsen, SI. April 14, 2003

THE JAZZ

▸ TWO FINALS APPEARANCES
▸ 25 PLAYOFF APPEARANCES

8

THE HEAT

FOUNDED 1988

❝In 1995 Pat Riley arrived to transform the seven-year old expansion franchise into a program built on his traditional values. Within 11 years the Heat was celebrating its first championship with Dwyane Wade, and more were to come with LeBron James.❞ —IAN THOMSEN

▸ THREE CHAMPIONSHIPS
▸ 18 PLAYOFF APPEARANCES

THE HEAT'S meeting with James in the IMG offices in downtown Cleveland lasted close to three hours, and Miami president Pat Riley was the star. Riley has seven NBA championship rings, and he has three copies of each—one gold, one silver, one platinum—to go with whatever he may be wearing on a particular day. He tossed the bag of rings on a table. "Like a weapon," as Riley would describe the scene later. "Hey," said Riley playfully, "try one on." They had spoken in other settings, and Riley knew he had James's attention. Early last week he was leaning toward Miami, but James insists he didn't make a final decision until a heart-to-heart with his mother, Gloria. Seven ringless years in the NBA had left James hungry to begin winning championships, even at the cost of his legacy. No doubt he found himself recalling the message Riley delivered: "The main thing is the main thing."

—*Ian Thomsen, SI. July 19, 2010*

James, Wade and Chris Bosh formed a winning trio.

9

THE SUNS

FOUNDED 1968

" For a franchise that has never won it all, the Suns have posted some impressive numbers, including 19 seasons of 50-plus wins. With a winning percentage of 55%, Phoenix is the most successful team never to win a title. " —CHRIS MANNIX

▸ NINE CONFERENCE FINALS APPEARANCES
▸ 29 PLAYOFF APPEARANCES

THE RUNNING Suns score more than any other team, take and make more three-point shots than any other team and, most important, set a sizzling pace in the standings: Their 36–10 record matched San Antonio for the league's best. Predictably, Phoenix also seems to be having more fun than any other team.

—Jack McCallum, SI, February 7, 2005

The Suns of the Steve Nash era were lively and loose.
PHOTOGRAPH BY JOHN W. MCDONOUGH

10

THE ROCKETS

FOUNDED 1967

" Built around bedrock centers, most notably Hakeem Olajuwon, the Rockets won two Western Conference titles in the 1980s and two championships in the '90s. " —LEE JENKINS

▸ TWO CHAMPIONSHIPS
▸ 28 PLAYOFF APPEARANCES

THEY ELIMINATED the three clubs with the best regular-season records in the league—the Spurs, the Jazz and the Suns—on their way to the Finals and were poised to add the fourth-best team to their list of victims by disposing of the demoralized Magic. It should be clear by now that Houston point guards Kenny Smith and Sam Cassell may look overmatched at times but one or the other of them will rise up to hit a three-point shot just when the Rockets are most desperate for it. It should come as no surprise anymore that Houston small forward Robert Horry transformed himself into a power forward simply because there was no other choice. There should be no further need to marvel at how Mario Elie, a CBA refugee, gives the Rockets a hard-as-nails attitude combined with a pillow-soft jump shot. "You look at that team on paper, and you might wonder how it wins," says Orlando's Penny Hardaway, "but that team has as much heart as anybody."

—*Phil Taylor, SI, June 19, 1995*

Olajuwon anchored Houston's title teams.

PHOTOGRAPH BY ANDREW D. BERNSTEIN/NBAE/GETTY IMAGES

10 THE

Best Dunks, Uniforms, Courtside Characters, Quotes, Moments,
Draft Surprises, International Scenes and the Full Results

FOR A WHILE DARKO MILICIC WAS KNOWN AS "THE HUMAN VICTORY CIGAR." WHEN THE DISAPPOINTING CENTER ROSE FROM THE BENCH AND CAME INTO THE GAME FOR THE PISTONS, EVERYONE KNEW THE GAME'S MEANINGFUL MINUTES WERE OVER. MILICIC, OWING TO HIS STATUS AS THE SECOND PICK OF THE RICH 2003 DRAFT, IS THE NOTORIOUS EXAMPLE OF THE END-OF-BENCH PLAYER WITH A FOLLOWING, BUT MANY A TEAM HAS HAD A PLAYER WHOSE INFREQUENT APPEARANCES BROUGHT A RISE FROM A CADRE OF LOYAL FANS. GREG BUTLER, WHO PLAYED FOR THE KNICKS FROM 1988–90, IS ANOTHER EXAMPLE.

THIS PHENOMENON SPEAKS TO HOW IN BASKETBALL, MORE SO THAN OTHER TEAM SPORTS, INDIVIDUALS ARE FRONT AND CENTER. ROSTERS ARE SMALL, AND ITS PLAYERS SO UNDRESSED—NO HELMETS, NO MASKS, JUST SHORTS AND A TANK TOP—THAT TO ATTENTIVE FANS, EVERY FACE BECOMES FAMILIAR.

IN THIS SECTION OUR PANELISTS EACH STEPPED INTO THE SPOTLIGHT, COMPOSING PERSONAL LISTS IN WHICH THEY CHOSE THE TOPIC AND HAD SOLE CONTROL OVER ITS RESULTS. THE SECTION OPENS WITH LEE JENKINS LISTING HIS FAVORITE SLAMS FROM THE ALL-STAR WEEKEND DUNK CONTESTS, WHICH IS AN APT TONE-SETTER. HERE THE TEAM GAME FALLS AWAY, AND OUR PANELISTS LET THEIR PERSONALITIES RULE THE DAY.

10 THE

BEST CONTEST DUNKS

SI senior writer LEE JENKINS holds up
a 10 card for the greatest jams ever at the
NBA's All-Star Weekend competition

1. VINCE CARTER, 2000, REVERSE 360 WINDMILL

Arguably the most powerful, innovative and athletic dunker of all time,
Carter, when he was a kid, used to study tapes of slam dunk contests.
He delivered one of the most memorable performances ever in Oakland,
with the "honey dip" dunk, in which he hung from the rim by the inside
of his right elbow. But even better than the honey dip was his reverse
360 windmill, an unparalleled blend of strength and agility.

2. MICHAEL JORDAN, 1988, FREE THROW LINE

A tribute to Julius Erving's unforgettable free throw line jam at the 1976
ABA dunk contest in Denver, Jordan took off from his home court at
Chicago Stadium, tongue extended, legs splayed, ball tucked fashionably behind his ear. There were more spectacular dunks, but none as
significant. Jordan's photogenic free throw line vault adorned a generation's bedroom walls.

3. JASON RICHARDSON, 2004, OFF-GLASS EAST BAY
FUNK DUNK

Richardson has authored so many memorable dunks—the lob along
the baseline in 2003, which he put between his legs and dunked on
the opposite side of the rim; the lob in '02, which he turned into a
windmill reverse—but the best was when he played for the Warriors
and took Isaiah Rider's famous East Bay Funk Dunk to new heights,
flipping the ball off the glass, between the legs and through the rim
in Los Angeles.

4. DWIGHT HOWARD, 2008, BEHIND-THE-BASKET WINDMILL

He wasn't wearing his Superman cape, but this was a superhero's dunk.
Howard stood behind the baseline in New Orleans, where the photographers usually sit, dribbled three times, and tossed the ball off the back
of the glass. Hurtling himself back inbounds, he caught the ball with
his left hand, and in one furious motion wrapped it around the basket,
throwing down a windmill with his off hand.

5. DOMINIQUE WILKINS, 1985, WINDMILL

The Human Highlight Film has spawned many imitators, young fliers
adding their own distinctive spin to his signature windmill. But there is
nothing like the original: Wilkins, eye-to-eye with the rim in Indianapolis,
beating Jordan in the finals for the first of his two titles. He invented
the windmill in the late 1970s, while goofing around with teammates
after a high school practice, and players still mimic it today.

To the question of "Windmill or 360?" Carter answered, why not do both?

Jordan's hometown free-throw-line slam became the stuff of posters.

6. SPUD WEBB, 1986, OFF-BOUNCE REVERSE

Yes, we are grading on a curve, as were the judges that day in Dallas. The 5' 7" Webb tossed a lob into the key, charged down the left wing, collected the ball and elevated for a thunderous two-handed reverse jam that dazzled the crowd and beat Wilkins, his teammate with the Hawks. In a dunk contest era dominated by Wilkins and Jordan, the smallest man in the league improbably rose above them all.

7. JAVALE MCGEE, 2011, THREE BALLS, ONE BASKET AND ALSO TWO BALLS, TWO BASKETS

The 2011 dunk contest in Los Angeles will be remembered for Blake Griffin levitating over a Kia Optima sedan while a choir sang in the background. But McGee's dunks were more difficult, including one in which he jammed three balls into the same basket, and another in which he simultaneously jammed two balls into two baskets, one off a lob to himself. He utilized all of his 7' 6" wingspan and 31½ inch vertical leap.

8. MICHAEL JORDAN, 1987, KISS THE RIM

He can't be on the list just once. Jordan's kiss-the-rim dunk in Seattle, while not quite as iconic as the free throw line jam in Chicago, is unmatched in terms of artistry. He glided down the left side of the court, pumped the ball and hung in the air long enough to smooch the hoop. His head hovered above the rim. With Jordan, the dunks were relatively simple, but he brought grace and flair to each one.

9. ANDRE IGUODALA, 2006, BEHIND-BACKBOARD ALLEY OOP

One of the most underrated dunkers ever, Iguodala set up behind the baseline in the deep right corner. His 76ers teammate, Allen Iverson, stood behind the backboard. Iverson threw the ball off the glass and Iguodala caught it with both hands while leaping back inbounds. He pulled off a nifty righthanded reverse dunk on the opposite side of the rim. Then he ran off the court and down the tunnel in Houston.

10. DEE BROWN, 1991, NO-LOOK

A feat of marketing as much as skill, Brown peddled countless pairs of Reebok Pumps at this contest when he bent down in the middle of the court to pump up his hightops. Leaping toward the basket in Charlotte, Brown dramatically covered his eyes with his right forearm mid-flight, and finished the dunk. It's hard to tell if he was peeking, but Brown definitely ushered in an age of dunk-contest creativity.

McGee's three-ball dunk involved putting through an alley-oop.

The 5' 7" Webb separated himself from the competition with his historic hops.

275

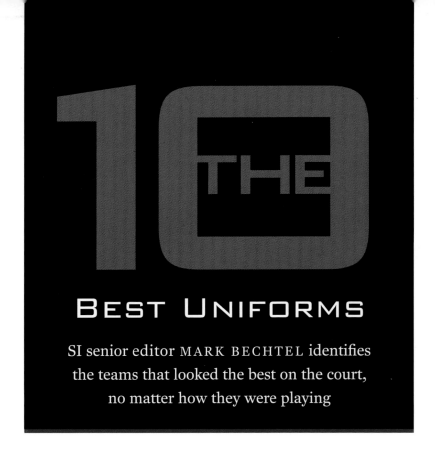

THE 10

BEST UNIFORMS

SI senior editor MARK BECHTEL identifies
the teams that looked the best on the court,
no matter how they were playing

1. SAN FRANCISCO WARRIORS, LATE 1960S

Leaving both the city and nickname off of a jersey is not unprecedented. Usually it's been done for the sake of saving room, most notably by the Minneapolis Lakers and Philadelphia Warriors, who truncated their city names to MPLS and PHILA, respectively. (Who knows what the Suns were thinking when they shortened Phoenix to PHX—the city's airport code—for their alternate jerseys from 2003 to '13?) A few seasons after the Warriors moved west, they decided to identify their hometown simply as The City. Any doubt which one that was was cleared up by the silhouette of the Golden Gate Bridge on the front and the cable cars that were incorporated into the numbers on the back. The result is the coolest uniform the league has seen, and also the boldest. ("We're not A city, we're THE city," they seem to say.) The Warriors brought the concept back for the 2010–11 season but modernized it: gone was the Golden Gate, replaced by the new East Span of the Bay Bridge, which connects the City with Oakland, where the team's home court is located.

2. HARLEM GLOBETROTTERS, TIME IMMEMORIAL

The sartorial equivalent of a mullet: business up top (classy blue jerseys with the team's name and, in its heyday, the word ORIGINAL), party down below (those candy-striped circus shorts). The bottoms are fitting for the clown prices of basketball; the tops strike the right note for a team that, when playing seriously in 1948, knocked off George Mikan's Minneapolis Lakers, the best team in the pros.

3. SPIRITS OF ST. LOUIS, EARLY 1970S

ABA uniforms were a decidedly mixed bag. Reasonable people can disagree about whether the Pittsburgh Condors' use of a giant vulture on the front of their jerseys was a good idea. The same can't be said of the Miami Floridians' abominable neon popsicle scheme. Hands down, the best of the ABA bunch belonged to the Spirits, a team named for aviator Charles Lindbergh's plane. As such, the front features a monoplane like Lindy's skywriting the team's name, a clever meta touch whose whimsy perfectly encapsulates what the ABA stood for.

4. BOSTON CELTICS, TODAY

No uniform has endured quite like the Celtics'. Save for a few minor modifications—Bob Cousy wore satin shorts, Larry Bird donned a darker shade of green—they've remained largely unchanged for al-

most seven decades. So what separates the C's current duds from the rest? A clean, bright green, and the simplest of adornments: a small shamrock on the back, above the player's name.

5. NEW YORK NETS, MID-1970S

The toughest decision on the list: Whose '70s star-spangled threads reign supreme? The Nets' or the Washington Bullets'? Erving's or Elvin's? At the end of the day, the Nets' look takes it, largely because it's impossible to look at these uniforms and not, in turn, see in one's mind's eye a majestically Afro'd Dr. J looking like the coolest cat there ever was.

6. SAN ANTONIO SPURS, TODAY

The Spurs have kept their look largely unchanged since the team moved in 1973 from Dallas (where it was known as the Chaparrals), and with good reason: They've got the best lettering in the league. The logo is perfectly integrated into the script, serving as the U in Spurs. The Jazz pulled off a similar trick from the '70s through the '90s (and again since 2010), melding a basketball and a musical note to form a J, but while that festooned some questionably colored duds (purple and green only work together if you're hosting Wimbledon or decorating for an Easter party), the Spurs monochrome is a perfect fit for the team's no-frills work ethic.

7. LOS ANGELES LAKERS, EARLY 1960S

When the Lakers adopted a new look in 1966, owner Jerry Buss, making reference to the team's new arena, insisted on calling the team's new colors Forum Blue and Gold, a peculiar choice given the fact that the former is most definitely purple. Perhaps he was trying to preserve a link to these two-tone blue beauties, worn for six years after the team moved from Minneapolis. The script is classy, but what makes these sing is the juxtaposition of light and dark blue, subtly evoking the sky and water enjoyed while spending a day on one of the bodies of water for which the team is named.

8. PORTLAND TRAIL BLAZERS, LATE 1970S

For a team whose nickname lends itself to nothing in particular, the Trail Blazers have always found a way to develop uniforms that somehow make sense—such as these jerseys with a vaguely futuristic lower-case font and what appear to be some sort of racing stripes. The entire ensemble is elevated by the fact that the stripes on the jersey flow into the stripes on the shorts. That kind of top-and-bottom integration is tough to find in other sports; baseball players slide around too much and football players tend to be too ungainly, but lithe hoopsters can pull it off. (The best example of this would be the Hawks' unis from 1982 to '92, omitted here on account of the fact that they were hideous.) Honorable mention to the Blazers for one of their current alternates, which take a page from the Warriors' book and identify the team as simply Rip City.

9. CLEVELAND CAVALIERS, LATE 1970S

The checkerboard pattern up the sides of the shorts and jerseys was a staple of DePaul's unis for years, and the Cavs weren't the only NBA team to borrow the look. The Bucks went with a similar design in the late '70s, too, but in a green-and-red color scheme that brought to mind an ugly Christmas sweater contest. What worked so well for the Cavs was the wine-and-gold combo, which stayed just on the right side of the line separating old-school cool from garishness.

10. BUFFALO BRAVES, EARLY 1970S

The franchise has enjoyed wretched results on the court, but give the Clippers this: They've usually looked great doing it. The best unis were worn by the team when it played in upstate New York, a simple baby blue get-up trimmed with black.

1. SAN FRANCISCO WARRIORS

2. HARLEM GLOBETROTTERS

3. SPIRITS OF ST. LOUIS

4. BOSTON CELTICS

5. NEW YORK NETS

6. SAN ANTONIO SPURS

7. LOS ANGELES LAKERS

8. PORTLAND TRAIL BLAZERS

9. CLEVELAND CAVALIERS

10. BUFFALO BRAVES

THE 10 BEST COURTSIDE CHARACTERS

SI senior writer ALEXANDER WOLFF selects the most memorable characters who surrounded, and occasionally took to, the court

1. LEON (THE BARBER) BRADLEY, PISTONS FAN

Sick of getting technicals for things Bradley said, Pistons players in the 1980s chipped in to move this former haircutter to behind the visitors' bench. The rest is history. Whether taunting Nuggets guard Lafayette Lever for failing to get off a shot at the end of a quarter (he waved his wristwatch at the huddle, saying, "Lever, you need this?") or a black ref for hosing the home team ("Capers, we marched to get you hired, we'll march to get you fired!"), Bradley was master of the silence-breaking interjection and a nonstop Redd Foxx routine.

2. DANCING HARRY, SIDELINE STRUTTER

Marvin Cooper was the guy at Bullets games in platform shoes and floppy hat who shucked and jived and, rising from a deep crouch while wiggling his fingers, put a hex on opponents. After Earl Monroe got traded to the Knicks, Harry followed his muse up I-95 and helped lead New York to its '73 title. Garden management never approved, and the next season barred him, so Cooper took his act to Nets and Pacers games. Not to be confused with Dancing Barry, who hoofed for the Rockets and Lakers.

3. DAVE ZINKOFF, SIXERS P.A. ANNOUNCER

The man who called Wilt Chamberlain's 100-point game in Hershey, Pa., could make "Two minutes, two minutes left in the quarter" sound world historical. Zink, who announced from 1946 to '85, delivered everything from concise alliteration ("Gola goal," "Mix makes" and "Dipper dunk") to impromptu coinages (Moses on a breakaway dunk was "MA-loooooone A-looooone"). But he'll be best remembered for the signature low roll of "ERRR-ving!"—and the kosher salami he passed out along press row and to fans and arena workers, which would have made him beloved even if he had never uttered a word.

4. SPIKE LEE, KNICKS FAN

No one begrudges this son of Brooklyn his seat in Row AA at the Garden, given his devotion, discernment and heavily borne disappointment when the home team let him down. He's best known for his back-and-forth with the Pacers' Reggie Miller during a 1994 playoff game. When Miller flashed a choke sign at the Knicks, Lee's response—"I thought the brother had more class"—got splashed all over the tabloids.

5. ROBIN FICKER, BULLETS FAN

For the dozen years he sat behind the visitors' bench in Washington, Ficker prepped each heckle like the litigator he was, getting under the skin of Bulls coach Phil Jackson (by reading sex-life passages from Jackson's memoir) or the Rockets' Lewis Lloyd (by recounting reports of delinquent child-support payments). The Suns' Charles Barkley flew Ficker to Phoenix for the 1993 NBA Finals, giving him a ticket behind the Bulls' bench—but security ejected him after he broke out oversized bills, cards and dice to lampoon Michael Jordan's alleged gambling habits.

6. THE BASELINE BUMS, SPURS FANS

Management has since turned them into a booster group with a philanthropic bent, but the Bums weren't nearly so domesticated in their ABA glory days at HemisFair Arena during the mid-1970s. Owner Red McCombs would pick up their pregame beer tab at a bar across the street; then they would encamp above the tunnel leading to the visitors' locker room. In 1975, after Nuggets (and future Spurs) coach Larry Brown derided their city as good for nothing but guacamole, the Bums pelted Brown with avocado.

7. THE GORILLA, SUNS MASCOT

In 1980 Henry Rojas, an employee of a singing telegram service called Eastern Onion, showed up at Phoenix's Veterans Memorial Coliseum in a gorilla suit to serenade a fan. A security official suggested he dance during a timeout to entertain the crowd, and Rojas kept coming back. This "five-foot-ape" graduate of "Fur-man" has since been inhabited by three successive suit-wearers who mimicked opposing coaches well enough, and trampoline-dunked with flair enough, to make the Gorilla (whose official name is Go) one of three inaugural inductees, along with baseball's Phillie Phanatic and San Diego Chicken, in the Mascot Hall of Fame.

8. JACK NICHOLSON, LAKERS FAN

The *One Flew Over the Cuckoo's Nest* star usually saw his Lakers get the better of visiting teams. But Trail Blazers reserve Lloyd (Ice) Neal once turned the tables on the guy in the shades and the linen suit. In *The Breaks of the Game*, David Halberstam describes the aftermath of Bill Walton's rising to block a Kareem Abdul-Jabbar shot: "They would not be beaten, not by Kareem, not by Los Angeles, not even by rich and celebrated actors, for there was Ice screaming at Nicholson, 'Take that, mother------ cuckoo!'"

9. TINY BB, BULLETS MASCOT

He wasn't the first canine mascot in the league, or even for his own team, as he succeeded Alex the Bullet, who in turn had relieved Buckshot. But this 7" high, 20-inch long dachshund—from "DePaw"—outlasted them all, presiding over the action from his basket at the end of the Bullets' bench as the team won its 1978 NBA title. After his death in 1987 he rejoined Alex and Buckshot in Rosa Bonheur Memorial Park, a pet cemetery in Elkridge, Md.

10. JIMMY GOLDSTEIN, SUPERFAN

A Milwaukee native who at 15 kept stats for the old Hawks' radio announcer, Goldstein used his fortune that began with a chain of Southern California trailer parks to pinball around the country to catch playoff games. He estimates he's seen 25–35 playoff games a season and more than 4,000 games total in the last 50 years. Though a longtime Lakers season-ticket holder (and now a Clippers one as well), Goldstein roots against them, preferring teams whose style he likes—recently, the Spurs and Suns. He's usually seen wearing animal-skin boots, a leather jacket, a wide-brimmed hat and a Russian model on one arm. The first thing he did upon buying his *Architectural Digest*–featured Beverly Hills home (which was showcased in *The Big Lebowski*)? Put up a hoop.

For the Gorilla, dancing led to dunking.

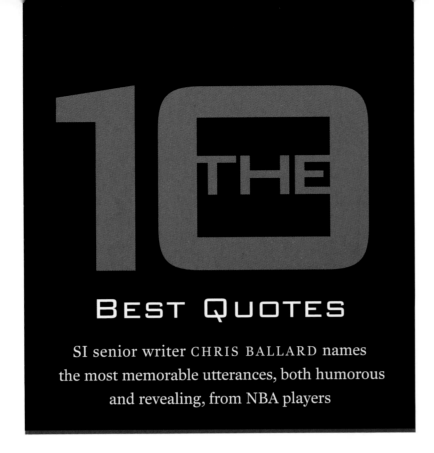

THE 10

BEST QUOTES

SI senior writer CHRIS BALLARD names the most memorable utterances, both humorous and revealing, from NBA players

1. "FO, FO FO."
Moses Malone, in April 1983, predicting three playoff sweeps for his Sixers. Concise, alliterative and (almost) right. The team went *fo, fi, fo* to win the title.

2. "CUZ THERE AIN'T NO FOURS."
Antoine Walker of the Celtics, when asked why he shot so many threes, during the NBA All-Star Game media availability in February 2003. The best part about this quote: Toine's just being honest.

3. "THE SHIP BE SINKIN'. "
Micheal Ray Richardson of the Knicks on the team's swoon in the 1981–82 season. The quote became a catchphrase, but the follow-up is just as good. Asked how far it might sink, he said "Sky's the limit."

4. "YOUNG MAN, YOU HAVE THE QUESTION BACKWARDS."
Bill Russell, asked if he would have feared playing Kareem Abdul-Jabbar.

Here we have one era's proud giant refusing to cede to the next's. Perfect.

5. "REPUBLICANS BUY SNEAKERS TOO."
Michael Jordan, on why he wasn't endorsing Charlotte mayor Harvey Gantt in his North Carolina senate race against Jesse Helms in 1990. This was around the time of the NBA's marketing boom, from the mouth of its greatest pitchman. Ali, he was not.

6. "I TOLD YOU I NEEDED TO FEED MY FAMILY. THEY OFFERED ME THREE YEARS AT $21 MILLION. THAT'S NOT GOING TO CUT IT."
Latrell Sprewell, outraged at a contract extension offer from Minnesota in November 2004. The quote, picked up and replayed, damaged the reputation of the league, and its players, with the general public.

7. "I CAN'T REALLY REMEMBER THE NAMES OF THE CLUBS WE WENT TO."
Shaquille O'Neal, in 1994, when asked if he'd been to the Parthenon during a trip to Greece. Most of the time Shaq was trying to be funny. Occasionally, it happened by accident.

8. "YOU GOT TO BELIEVE IN YOURSELF. HELL, I BELIEVE I'M THE BEST-LOOKING GUY IN THE WORLD, AND I MIGHT BE RIGHT."
Charles Barkley, on Charles Barkley. Just one of many gems from the most quotable NBA player in history.

9. "I WANT ALL OF YOU TO KNOW I'M WINNING THIS THING. I'M JUST LOOKING AROUND TO SEE WHO'S GOING TO FINISH UP SECOND."
Larry Bird to his fellow competitors, before the inaugural NBA All-Star Three-Point Shootout in February 1986. Bird, one of the greatest trash-talkers in league history, backed up the boast with a win. In fact, he took the contest three years in a row.

10. "PRACTICE? WE TALKIN' 'BOUT PRACTICE, MAN. WE TALKIN' 'BOUT PRACTICE. WE TALKIN' 'BOUT PRACTICE. WE AIN'T TALKIN' 'BOUT THE GAME, WE TALKIN' 'BOUT PRACTICE, MAN. . . . "
Allen Iverson in May 2002, in response to criticism of his practice habits. One of the more mimicked NBA quotes ever, with good reason. The speech was Iverson, and a whole breed of NBA scorer-types, in a nutshell.

Walker's line about four-pointers was endearingly candid.

The "practice" quote haunts Iverson, our No. 6 shooting guard.

1. MICHAEL JORDAN'S GAME WINNER, NBA FINALS, GAME 6, JUNE 14, 1988

Down a point with less than 10 seconds left, Jordan sprang himself with a crossover and a (cough, cough) push-off of Bryon Russell. Jordan's jumper sealed the Bulls' sixth title, punctuating a dynasty and Jordan's career, simultaneously. Sort of. We're choosing to forget about those two years with the Wizards.

2. LARRY BIRD'S STEAL, EASTERN CONFERENCE FINALS, GAME 5, MAY 26, 1987

The game was over. Five seconds left, Pistons' ball, up a point. That is until Bird swooped in to steal Isiah Thomas's inbounds pass. With the Boston Garden crowd in a frenzy, Bird laced a pass to a cutting Dennis Johnson for a layup and a one-point Celtics win.

3. KAREEM ABDUL-JABBAR BREAKS WILT CHAMBERLAIN'S NBA CAREER SCORING RECORD, APRIL 5, 1984

With an effortless flip of the wrist, Kareem's fourth-quarter skyhook against the Jazz in 1984 bumped him past Wilt Chamberlain's 31,419 on the NBA's alltime scoring list. Abdul-Jabbar finished his career with 38,387 points, a mark that looks as if it will stand for a long time.

4. REGGIE MILLER'S EIGHT POINTS IN 11 SECONDS, EASTERN CONFERENCE FINALS, GAME 1, MAY 7, 1995

With the Pacers down six with 18.7 seconds left, Miller drained a three, stole an inbounds pass and buried another triple to tie it, all in a dizzying 3.1 seconds. His free throws with 7.5 seconds left gave Indiana the win.

5. JERRY WEST'S 60-FOOT PRAYER, NBA FINALS, GAME 3, APRIL 29, 1970

A Dave DeBusschere jumper with three seconds appeared to seal a Knicks win, that is until West launched a 60-foot missile from well beyond halfcourt that found the basket. The good news? West's shot tied the game, sending it into overtime. The bad? Because the three-point line had not yet been instituted, it didn't win it, and L.A. lost in OT.

6. WILLIS REED WALKS OUT ON TO THE COURT, NBA FINALS, GAME 7, MAY 8, 1970

Statistically, Reed's impact on Game 7 was negligible—four points in 27 minutes—but his inspirational boost, teammates would swear years later, was a driving force behind the Knicks' win.

7. MAGIC JOHNSON'S RUNNING HOOK, NBA FINALS, GAME 4, JUNE 9, 1987

Down a point with seven seconds left, Magic drove into the teeth of the Boston defense and let fly a picture perfect baby hook, giving the Lakers a 3–1 series lead. It was one final signature moment in what would turn out to be the last title clash between Magic's Lakers and Bird's Celtics.

8. MICHAEL JORDAN BEATS CRAIG EHLO, OPENING ROUND PLAYOFFS, GAME 5, MAY 7, 1989

Known in Cleveland simply as "The Shot." With three seconds left, Jordan collected an inbounds pass, evaded Ehlo with two dribbles and knocked down a jumper to give Chicago the game and the series.

9. MAGIC JOHNSON'S RETURN, NBA ALL-STAR GAME, FEBRUARY 9, 1992

Magic retired at the start of the 1991–92 season, after discovering he had contracted HIV. Fans voted him into the All-Star Game anyway, and Johnson elected to participate. In an emotionally charged evening, Johnson scored 25 points, handed out nine assists and was named the game's MVP. Johnson went on to play 32 games for the Lakers in '95–96, but the '92 All-Star Game is still considered his NBA farewell.

10. DOMINIQUE WILKINS VS. LARRY BIRD, EASTERN CONFERENCE SEMIFINALS, GAME 7, MAY 22, 1988

Bird's last bucket—a driving layup past Wilkins—sealed a Celtics win and prompted play-by-play man Brent Musburger to utter the famous line, "You are watching what greatness is all about."

THE 10
BEST MOMENTS

SI senior writer CHRIS MANNIX breaks down the shots, sequences and simple appearances that define NBA history

Magic delighted with an All-Star show after his HIV diagnosis.

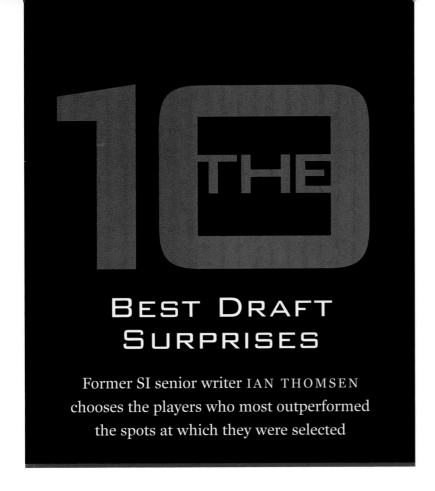

THE 10

BEST DRAFT SURPRISES

Former SI senior writer IAN THOMSEN chooses the players who most outperformed the spots at which they were selected

1. KOBE BRYANT, NO. 13, 1996

As a skinny guard entering the draft out of high school, Bryant was viewed as a gamble when the Hornets traded his rights to Los Angeles for Vlade Divac. Bryant became his era's biggest winner while leading the Lakers to five NBA championships.

2. MANU GINÓBILI, NO. 57, 1999

He was a guard in the Italian second division when the Spurs picked Ginóbili late in the second round. They would not have won their four titles in the new millennium without him.

3. DENNIS JOHNSON, NO. 29, 1976

He hardly played in high school, spent time in junior college before Pepperdine and was a second-round pick by the Sonics. He became a NBA Finals MVP and a Hall of Famer who won three championships.

4. JOHN STOCKTON, NO. 16, 1984

In an era of big NBA backcourts, Stockton was a small guard (6' 1") from a small school, Gonzaga. The Spokane native would play every game in 17 of his 19 seasons with Utah and retire as the NBA's alltime leader in assists and steals.

5. KARL MALONE, NO. 13, 1985

After three years at Louisiana Tech, "The Mailman" joined Stockton in Utah to form a devastating pick-and-roll partnership. Malone played in 19 straight postseasons and two Finals while finishing as the NBA's alltime No. 2 in points scored.

6. TONY PARKER, NO. 28, 2001

After his first predraft workout, the French point guard was rejected as "soft" by Spurs coach Gregg Popovich. But a second workout earned Popovich's respect, and that was followed by four NBA championships, not to mention a Finals MVP in 2007.

7. STEVE NASH, NO. 15, 1996

Santa Clara was the only school to offer a college scholarship to Nash, a Canadian who was then drafted by the Suns to be their No. 3 point guard. After six seasons with the Mavericks, Nash returned to Phoenix to win back-to-back NBA MVP awards.

8. TINY ARCHIBALD, NO. 19, 1970

A troubled childhood and poor grades threatened to prevent Archibald from even attending college. Eventually, he played at UTEP, was picked in the second round by Bob Cousy's Royals, and went on to win a championship with Larry Bird's Celtics on his way to the Hall of Fame.

9. JOE DUMARS, NO. 18, 1985

Pistons general manager Jack McCloskey had targeted the senior guard from tiny McNeese State, but he doubted that Dumars would slip to him in the draft. He went on to form a Hall of Fame backcourt with Isiah Thomas.

10. MICHAEL JORDAN, NO. 3, 1984

He was a national champion, but no one imagined that Jordan would become the greatest player of modern times. The Rockets and Trail Blazers drafted centers for need rather than gamble on a guard with an iffy jump shot.

Ginóbili is one of the many talents that the Spurs have discovered abroad.

Archibald in the only player to lead the NBA in scoring and assists the same season.

1. TOURNAMENT OF THE AMERICAS OLYMPIC QUALIFIER, JUNE 28, 1992, PORTLAND

First game for the Dream Team. They ran out for the first time together and their opponents from Cuba stopped warming up and rushed over to take photos, before getting beat 136–57. Best. Pregame. Scene. Ever.

2. FIBA WORLD CHAMPIONSHIP FINAL, SEPTEMBER 12, 2010, ISTANBUL

Team USA was primed for defeat, facing a formidable host team and a deliriously partisan crowd. But Kevin Durant scored 20 first-half points, firing up perimeter jumpers as if he were practicing in his backyard, and the Americans went on to a 81–64 victory.

3. MCDONALD'S OPEN, OCTOBER 21 & 23, 1988, MADRID

The Boston Celtics won both of their games, against Yugoslavia and Real Madrid, and Larry Bird described a trip to the Palacio de la Zarzuela (Spain's royal palace) as "the King thing." For Real Madrid, future NBA guard Drazen Petrovic was dazzling in defeat.

4. OLYMPIC FINAL, AUGUST 12, 2012, LONDON

Spain, the second best team in the tournament and a tough final foe in 2008 in China, was threatening down the stretch against the U.S. But LeBron James and Durant preserved a 107–100 gold-medal win, giving James an NBA title, regular-season MVP, NBA Finals MVP and Olympic gold in the same year.

5. OLYMPIC BASKETBALL MEDAL PRESENTATION, AUGUST 8, 1992, BARCELONA

As Team USA marched out, everyone wondered what Nike endorser Michael Jordan would do to cover up the Reebok logo on his medal ceremony jacket, which was a subject of much pregame attention. He and Nike stablemates Magic Johnson and Charles Barkley emerged wearing flags that covered up the top part of their jackets.

6. ATLANTA HAWKS EXHIBITION TOUR IN THE SOVIET UNION, JULY 1988, A DOCK IN SUKHUMI ON THE BLACK SEA

Soviet star Sarunas Marciulionis, a true believer in Glasnost-through-hoops and later an NBA player with the Golden State Warriors, serenaded American visitors, including a couple of members of the Hawks, with Lithuanian folk songs.

7. MCDONALD'S OPEN, OCTOBER 18 & 19, 1991, PARIS

Monsieur Magique (Johnson) was the star attraction during the Lakers' visit, dishing 21 assists in his first game, against Limoges. But L.A. came close to losing in the final, nipping Joventut Badalona 116–114. Once back in the States, something more eventful happened—Magic announced that he had contracted HIV.

8. OLYMPICS, JULY 27, 1992, BARCELONA

Steamed that Bulls general manager Jerry Krause had pursued young Yugoslavian star Toni Kukoc, Dream Teamers Scottie Pippen and Michael Jordan vowed to make life miserable in Team USA's game against Croatia. They did. Kukoc went 2 for 11 with seven turnovers in a 103–70 loss. A year later Kukoc was a member of the Bulls. Two decades later, the Dream Teamers still referred to it as "the Kukoc game."

9. NBA EUROPE LIVE TOUR, OCTOBER 2006, SOMEWHERE OVER RUSSIA

Commissioner David Stern awoke from a few hours of light sleep on his private plane and began reciting, in liturgical fashion, names of old New York Knicks players.

10. ATLANTA HAWKS EXHIBITION TOUR IN THE SOVIET UNION, JULY 30, 1988, MOSCOW

The Soviet national team beat the Hawks 132–123 and the basketball world was stunned. Nobody traveling with the team, however, was stunned: The Hawks just wanted to get home.

10 THE
BEST INTERNATIONAL SCENES

Much-traveled SI special contributor JACK MCCALLUM recalls his favorite moments, on the court and off, from the world of global hoops

Barkley displayed the U.S. flag—and covered the Reebok logo—on the medal stand.

THE FULL RESULTS

IF THEY WERE LISTED ON A PANELIST'S BALLOT, THEY MAKE IT HERE TOO, IN THIS FULL RANKING OF EVERYONE WHO RECEIVED A VOTE IN EVERY CATEGORY

POINT GUARD

1. MAGIC JOHNSON
2. JOHN STOCKTON
3. ISIAH THOMAS
4. OSCAR ROBERTSON
5. JASON KIDD
6. BOB COUSY
7. STEVE NASH
8. WALT FRAZIER
9. GARY PAYTON
10. CHRIS PAUL
11. JERRY WEST
12. LENNY WILKENS
13. TINY ARCHIBALD
14. MAURICE CHEEKS
15. MARK JACKSON
16. TONY PARKER

SHOOTING GUARD

1. MICHAEL JORDAN
2. KOBE BRYANT
3. JERRY WEST
4. DWYANE WADE
5. CLYDE DREXLER
6. ALLEN IVERSON
7. GEORGE GERVIN
8. OSCAR ROBERTSON
9. SAM JONES
10. REGGIE MILLER
11. WALT FRAZIER
12. RAY ALLEN
13. PETE MARAVICH
14. EARL MONROE
15. MANU GINÓBILI
16. JOE DUMARS
17. BILL SHARMAN
18. GAIL GOODRICH
19. JOHN HAVLICEK
20. SIDNEY MONCRIEF

SMALL FORWARD

1. LARRY BIRD
2. LEBRON JAMES
3. JULIUS ERVING
4. SCOTTIE PIPPEN
5. ELGIN BAYLOR
6. JOHN HAVLICEK
7. RICK BARRY
8. JAMES WORTHY
9. DOMINIQUE WILKINS
10. PAUL PIERCE
11. KEVIN DURANT
12. BERNARD KING
13. CHRIS MULLIN
14. PAUL ARIZIN
15. ALEX ENGLISH

POWER FORWARD

1. KARL MALONE
2. TIM DUNCAN
3. CHARLES BARKLEY
4. KEVIN GARNETT
5. DIRK NOWITZKI
6. BOB PETTIT
7. KEVIN MCHALE
8. ELVIN HAYES
9. DOLPH SCHAYES
10. ELGIN BAYLOR
11. DENNIS RODMAN
12. DAVID ROBINSON
13. TOM HEINSOHN
14. BOB MCADOO
15. KEVIN DURANT
16. PAU GASOL
17. WES UNSELD

CENTER

1. BILL RUSSELL
2. KAREEM ABDUL-JABBAR
3. WILT CHAMBERLAIN
4. HAKEEM OLAJUWON
5. SHAQUILLE O'NEAL
6. MOSES MALONE
7. DAVID ROBINSON
8. GEORGE MIKAN
9. WILLIS REED
10. BILL WALTON
11. PATRICK EWING
12. TIM DUNCAN
13. BOB LANIER
14. ROBERT PARISH
15. NATE THURMOND

COACH

1. PHIL JACKSON
2. RED AUERBACH
3. PAT RILEY
4. CHUCK DALY
5. GREGG POPOVICH
6. LARRY BROWN
7. RED HOLZMAN
8. JOHN KUNDLA
9. JERRY SLOAN
10. LENNY WILKENS
11. JACK RAMSAY
12. DON NELSON
13. BILL FITCH
14. TOM HEINSOHN
15. ALEX HANNUM
16. RUDY TOMJANOVICH
17. BILL SHARMAN

SIXTH MAN

1. MANU GINÓBILI
2. JOHN HAVLICEK
3. VINNIE JOHNSON
4. KEVIN MCHALE
5. MICHAEL COOPER
6. DETLEF SCHREMPF
7. BOBBY JONES
8. TONI KUKOC
9. RICKY PIERCE
10. FRANK RAMSEY
11. JASON TERRY
12. FRED BROWN
13. BILL WALTON
14. RAY ALLEN
15. BILLY CUNNINGHAM
16. BOB MCADOO
17. EDDIE JOHNSON
18. JOHN STARKS
19. JAMAL CRAWFORD

THREE-POINT SHOOTER

1. RAY ALLEN
2. REGGIE MILLER
3. LARRY BIRD
4. STEVE KERR
5. STEVE NASH
6. DALE ELLIS
7. GLEN RICE
8. STEPHEN CURRY
9. PEJA STOJAKOVIC
10. ROBERT HORRY
11. KOBE BRYANT
12. MARK PRICE
13. PAUL PIERCE
14. CHAUNCEY BILLUPS
15. DEREK FISHER
16. LOUIE DAMPIER
17. RICK BARRY
18. DELL CURRY
19. MIKE MILLER
20. DAN MAJERLE
21. MITCH RICHMOND
22. MICHAEL ADAMS
23. DANA BARROS
24. DIRK NOWITZKI

REBOUNDER

1. WILT CHAMBERLAIN
2. DENNIS RODMAN
3. BILL RUSSELL
4. MOSES MALONE
5. JERRY LUCAS
6. WES UNSELD
7. CHARLES BARKLEY
8. NATE THURMOND
9. BOB PETTIT
10. KAREEM ABDUL-JABBAR
11. ELVIN HAYES
12. TIM DUNCAN
13. BILL WALTON
14. SHAQUILLE O'NEAL
15. MEL DANIELS
16. DAVE COWENS
17. ELGIN BAYLOR
18. WALT BELLAMY
19. GUS JOHNSON
20. KARL MALONE

CLUTCH PERFORMER

1. MICHAEL JORDAN
2. LARRY BIRD
3. MAGIC JOHNSON
4. BILL RUSSELL
5. JERRY WEST
6. KOBE BRYANT
7. REGGIE MILLER
8. SAM JONES
9. ROBERT HORRY
10. ISIAH THOMAS
11. JOHN HAVLICEK
12. KAREEM ABDUL-JABBAR
13. LEBRON JAMES
14. JAMES WORTHY
15. DIRK NOWITZKI
16. RICK BARRY
17. DWYANE WADE

The Full Results

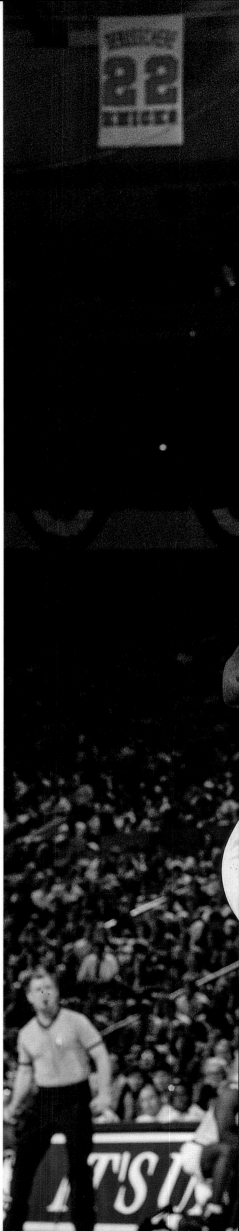

DEFENDER

1. BILL RUSSELL
2. MICHAEL JORDAN
3. HAKEEM OLAJUWON
4. DENNIS RODMAN
5. GARY PAYTON
6. SCOTTIE PIPPEN
7. TIM DUNCAN
8. LEBRON JAMES
9. KEVIN GARNETT
10. DIKEMBE MUTOMBO
11. KAREEM ABDUL-JABBAR
12. BEN WALLACE
13. MICHAEL COOPER
14. WALT FRAZIER
15. DAVID ROBINSON
16. DAVE DEBUSSCHERE
17. DENNIS JOHNSON
18. BRUCE BOWEN
19. SIDNEY MONCRIEF
20. NATE THURMOND
21. WILT CHAMBERLAIN
22. MAURICE CHEEKS
23. JOHN HAVLICEK
24. DWIGHT HOWARD
25. METTA WORLD PEACE

MOST ENTERTAINING

1. MICHAEL JORDAN
2. JULIUS ERVING
3. PETE MARAVICH
4. MAGIC JOHNSON
5. LEBRON JAMES
6. LARRY BIRD
7. ALLEN IVERSON
8. CHARLES BARKLEY
9. GEORGE GERVIN
10. EARL MONROE
11. MANU GINÓBILI
12. DOMINIQUE WILKINS
13. WILT CHAMBERLAIN
14. BOB COUSY
15. STEVE NASH
16. DAVID THOMPSON
17. KOBE BRYANT
18. JASON KIDD
19. CALVIN MURPHY
20. VINCE CARTER
21. OSCAR ROBERTSON
22. JERRY WEST
23. ELGIN BAYLOR
24. SHAQUILLE O'NEAL
25. BILLY CUNNINGHAM
26. SHAWN KEMP
27. ISIAH THOMAS
28. RICK BARRY
29. DERRICK ROSE

GAME

1. 1976 FINALS, GAME 5 (CELTICS-SUNS 3OT)
2. 2013 FINALS, GAME 6 (HEAT-SPURS)
3. 1987 EASTERN CONFERENCE FINALS, GAME 5 (BIRD STEALS INBOUNDS VS. DETROIT)
4. 1970 FINALS, GAME 7 (WILLIS REED GAME)
5. 1962, MARCH 2, WILT CHAMBERLAIN 100-POINT GAME
6. 1998 FINALS, GAME 6 (BULLS-JAZZ)
7. 1957 FINALS, GAME 7 (CELTICS-HAWKS)
8. 1988 EASTERN CONFERENCE SEMIFINALS, GAME 7 (BIRD-WILKINS DUEL)
9. 1980 FINALS, GAME 6 (MAGIC JOHNSON STARTS AT CENTER)
10. 1986 EASTERN CONFERENCE FIRST ROUND, GAME 2 (JORDAN SCORES 63 VS. CELTICS)
11. 1987 FINALS, GAME 4 (CELTICS-LAKERS)
12. 1995, MARCH 28, JORDAN SCORES 55 AGAINST KNICKS
13. 1993 FINALS, GAME 5 (BULLS-SUNS)
14. 1965 EASTERN DIVISION FINALS, GAME 7 (76ERS-CELTICS)
15. 1997 FINALS, GAME 5 (BULLS-JAZZ)
16. 1962 FINALS, GAME 7 (CELTICS-LAKERS)
17. 1995 EASTERN CONFERENCE SEMIFINALS, GAME 5 (PACERS-KNICKS)
18. 1969, NOV. 28, KNICKS WIN 18TH STRAIGHT GAME
19. 1970 FINALS, GAME 3 (LAKERS-KNICKS)
20. FINALS, GAME 7 (CELTICS-LAKERS)
21. 2004 WESTERN CONFERENCE SEMIFINALS, GAME 5 (LAKERS-SPURS)
22. 1984 FINALS, GAME 4 (CELTICS-LAKERS)
23. 1989 EASTERN CONFERENCE FIRST ROUND, GAME 5 (BULLS-CAVALIERS)
24. 1995 EASTERN CONFERENCE SEMIFINALS, GAME 1 (PACERS-KNICKS)
25. 1987 WESTERN CONFERENCE SEMIFINALS, GAME 4 (LAKERS-WARRIORS)
26. 2012 EASTERN CONFERENCE FINALS, GAME 6 (HEAT-CELTICS)

SINGLE-SEASON TEAM

1. 1995–96 BULLS
2. 1971–72 LAKERS
3. 1985–86 CELTICS
4. 1966–67 SIXERS
5. 1982–83 SIXERS
6. 1986–87 LAKERS
7. 1964–65 CELTICS
8. 1991–92 BULLS
9. 1969–70 KNICKS
10. 1988–89 PISTONS
11. 2012–13 HEAT
12. 1970–71 BUCKS
13. 2000–01 LAKERS
14. 1959–60 CELTICS
15. 1999–2000 LAKERS
16. 1976–77 BLAZERS
17. 2008–09 LAKERS
18. 1968–69 CELTICS

FRANCHISE

1. CELTICS
2. LAKERS
3. SPURS
4. BULLS
5. 76ERS
6. PISTONS
7. JAZZ
8. HEAT
9. SUNS
10. ROCKETS
11. KNICKS
12. TRAIL BLAZERS
13. SONICS/THUNDER
14. PACERS
15. WARRIORS
16. BUCKS

Patrick Ewing, an 11-time All-Star, was our 11th-ranked center.

ACKNOWLEDGMENTS

THIS BOOK DRAWS FROM THE efforts of a legion of SPORTS ILLUSTRATED writers, editors, reporters and photographers who have covered professional basketball since the magazine's inception in 1954; BASKETBALL'S GREATEST would not have been possible without them. Special thanks also goes to Stephen Cannella, Karen Carpenter, Prem Kalliat, Joe Felice, George Amores and Will Welt for their generous help; and to Geoff Michaud, Dan Larkin and the rest of the SI Premedia group for their tireless work on this project.

PHOTO CREDITS

COVER: FRONT (left to right, from top): John G. Zimmerman, Greg Nelson, Al Tielemans, John W. McDonough, Greg Nelson, John Biever, John G. Zimmerman, Andy Hayt, John Biever, Richard Mackson, David E. Klutho, John W. McDonough, Richard Mackson, John W. McDonough. **BACK** (left to right, from top): Greg Nelson, Manny Millan, Bob Rosato, John W. McDonough, David E. Klutho, John Biever, John W. McDonough, Long Photography Inc., Manny Millan, Damian Strohmeyer, Richard Mackson, Sam Forencich/NBAE/Getty Images, Steve Lipofsky/Basketballphoto.com. **BACK FLAP:** Hy Peskin.

SECTION OPENERS: Page 22: Greg Nelson; Page 38: Greg Nelson; Page 54: Walter Iooss Jr.; Page 70: David E. Klutho; Page 86: John W. McDonough; Page 102: Greg Nelson; Page 118: Phil Huber; Page 134: Greg Nelson; Page 150: John W. McDonough; Page 166: John W. McDonough; Page 182: John W. McDonough; Page 198: Brian Lanker; Page 214: John W. McDonough; Page 236: John W. McDonough; Page 252: Doug Benc/Getty Images; Page 270: James Drake.

ADDITIONAL CREDITS: Page 7: John W. McDonough; Page 8: Dick Raphael/NBAE/Getty Images; Page 9: Walter Iooss Jr.; Pages 20-21: Greg Nelson; Pages 272-273: John W. McDonough; Page 274: Walter Iooss Jr.; Page 275 (from left): Robert Beck, Andrew D. Bernstein/NBAE/Gerry Images; Page 277 (left to right, from top): Long Photography Inc., Heinz Kluetmeier, Manny Millan, John Biever, Dick Raphael/NBAE/Getty Images, John W. McDonough, Focus on Sport/Getty Images, John W. McDonough, Manny Millan, Dick Raphael/NBAE/Getty Images; Page 279: John W. McDonough; Page 280 (from left): Joe Murphy/NBAE/Getty Images, Damian Strohmeyer; Page 281: Damian Strohmeyer; Page 282 (from left): John W. McDonough, Neil Leifer; Page 283: John W. McDonough; Page 285: Layne Murdoch/NBAE/Getty Images; Pages 286-287: Manny Millan; Page 288: Walter Iooss Jr.

ENDPAPERS: FRONT SPREAD AND FRONT SINGLE: Greg Nelson. **BACK SPREAD AND BACK SINGLE:** John W. McDonough.

TIME HOME ENTERTAINMENT: Jim Childs, PUBLISHER; Vandana Patel, VICE PRESIDENT, FINANCE; Carol Pittard, EXECUTIVE DIRECTOR, MARKETING SERVICES; Suzanne Albert, EXECUTIVE DIRECTOR, BUSINESS DEVELOPMENT; Susan Hettleman, EXECUTIVE DIRECTOR, MARKETING; Megan Pearlman, PUBLISHING DIRECTOR; Courtney Greenhalgh, ASSOCIATE DIRECTOR OF PUBLICITY; Simone Procas, ASSISTANT GENERAL COUNSEL; Ilene Schreider, ASSISTANT DIRECTOR, SPECIAL SALES; Susan Chodakiewicz, SENIOR BOOK PRODUCTION MANAGER; Bryan Christian, SENIOR MANAGER, CATEGORY MARKETING; Isata Yansaneh, MARKETING MANAGER; Alex Voznesenskiy, ASSOCIATE PREPRESS MANAGER; Hillary Hirsch, ASSISTANT PROJECT MANAGER; Stephen Koepp, EDITORIAL DIRECTOR

Wilt Chamberlain stood tall in the Boston Garden in 1967.

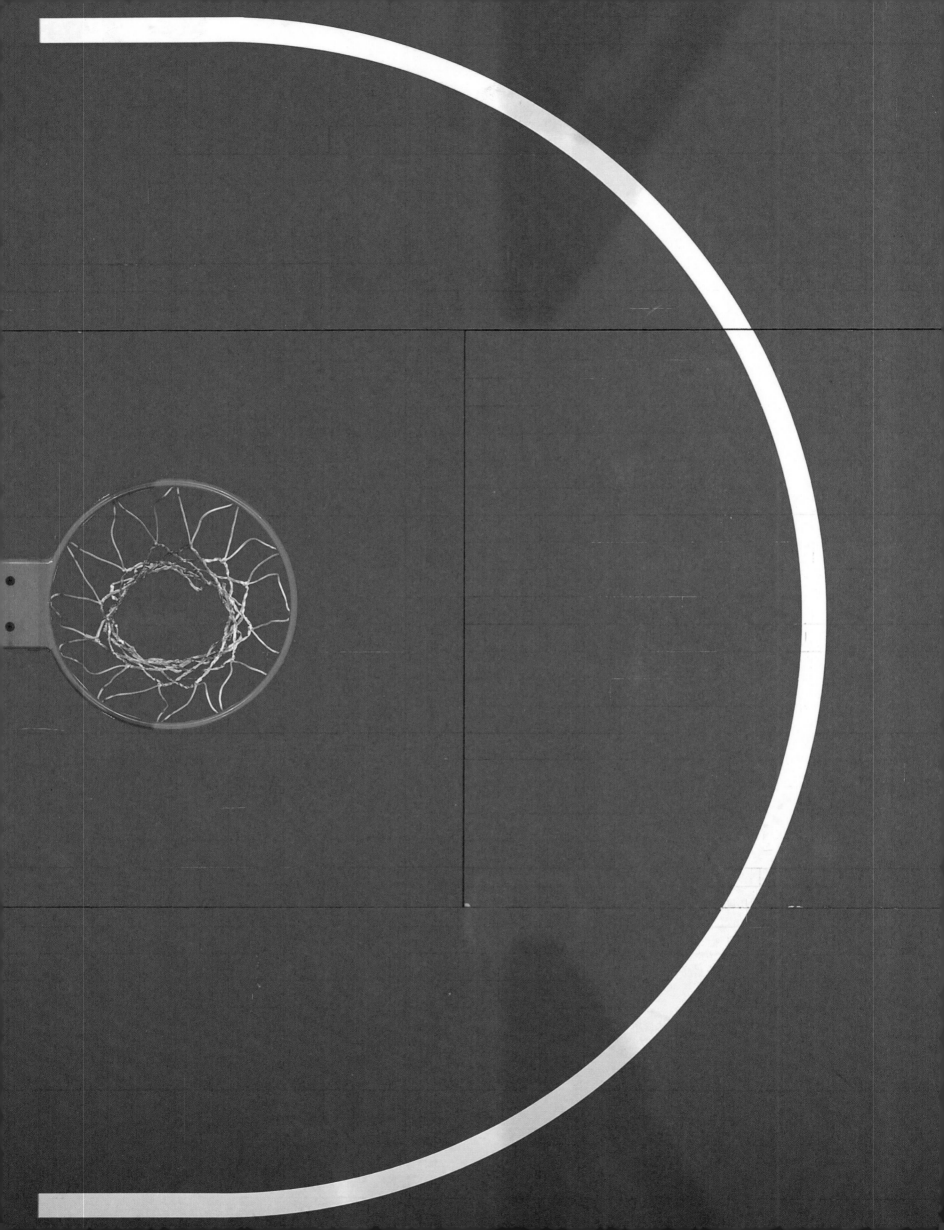